D0049381

UNDERSTANDING SHAME

COMMENTARY

"Dr. Carl Goldberg's book *Understanding Shame* is a scholarly and comprehensive examination of the role of shame in human behavior and in the therapeutic process. He makes a clear distinction between guilt and shame that will advance the effectiveness of psychotherapy in innumerable ways. Dr. Goldberg makes countertransference come to life in his self-revelation in the therapeutic process, and the case histories are brilliantly illuminated. Although he explores the theoretical and philosophical concept of shame, his orientation is focused on the patient and his problems. This is an excellent and long-overdue review of the significant role of shame in undermining the human potential and an indispensable tool for the therapist. It should become required reading for all therapists, psychologists, social workers, and psychiatrists."

—Leon Salzman, M.D.

"In *Understanding Shame*, Carl Goldberg presents a cogent critique of psychoanalytic theories that have assigned central importance to guilt and have ignored shame. Dr. Goldberg redresses this imbalance by refocusing on shame as 'the master emotion.' With a personal candor rare in clinical writing and a voice refreshingly free of professional jargon, Goldberg presents an approach to shame-dominated persons based on the therapist's willingness to confront his own shame. Although some of Goldberg's recommendations are certain to be controversial, everyone interested in shame or in simply doing better psychotherapy will benefit from reading this book."

—Francis Broucek, M.D.

"Noted psychoanalyst Carl Goldberg expands our horizons by providing brilliant insights into the devastating, long-neglected emotion of shame. Using a backdrop of clinical thought, philosophy, mythology, literature, and biblical writings, he weaves a portrait of an emotion that can be both corroding and enhancing to the human spirit. Going beyond guilt, we are led through absorbing portraits of patients suffering shame whose lives and experiences are linked with those of the author in the ongoing search for meaning. This erudite work reads like a novel. Its applicability is far-reaching in cutting across diagnostic lines to penetrate the soul of the human condition. 'Healing' takes on new meaning. This book's impact is truly extraordinary."

—Marcella Bakur Weiner, PH.D.

"Therapists can make contact with the most profound aspects of the shame experience in their patients only when they are in touch with their own shame. Dr. Goldberg is unsparing in his honesty regarding his own shame, both in the clinical setting and outside of it. This allows him to reach deeply troubled and shame-ridden individuals in a manner that is at once intimate and compassionate. It is also in the best tradition of analytic therapy."

—John O'Leary, PH.D.

UNDERSTANDING SHAME

CARL GOLDBERG, PH.D.

JASON ARONSON INC.
Northvale, New Jersey
London

Production Editor: Bernard F. Horan
Editorial Director: Muriel Jorgensen

This book was set in 11 point Bookman by Lind Graphics
and printed and bound by Haddon Craftsmen.

Library of Congress Cataloging-in-Publication Data

Goldberg, Carl.
    Understanding shame / by Carl Goldberg.
      p. cm.
    Includes bibliographical references and index.
    ISBN 0-87668-541-6
    1. Shame. 2. Psychotherapy. I. Title.
    [DNLM: 1. Psychoanalytic Theory. 2. Shame. BF 575.S45 G618u]
RC455.4.S53G65   1991
152.4—dc20
DNLM/DLC
for Library of Congress   91-13935

Manufactured in the United States of America. Jason Aronson Inc. offers books and
cassettes. For information and catalog write to Jason Aronson Inc., 230 Livingston
Street, Northvale, New Jersey 07647.

*This book is dedicated
to my mother, who encouraged me
to know myself*

CONTENTS

PREFACE

Shame opens a path to ourselves.

—Max Scheler

The need for a book on the treatment of shame is clinically evident. Despite decades of psychological insight into the etiology of emotional disturbance and the development of a wide array of innovative treatment methodologies, many patients in psychological conflict are not being sufficiently helped by psychotherapy. Currently, there are conceptual gaps in our understanding of the causes and the appropriate treatment of human suffering.

It is not only my own clinical experience, but that of an increasing number of other practitioners, that the troublesome inner doubts and self-recriminations that daily pervade our patients' thoughts and communications are evoked by the syndrome of shame. For many people shame is not a single, isolated event in their lives. The self-condemnation and self-loathing that shame precipitates are part and parcel of a pervasive, persistent, and destructive set of emotions that grips the sufferers with a crippling sense of terror and pessimism, preventing them from living harmoniously and confidently. The terror of shame leads to a lifetime of secrecy and attempted cover-ups of one's true feelings. Chronic, toxic shame breeds the helpless despair that characterizes one of the most unbearable of human experiences.

Shame is also an ironic emotion. Despite how intensely afflicted sufferers of shame are, rarely can they do anything about their despair because they lack the awareness that their suffering is rooted in shame. Few people are able to express articulately the misery derived from shame. No matter how deeply shaken they are by a shaming reaction, rarely are they able to tell themselves, much less anyone else, just what is so tenaciously gripping their psyche.

A full examination of the etiology and clinical implications of shame is a neglected area of psychological investigation. The *Psychological Abstracts* does not have a separate subject category for it, placing this elusive affect under the category of guilt. In short, shame and its variants are the most seriously neglected and misunderstood emotions in contemporary society.

We have traditionally attributed much of our most complex and difficult clinical cases of shame and despair to the agent of guilt rather than to the steward of shame. Due to an overabundance of clinical studies of guilt, the emotional workings of shame have only recently received some of the careful psychological investigation they deserve. Going back to Sigmund Freud, there has been a shame about studying shame in the psychoanalytic and psychotherapeutic fields. Only in recent years has this stigma been lifted.

I present in this book a thesis about the vital role shame plays in human misery that modifies the psychoanalytic view—that the remote shadows of childhood guilts are the major source of unhappiness. The limitation of this moral masochism (guilt) view of human suffering is that it has seriously neglected how people unknowingly shame themselves and the ways they allow others to humiliate them in their daily adult interactions.

As a psychoanalyst I have always had trouble reconciling the psychoanalytic theories that I had been taught about the causes of human suffering with my own life experiences. Moreover, I also have had difficulty applying these psychological notions to the patients I have worked with for the past twenty-five years.

My psychoanalytic training taught me that unconscious guilt, usually of an incestuous origin, was the major cause of human unhappiness. Yet I recognized from the beginning of my clinical practice that there were real differences between those people I treated who had identifiable guilt issues and those my colleagues and I found the most perplexing in understanding and clinically treating. I have come to realize that our clinical and psychological theories have unwittingly, but seriously, misled both the public and practitioners about the causes of human unhappiness.

I have found in my own clinical work, and in that of my students, that whenever the themes of shame, humiliation, and embarrassment have been indicated and openly examined during therapy, these manifestly resistant patients take a discernible interest in trying to understand themselves that was not evidenced heretofore.

In proposing that shame and its everyday consequences are a major source of human suffering, I am not claiming that shame is the only emotion peculiar to human suffering. Other emotions, such as guilt, anger, envy, fear, and so forth have often been identified as major themes in the pathos of suffering. Shame, however, has too often been overlooked.

I will discuss in this book why Sigmund Freud neglected the terrifying experiences of shame and despair, while at the same time emphasizing the monocausal role of guilt in the experience of suffering. I also will examine Freud's rationale in choosing the Oedipus myth as the cornerstone of psychoanalysis. By relating Freud's interpretations of *Oedipus Rex* and *Hamlet* to the role the concepts of guilt and shame have played in the history of ideas, I will demonstrate that shame and its existential consequences, rather than guilt, lie at the heart of our difficulties in understanding complex manifestations of human suffering far more often than the psychoanalytic literature suggests. Understanding those features

of the Sophocles and Shakespeare dramas that Freud neglected enables us to make improvements in the therapeutics of shame.

Fortunately, the practice of psychoanalysis does not rest
upon the acceptance of all of Freud's theories. Despite
Freud's mistaken notions about guilt and human misery, he
has provided us with a powerful and sensitive instrument to
study the exquisite nuances of human emotion and complexity. Indeed, it was from clinical, psychoanalytic practice
that some fellow practitioners and I have come to appreciate
the crucial nature of shame in human experience.

The treatment of shame requires a continuous self-
examination by the practitioner. Any clinician who is interested in the treatment of shame probably has his own
personal story about the role it has played in his own life. In
the clinical chapters of this book I discuss how by being
confronted by difficult-to-treat patients I was forced to come
to terms with what had been up to then my unrecognized
feelings of shame. Although I had always been deeply
affected by my sensitivity to shame, I had not understood
my feelings as such. By discovering the presence of shame
in my own life, I was for the first time clinically able to
understand the devastating role shame plays in the lives of
my patients and respond to their muffled cries for help.

The examination of my own feelings helped me recognize that in treatment situations we are always concerned
with issues of shame. The shame we need to be concerned
with emanates not only from the patient's history and the
deleterious relationships that bring him to our consulting
room. This book is intended to help the clinician recognize
that, inevitably, the psychotherapeutic session itself is an
experience of shame.

Coming to terms with the sources of shame in the
therapeutic situation can be a difficult task. Therapists must
often actively seek out their patients' shame from a minimum of clues (Robertiello and Gagnier 1990). There are
several ways we need to recognize the presence of shame in
psychotherapy. First, the very position of being a psychotherapy patient is perceived as a humiliating one by many in

contemporary society. It implies that one is incapable of living competently without someone else's help. For this reason most people eschew psychotherapy unless compelled by desperation.

Second, the very distressing symptoms that are brought to us by patients are deeply implicated with shame. Lewis (1987a) indicates that closely examining the dynamics of shame reveals that it is the key to what Freud (1923) identified as the "archaic" or "irrational" guilt that breeds neurotic and psychotic symptoms. From her long-standing clinical concern about shame, Lewis has shown that a protracted empathic immersion into the affective state of all patients in psychotherapy uncovers deep and painful feelings of shame. They are usually difficult to detect because of the protective overlay of defense mechanisms, such as grandiosity, that cover the gripping sense of defeat, failure, and emptiness that has spurned shame and despair.

In Chapter 3, I chart the levels of defenses against and the responses to shame. In this way, I show the role that shame and despair play in obsession and paranoid conditions and how it is deeply involved in clinical descriptions of narcissistic and borderline personalities. Shame also is at work in the self-blame and self-loathing that foster low self-esteem and create depression. Several investigators (Binder 1970, Crouppon 1977, Harder and Lewis 1987, Hoblitzelle 1982, Smith 1972) have shown that shame enacts a greater role in depression than does guilt. Shame, as a chronic mood, decisively sours one's everyday activities and life plans. Since shame is closely associated with the bitterness and animosity people direct toward themselves when they realize that they are living a futile life, it is small wonder that the patient who faces us in psychotherapy feels ashamed.

Third, understanding the role shame plays in human development enables us to correct misappropriate treatment of conditions previously labeled as afflictions of guilt. What we have called pathological guilt is in most instances pathological shame. There is probably no such actual entity as pathological guilt (Fisher 1985). This is to say, people who are unable to resolve feelings of guilt are, in fact, unable to make the distinctions between a "bad" act and a "bad" person. For example, many parents are unable to make a separation between their child's improper behavior and the child being a "bad" child—either in their own thinking or in statements to the child. The operating belief is that only inherently bad children can do bad things. Consequently, when the child is punished and the focus of the punishment is the child's character rather than his specific behaviors, shame, not guilt, is fostered.

Fourth, despite his best efforts, it is difficult for the practitioner to avoid augmenting his patient's shame. The therapist's presence during the recitation of the patient's secrets evinces mortifying aspects of the patient.

Fifth, shame plays an especially crucial and often disguised role in the lives of our male patients. It probably has an even more dysfunctional position with males than with most female patients. But, whether or not sex differences actually exist in our patients' proneness to guilt and shame, clinical studies have indicated that shame-debilitated patients require a different treatment focus than do those who are more guilt-sensitive (Harder 1990).

Finally, as I previously mentioned, clinicians cannot avoid the issue of shame in effective clinical practice because they are themselves subject to being shamed as part and parcel of their daily clinical endeavors. I am concerned in the treatment chapters of this volume with the intersubjectivity of shame. This is because the ashamed patient has the proclivity, in turn, to humiliate the practitioner. The caring and concerned practitioner is susceptible to shame to the extent that he can not meaningfully reach and help to heal his suffering patient. The inexorable shaming of the therapeutic encounter awakens unresolved personal concerns and conflicts on the part of the practitioner.

To this point I have discussed shame in somewhat pessimistic terms. Shame, traditionally, has been viewed as a negative emotion to avoid. This perspective on shame is inaccurate and does us a disservice. Like Broucek (in press) I believe that if one understands shame, one not only knows

a great deal about psychopathology, but also quite a bit
about health. A sensitivity to the workings of shame results
in the recognition of the processes that make us human
(Schneider 1977). Shame is one of the most complex and
contradictory emotions with which the human race must
come to terms. Shame cannot be accurately reduced to
simply the foreclosure of despair, or to a desperate flight
from our tragic human condition. The message I emphasize
in this book is that shame takes various forms. In different
manifestations and contexts, it may be either constructive,
restraining, or pathological. Therefore, whereas it is true
that pathological shame is the harbinger of hopelessness,
healthy shame is the crucible of freedom. It spurs our
greatest human achievements by making us aware of the
conditions necessary in our lives for self-improvement and
self-realization.

Fortunately, like other contexts in which shame arises,
therapeutic shame has a constructive potential. As the
clinical studies in this book will demonstrate, the mutual
shaming between patient and therapist does not necessitate
a therapeutic misalliance. I will give numerous clinical
examples and vignettes to delineate how this happens only
to the extent that the therapeutic participants fearfully
avoid exploring therapeutic shame in order not to lose the
magical hope that the self can psychologically thrive
without excoriating its psychic vulnerabilities. The presence of therapeutic shame provides the sine qua non for a
meaningful and humanizing examination by the therapeutic participants of their existential dilemmas. In short,
there is a crucial interrelationship between how therapists
use their own shame and their patients' willingness to
express and to work through despair.

As therapists, we realize, idealistically at least, that by
using a deeply subjective understanding of ourselves we
possess the most potent human instrument available for
understanding and responding to the hurt and suffering of
our fellow beings. Yet the lessons learned from examining
the human psyche can be seen as a two-way street. We
cannot afford to set aside our humility in sharing with our

patients the frailties of being merely human in an imperfect world. We need to learn wisely from even those we cannot reach. Whatever wisdom I have brought to the analytic hour was only partially shaped by my professional education and clinical training. Just as important, my own maturity both as a person and as an analyst was augmented by witnessing and participating in my analysands' struggles as well as those of people I have encountered outside of my practice. I have tried during my career to act in accordance with the wise humility contained in the belief of the pioneer American psychiatrist William A. White, who reportedly said, "I have never met a man I could not learn from."

It is unsettling to me as a practitioner that we have not yet formulated a therapeutic model that emphasizes the values of sharing and cooperating rather than highlighting the obstacles of fear and resistance to effective psychotherapy.

Psychotherapy has yet to establish an effective model for interpersonal competence. Traditionally, transference analysis has been regarded as the most powerful tool available for personality modification. We now have come to realize that there is an inherent limitation to the usefulness of examining historical material in psychotherapy. As the cases in this volume will demonstrate, the transference model precludes the practitioner from demonstrating certain essential psychosocial behaviors necessary for shame-imbued patients to realize the skills required for satisfying interpersonal activity.

In search of a model for effectively working with shame-sensitive patients I have turned from focusing on psychopathology to the study of normal and creative lives. A major theme of this volume is that the healing of shame requires the opportunity for genuine friendship. One of the most notable observations of human affairs is the recognition that the social and emotional basis of a life lived well is friendship (Levinson 1978). Since we live in the community of others and generally achieve our greatest satisfactions in other people's company, the highest aim of humanity, as Aristotle long ago indicated, is found in genuine friendship. People who lack or lose trusted friendships are vulnerable to the devastating effects of shame. The central importance of friendship in this book is unique for a volume dealing with the subject of psychoanalysis. I know of no other analytic position, with the possible exception of the work of Harry Stack Sullivan, that has not seriously neglected the importance of friendship in human satisfaction.

DIFFERENT KINDS OF SHAME

Insofar as only a minority of experiences of shame are consciously recognized as such, it is necessary to define the different manifestations of shame I will be employing in this book. Most writers on the subject of shame have not made these distinctions. The term "shame" is often too vaguely defined in the literature. I will be referring to shame and its variants in the following ways: first, the word "shame" will designate internalized and unrecognized shame as well as feeling ridiculous, embarrassed, humiliated, chagrined, mortified, shy, reticent, painfully self-conscious, inferior, and inadequate; second, an important differentiation needs to be made between recognized and unrecognized shame. A "sense of shame" will denote the awareness of the source of feelings of self-blame, and "being shamed" will describe a lack of awareness of the precise emotion being experienced; third, a distinction also needs to be made between being humiliated and shamed by someone else and those incidents in which the person himself is the major source of criticism and assault on self-esteem. I will refer to the latter as "being ashamed." This consideration is in keeping with Loevinger's (1976) critique of cognitive and moral development in which she contends that "to be ashamed implies a more self-administrative put-down than to be shamed" (p. 398). Fourth, I will refer to "discretionary shame" (Schneider 1977) as those experiences in which a person is aware that the behavioral options before him involve moral and value choices. Therefore, whereas some forms of shame operate beyond our awareness, other experiences make us pause before saying or doing something that would arouse

painful self-rebuke if pursued. Finally, I will make distinctions between healthy, constructive aspects of shame,
trying to clearly differentiate them from pathological and
debilitating shame.

THE AUTHOR'S POINT OF VIEW

I approach the study and treatment of shame from a
different perspective than most others who have written
about shame in recent years. Other theorists have focused
largely on the experience of shame during childhood. They
attribute the problems of adulthood to how a parent, usually
a mother, has fostered a depreciative sense of self in her
child by means of shaming and blaming. I agree with
Broucek (in press) that this view of the fostering of shame
"misses the dynamic complexity of self-development, its
continuities as well as its discontinuities." I will show how
the development of shame is a continuous process and how
to effectively treat its devastation.

In conclusion, this volume provides a guide for dealing
with the conditions that cause shame. It indicates the
necessary steps for identifying and constructively using the
sensitive and vulnerable feelings of shame to enable individuals to foster a more satisfying and meaningful existence. I
present the clinical material from a phenomenological approach that avoids abstract, mechanical, and dehumanized
terms to describe patients and their interactions with others. The identities of patients and of colleagues have been
changed in the case studies.

This work is intended to enable clinicians and other
behavioral scientists to view shame differently from the way
it has been traditionally regarded. My hope is to enable
therapists to be in a better position to treat the devastation
of shame and despair. It also should help behavioral scientists understand how shame plants the seeds for our hei-
nous societal maladies. The shame to be examined in the
proposed work has direct relevance to the seemingly insol-
uble problems of the homeless, addictions, violence, abuse,
political unrest, and the malodorous corruption of nearly
every fiber of our contemporary society.

Finally, I wish to express my appreciation to the fol-
lowing colleagues of mine who contributed to this volume:
Herman VanPraag, M.D., Chairman of the Department of
Psychiatry at Albert Einstein College of Medicine, who first
encouraged me to write this book; my publisher, Jason
Aronson, M.D.; Virginia R. Crespo, M.S.W., Harold Frank,
Ph.D., John O'Leary, Ph.D., Marcella Weiner, Ph.D., Tom
Robischon, Ph.D., and Hillel Swiller, M.D., who were helpful
in revising an earlier draft of this book.

PART I

THE PROBLEM OF SHAME

1

UNRECOGNIZED SHAME IN THE DAILY LIVES OF OUR PATIENTS

> There is a shame that bringeth sin and there is a
> shame which is glory and grace.
> —*Ecclesiastes*

SHAME AND PERSONAL IDENTITY

An individual's *personal identity* is a complex enterprise. It consists not only of the sense of who one currently is, but also includes beliefs and desires about who one should be and what one can become. From this context, every action and interaction on one's part may be judged in terms of the information it provides for either substantiating or disconfirming the self one desires to be. Where there is a congruent fit between the experience of one's *tested self* (e.g., the import of one's senses about the circumstances of one's life) with the images, fantasies, and intentions of one's *desired identity*, a feeling of competence accompanies these experiences. According to White (1963), competence is an expression of the ability, fitness, and capacity to live effectively and well. Being shamed, in contrast, always involves a sense of incompetence.

3

The potential for shame anxiety, therefore, is present when there is a disparity between the tested self and the desired self (Bilmes 1967). As such, a useful way to view being *shamed* is to regard it as a powerful, but unquestioned, conviction that in some important way one is flawed and incompetent as a human being.

SUSCEPTIBILITY TO SHAME

It would be unrealistic to assume that an individual could be the ideal self all the time. Even with the kindest of parents, the best of life experiences, and an ability to convey a presence of competence and self-confidence, anyone is vulnerable to critical assaults on one's self-worth by significant people in that person's life (Potter-Efron and Potter-Efron 1989). Even worldly success doesn't necessarily shield a person from the insecurity of shame. That grand dame of the mystery tale, Agatha Christie, only once in her life attended a party to celebrate the rave reviews of her books and plays. Her grandson reported that she was a painfully shy person, who was afraid of making a fool of herself. The shyness Dame Christie was demonstrating is a shrinking-away from one's full presence in the world. A depleted sense of personal identity is an essential characteristic of shame.

Moreover, being painfully ashamed doesn't happen to only the unfortunate few. *The New York Times* carried a story about the humiliating experience of a health care–system manager who is a chain smoker. Said the executive:

> I'm responsible for overseeing about one billion dollars a year and sometimes I think maybe the fact that I am ruled by this one thing—cigarettes—means the wrong person is sitting in this chair. Sometimes I think the kid in the stockroom who doesn't smoke is brighter than I am.

This executive goes to great lengths to avoid being seen smoking by his own employees. The Indo-European origins of the word "shame" comes from "schame," which means "to hide" or to "cover up."

Many people grow up with masks to hide their humiliation and hurts. Many of these masks pretend to laugh or smile, as if their bearer harbored no psychic pain inside. However, no one is effectively immune to shame. Everyone experiences shame at different moments of their lives about some aspect of their selves. People are as likely to be shamed silently as in a direct, verbal way. Having someone one knows walk by in the street without speaking, smiling, or acknowledging one's presence can leave one with the unsettling sense of being uninteresting and unattractive to other people. During times of stress in a person's life, it does little good to tell oneself that perhaps the acquaintance was preoccupied and didn't notice the person being passed by. The ashamed is convinced that he has been intentionally slighted. In viewing himself as disregarded he experiences shame.

For some people, being ashamed is only an occasional incident in their lives. For still others it is a continual sense of their being in the world. When our patients habitually feel taken advantage of on the job and in their significant relationships, but feel powerless to change these situations because they fear that if they protested they would lose their livelihood or the relationships that they feel dependent upon, they are victims of debilitating shame. Painful shame threatens the integrity of personal identity. In the throes of debilitating shame, people feel that life is happening to them and that they are helpless in the wake of what is happening (Middleton-Moz 1990). Debilitating shame leaves one with doubts about one's competence and self-worth. It leads to what Erikson (1980) has called a *negative personal identity*—a contemptuous sense of oneself in which one feels scornful and hostile "towards the roles offered as proper and desirable in one's family or immediate community."

THE SOURCES OF SHAME

Zimbardo and colleagues (1974) found in a survey of 800 high school and college students that 82 percent regarded themselves as having been "dispositionally shy" at times in their lives. Only 1 percent denied ever having been shy.

Being shy is but one variant of the shame syndrome. Actually, there are so many sources for creating shame in a person that it is virtually impossible to categorize them all. A person could be ashamed of almost anything about himself—his appearance, manners, dress, physique, personality, and so forth. Moreover, he may be ashamed at not only what he is or has done, but also with what he identifies with—his family, his ethnic origins, his country's politics, his parents' religious practices, and so forth (Broucek, in press). However, what is shameful differs among people. The situations that evoke shame in one may cause anger and aggression in another, distress and fear in a third, and challenge and excitement in still others (Izard 1977). The issues over which one can be shamed correspond directly to the composite of concerns with which a person specifically identifies. In any area in which one feels or is treated as unworthy, inferior, or incompetent, a potential for shaming is present, unless, as William James (1890) noted, it is an endeavor or status outside of one's personal world. Consequently, as Broucek (in press) indicates:

> One may feel shame over failures to be accepted or valued by any person or group whose acceptance is desired. One may feel shame over a lack of competence or the loss of previously acquired competence as might occur with illness or aging. Any loss of control over one's body, mental functions, or emotions may elicit shame. Shame often has to do with matters of exposure and privacy. When personal boundaries are not respected by others, shame and shame rage are apt to be the result. Shame also has to do with one's relationship to one's bodily functions and may be elicited under certain circumstances in association with eating, excretion, and sexuality. Any time the self experiences itself as ruled by some "lower" passion, the self may be vulnerable to shame.

What is so unsettling in trying to understand the dynamics of shame is that shameful feelings include matters and circumstances over which the ashamed may have had no responsibility or control. Therefore, a person may be ashamed to find out that his grandfather was a convicted rapist, an uncle an alcoholic, or even that a cousin of his wife cruelly mistreated her pets.

Shame occurs at every phase of human development. But it takes diverse forms and has a variety of different sources in each period of life. The five major sources in the fostering of shame to be discussed in this book are (1) genetic and biochemical disposition; (2) family of origin; (3) self-shaming thoughts and feelings orchestrated by one's narrative self; (4) current humiliating relationships; and (5) contemporary American culture.

THE DESTRUCTIVE ROLE SHAME PLAYS IN PERSONAL IDENTITY

Each shaming experience, especially those that involve disregard and mistreatment, depletes a person's sense of self-worth. An inability to secure proper treatment and respect from others renders a shame-sensitive person vulnerable to feelings of self-blame and self-loathing, the emotive forces that cause the feelings of misery and unhappiness that bring people to seek psychological help. These contemptuous feelings inform the sufferer in destructive and painful ways that he is incompetent, inadequate, and unwanted. As such, they undermine the sufferer's interpersonal relationships and his feelings of self-regard, well-being, and security. Chronic shame, because it diminishes one's sense of self-worth, prevents one from defining oneself constructively to others, leaving the person vulnerable to further abuse and neglect by others.

What makes shame such an unfathomable experience is that people subject to shame are often unable to identify the precise cause of their uneasy feelings. Consequently, when experiencing shame they have a great deal of difficulty finding language to communicate their painful experience. There is a temporary difficulty in thinking logically and effectively and a loss of words, particularly the appropriate words and concepts to express one's painful and confusing plight. Moreover, during debilitating shame the victim experiences a loss of connection with what is familiar and safe. He senses that his true self has now been exposed forever. He feels a desire to hide and to get out of the interpersonal situation or existential situation in which he finds himself. But he also feels stuck and unable to control or to escape the painful present moment. There seems to be no refuge from his vulnerable feelings—no place to hide.

Because shame and self-contempt usually go together (Tompkins 1978), seemingly trivial matters can be as painfully shameful as ostensibly more significant concerns. One of Larry's most painful memories from childhood was of a series of interactions with a candy-store proprietor, who continually promised the young boy that he would soon have available packets of basketball cards and bubblegum. The cards were prized because they were difficult to find. Few stores carried them. They consisted of photographs of professional basketball players, with their performance statistics. Larry and his friends swapped these cards as they avidly listened together to basketball games on the radio. Even as an adult Larry could not understand why the storekeeper continually lied to him. Each day during that humiliating period of his childhood Larry walked out of the store empty-handed and dejected. He felt foolish and assumed that, in some way he could not figure out, he was responsible for this unkind man treating him shabbily.

Debilitating shame prevents a person from facing life courageously, honestly, and with the full confidence in his ability to competently deal with life's problems and opportunities. Debilitating shame is an alienating feeling. It conveys an anxiety that all is not right with one's life, that one's existence is not safe and harmonious. It carries the opprobrium that the sufferer is unlovable and should be cast out of human company. The shame-bound person has learned from others and now accuses himself of the "crime" of being surplus, unwanted, and worthless.

Alicia unhappily returned home alone that night. Earlier in the evening she had attended an office party, celebrating the festivities of the winter season. As was her custom, Alicia stood alone in the shadows of the merrily decorated, candle-lit reception room, apart from her colleagues engaged in animated conversations. A very attractive man in a three-piece suit, with a drink in each hand, approached Alicia. With an inviting smile, he offered her eggnog. She had never seen him before. She was immediately aware of how differently he carried himself than the short, balding, bearded men with meager physical stamina with whom she had spent so many dreary hours in her life. He had the quiet poise of a confident athlete. Alicia, a slim and attractive woman, whose face is encompassed with rather long, dark and wavy hair, is now close to forty. She has never married. She has had a number of long-term relationships with boring men. These affairs have not held a central place in her life. Alicia and the man she found so charming and attentive spoke for a long while. They are both magazine writers and were currently romantically unattached. As they conversed, Alicia found herself moving to his bodily movements as if he were leading her in a sensual dance. When it was apparent that the party was drawing to a close, with an eager smile and a tender caress of her hand, he asked Alicia if she would like to leave and continue their conversation over coffee. In a subdued voice, Alicia confessed that she found him attractive and charming. But if they dated, she told him with a deep sigh, she would continually feel anxious about him. She was certain, she added, lowering her eyes and looking away, that he would eventually lose interest in her. He stood there motionless for a while, as if he were stunned. Then he shrugged his shoulders, turned, and walked away.

Alicia has a foolproof method for avoiding getting involved with men she responds to strongly. In their presence she outrightly rejects herself. Alicia is an unknowing victim of debilitating shame.

Shame has its tragic and violent side, as well, as its debilitating passivity.

THE TRAGIC CONSEQUENCES OF SHAME

At the time I began writing this book the tragic Lisa Steinberg story was prominent in the concerns and conversations of my patients. The unfortunate Steinberg situation epitomizes some of the worst fears my patients harbored about themselves and those they care about. At the same time, the Steinberg saga had all the elements of a puzzling mystery.

Joel Steinberg and Hedda Nussbaum appeared to have everything going for them. He was a bright, wealthy, and busy attorney, with a compelling personality. She was a respected children's book editor, a former schoolteacher, who, according to the pictures shown on television, was quite attractive at the time she met Steinberg. Together, although not legally married, they were the adoptive parents of two bright and engaging young children. They had a wide assortment of friends with whom they associated.

But something went horribly wrong in their lives. It led this advantaged couple to physical, emotional, and spiritual corruption. Whatever went amiss resulted in Steinberg developing a paranoiac reaction to being stared at, along with a lack of control of his own rage. Correspondingly, Nussbaum became passive and reclusive. Finally, one of the most deplorable human acts imaginable took place in their Greenwich Village home—the brutalization and murder of a young child.

As we all know, Steinberg has been convicted of striking Lisa three times with his fist after, allegedly, his customary evening of smoking cocaine. Medical experts have testified in court that Steinberg's forceful blows produced a brain hemorrhage that caused Lisa's death four days later.

As outraged as my patients were with Steinberg's violence, they were no less baffled by Nussbaum's suppression of her maternal instincts. Each among them was stunned to learn that she had allowed her mortally injured child to remain neglected in a coma for about twelve hours. Her pathetic response to why she had not summoned medical help for Lisa was "I expected Joel to do that." What manner of sadistic monsters reside in our midst, cloaked with middle-class respectability? they asked me.

My patients were troubled because no simple under-standing of the Steinberg-Nussbaum murderous affair was provided them. Nussbaum's psychiatrists confounded the already sordid and bizarre details of the Steinberg case. They testified that Nussbaum was so physically and men-tally battered by Steinberg that she was incapable of pro-tecting herself, let alone aiding Lisa. They indicated that so thorough was Steinberg's control over Nussbaum, that de-spite his brutalization of her, she continued to worship him. Take, for instance, their dining rituals. If she dared to eat before asking and receiving his permission, he commanded her to draw and enter a bathtub of ice water. She would do so, it was alleged, rarely protesting, or even becoming angry at what any of my patients regarded as cruel and bizarre treatment. Nussbaum even admitted to lying to police to protect Steinberg after Lisa died.

The Steinberg case was disquieting for my patients because they suspected that both Steinberg and Nussbaum represent parts of themselves that they do not really under-stand. They sensed that what caused Steinberg and Nuss-baum's tragic fall from a life that had all the trimmings of security and stability could also happen to any of them.

From listening to my patients speak of the Steinberg affair, I suspect that in order to psychologically distance themselves from their uneasy identification with the couple, they were reaching out for some explanation of their be-havior that would clearly differentiate themselves from Steinberg and Nussbaum. Psychoanalysis has helped in this fugitive endeavor. We have been tutored by decades of analytic explanation to account for the behavior of any person (especially a woman) who would submit to repeated beatings as being masochistic. Correspondingly, we have been taught to render the person (usually a male) who inflicts the abuse the judgment of being either sadistic or crazy. Clinical theory has evolved from the original conten-tion of Freud that the Nussbaums get involved with the Steinbergs to relieve themselves of guilty consciences, to the

even more outrageous belief, held by many psychotherapists, that the Hedda Nussbaums seek out mistreatment
because the pain itself has become a perverse pleasure.

I hope to convince you by the time you have finished this
book, in case your own clinical experience has not done so
already, that the deployment of clinical concepts, such as
"masochism," "sadism," and a "guilty conscience" rarely
have verifiable evidence. My own clinical experience, as I
will share with you in several chapters of this book, strongly
suggests that these Freudian concepts do little more than
heap blame on the sufferer. It is for this reason that the
person suffering pathological shame is frequently misunderstood and, as a result, inadequately clinically treated.

The Steinberg case itself gives us evidence that a guilty-
conscience explanation hinders our understanding of complex psychological events. Neither in the Steinberg case, nor
in any of the other cases I will discuss in this book—which
include the story of Roy, a person who had spent most of his
life in forensic hospitals and prisons, and Vincent, who
blamed himself for the death of his own infant son—do any
of the perpetrators of violence express, in any way that I
could discern, the feeling that a guilty conscience led them
to their grievous misfortunes. Are these people without a
moral conscience? No, I don't believe that any of them were
heartless, cynical people—at least they weren't at the time
their fall began from a vibrant life. Consequently, there
must be something more devastating at work in their psy-
ches than that of pathological guilt.

In order to better understand the causes of the conflictual lives of people like Steinberg and Nussbaum, I would
like to direct your attention to some important information
about Hedda Nussbaum to which I don't believe the media
gave sufficient attention. I am referring to Nussbaum's
explanation for why she believed that Steinberg had ruined
her life.

I find it revealing that she did not claim that her life had
been destroyed because Steinberg robbed her of her youth,
her health, or her well-being. Nor did she say that he made

it impossible that their home be a place of mutually respectful and caring relationships. She did not even mention the loss of her adopted children.

What did Hedda Nussbaum most grieve about? According to Judith Liebman, Nussbaum's sister, Nussbaum expressed her strongest emotions about her sorry situation when she deplored the fact that she had allowed herself to believe every lie and every exaggeration Joel Steinberg had ever told her. She reportedly conveyed considerable humiliation in saying that she had accepted without question Steinberg's contentions that she had been involved in witchcraft, cults, and illicit sexual practices that also included Lisa. In short, what seemed to have most unhinged Hedda Nussbaum after their arrest was the shocking realization of the tremendous reliance she had on Steinberg and the lying and betrayal that resulted from her misplaced trust in him.

In realizing that one has been repeatedly lied to and betrayed by others, the shame-debilitated person is compelled to recognize that he is living a futile and fictional existence. This painful realization annihilates the purpose and meaning that have, heretofore, guided one's life. This speaks to the conflicts of personal identity I am concerned with in this book.

People who suffer the terrors Hedda Nussbaum has experienced do not passively accept their mistreatment because they are crazy or because they feel they deserve or enjoy suffering. This is the argument that Steinberg's lawyer, Ira London, nevertheless tried to persuade the jury of in explaining Hedda Nussbaum's behavior.

I believe that Hedda Nussbaum's helpless passivity came from having to face the gradual realization that her life had been a lie. During her relationship with Steinberg, she needed to believe that Steinberg loved and cared about her. And as long as she assumed he did, she could rationalize his brutality as his stern zeal in trying to enable her to become a better person. People like Nussbaum, who passively accept repeated mistreatment, internalize their humiliations as deserved. Not, however, because they feel morally guilty

about unacceptable urges toward other people, but rather
because they feel that they are incompetent to take better
care of themselves.

However, in realizing that Steinberg had repeatedly lied
to her, Nussbaum startlingly recognized that despite her
sense of incompetence and poor judgment, trusting Steinberg was patently absurd. The stupid and fictitious existence that she had gone along with had resulted in the death
of her child.

Ironically, Steinberg also was a victim of shame. To
continue an intimate relationship with a woman who allowed him to debase her in the way Nussbaum tolerated
could only be savored by a man who himself had considerable self-contempt. Joel Steinberg's concealed self-
deprecation, no less than his manic demandingness of other
people, would be intolerable to a woman who had good
self-esteem. Brownmiller (1989) suggests that his contempt
for Nussbaum may have been continually fueled by being
compelled to recognize that he could only make it with a
woman who allowed him to abuse and take advantage of
her. Not surprisingly, the woman with whom Steinberg
lived before Nussbaum claimed that Steinberg also routinely beat her.

Joel Steinberg fulfills the classic characteristics of the
"shameless" personality. In the throes of their shamelessness, people do not only become insensitive to the griefs and
sensitivities of other people, but lose touch with their own
feelings as well. However, the appellation of "shamelessness" to describe people like Joel Steinberg, as I will demonstrate in Chapter 4, is misidentified. The statement of
another well-known murderer offers additional evidence for
this point of view. William Mosely, the murderer of Kitty
Genovese, told the police that he felt no remorse for his
actions. When led by the police past a battery of camera-
men, however, he was quoted to have said: "I have a father
out there. I also have a wife, and this is a pretty shameful
thing. Would it be alright with you people if I covered up my
face?" (Bilmes 1967).

Shame is a more profound, serious, and disturbing issue

than we, as clinicians, have realized until recently. It is the source of many of the psychological problems that we have attributed to guilt in the past.

UNRECOGNIZED SHAME

Until quite recently clinicians' view of human behavior seriously neglected how people unknowingly shame themselves and the variety of ways that they allow others to humiliate them in their daily interactions. Shame is a cloaked emotion. Like an unseen powerful electric current, shame may cause a person serious harm without his being aware of its presence. An understanding of shame is complicated by the indirect consequences and the delays in responding to a shame stimulus.

I estimate that more than 90 percent of everyday experiences of being shamed lie buried beneath the surface of one's conscious awareness. During moments of being seriously shamed, the powerful hurt and the person's ability to identify the emotion that he is experiencing may be "bypassed." Instead of being aware of what has happened to cause him to feel badly about himself, the emotional wound is registered on his psyche physiologically as a "wince," or as a "jolt" (Lewis 1971), or on the other hand, the sensation may be confused and misidentified as some other emotion. The complex interplay of emotions with which shame is involved is discussed in Chapter 3.

THE SUBTLETIES OF SHAME

Shame has its more subtle personal and social manifestations, as well as its explosive aspects.

Jessica is a lovely, hardworking and well-educated businesswoman. Yet there is something that prevents her from being successful in her career. It causes her to obsess constantly about her faults and her limitations. When she is alone she calls herself harsh and horrible names, as if she had committed some unknown and unpardonable crime. Due to her feelings of self-loathing, she will not wear the expensive clothes in her closet or drive the new car given to her by her father to try to cheer her up. Jessica is more concerned about damaging her possessions than with their enjoyment. She walks with her shoulders hunched, although she is a tall and striking woman, as if she needed to protect herself from an unexpected attack at any moment.

Shame, research has shown, is conveyed by specific facial muscle contractions and the visual posture of the person (Hoblitzelle 1987). This can be seen in Jessica's stance toward the world. She averts her eyes continually. She cannot look someone in the eye, even a familiar person, for more than a moment. Jessica is impinged also by troublesome bodily sensations during most interpersonal interactions—she frequently blushes, readily perspires, and is always close to tears. Correspondingly, there are tell-tale signs of shame in her speech—abrupt changes of topic, hesitations, and flat affect.

Jessica's shrinking-back from her full presence in her interpersonal transactions is not only distressing to her. The acute sense of embarrassment and inferiority that she manifests produces negative "vibes"—such as feelings of irritation, annoyance, and flushes of facial warmth and discomfort—in the person she is involved with in a social or business interaction.

Shame is a very contagious emotion. The strong negative reaction that Jessica produces in other people is a very important aspect of shame that clinicians are still learning about. In most events in which shaming occurs, both victim and shamer are mutually being shamed and affected by the other person's innermost feelings. Rarely is either aware of what is adversely affecting them. I refer to this mutual shaming as "the intersubjectivity of shame." Chapter 4 examines this very important concept in detail. However, a common occurrence of mutual shame may be illustrative here.

An ubiquitous manifestation of mutual shame takes place between disappointed lovers. A typical scenario is as follows: the male finds himself having sexual difficulty in a romantic encounter. He physically and emotionally with-

draws, brooding over whether his difficulty is a fluke misfortune or to be his continual future fate. Correspondingly,
he feels angry at his partner because she has "embarrassed" him by witnessing his inability to exhibit masculine
competence. In turn, the female feels humiliated and disregarded. Her lover had begun the romantic interlude by
expressing considerable caring and attraction for her. Now
she feels betrayed. She interprets his impotence as a statement that he actually finds her sexually undesirable. Furthermore, she regards his self-centered brooding as his lack
of concern and interest in her after the sexual moment has
passed.

The Interpersonal Context of Shame and Humiliation

Not surprisingly, the most powerful adult experiences of
being shamed are based upon the types of humiliation that
were suffered during one's tender, developmental years.

Few interpersonal behaviors cause more pain than does
the blaming and shameful reproaches of a parent to a child.
When Paul was 10 years of age, his loud, foulmouthed uncle
asked the child to show him his favorite possession, a small
collection of rare coins. The boorish man grabbed half a
dozen of the child's coins and put them into his pants
pocket. He mocked the boy's dismay, refusing to return the
coins. When told by her sobbing son what had happened,
Paul's mother responded by indicating that he should be
ashamed of himself for being selfish. "After all," she pointed
out, "you have more coins and he *is* your uncle."

Each of us has a "shame button" by which we can be
psychologically manipulated and "blackmailed" (English
1975) into acting in ways that other people want of us.
Leveton (1962) indicated that reproach in family relations is
a form of "pseudo-mutuality," in which the energies of
family members are directed toward maintaining an
appearance of reciprocal fulfillment rather than genuine
caring. Being shamed also can be viewed as one person's

attempt to "shut up" another and force the sufferer to bear
his hurt alone (Edwards 1976). Shame leads to self-
destructive behavior. Suicide is one of the most powerful
statements of being trapped and helpless by feelings of
shame. There was recently a news story that reported that
the Internal Revenue Service had driven a taxpayer to
suicide. His wife claimed that the IRS had taken her
husband's dignity and desire for life away. She said that he
was compelled to take his own life as the only way to escape
the hounding of the government's tax investigators.

The younger and the more often the child is shamed, the
more pliant he becomes to unfair and abusive treatment
from his caretakers. As we shall learn in the next chapter,
shame represents a special fear. It operates similarly to how
instincts for self-preservation function for lower animals.
The issues that evoke shame in the child are experienced as
threatening to the survival of the child at a period of
development in which the child is not capable of an accurate
assessment of reality. During adult shaming the person
returns to the feelings of fear of abandonment by his caretakers that he experienced as a child. At that excruciatingly
painful moment—whether in adulthood or childhood, the
shamed person feels small, helpless, and worthless. Time
seems large and endless. He experiences no way to escape,
because he senses no moment in the future when he expects
to be beyond the present painful moment.

For Paul, being called "selfish" was his shame button.
Following his mother's scolding he no longer consciously
pursued the matter of the stolen coins. Nevertheless, he felt
miserable for many months after the hurtful incident, but
was not able to associate his upset feelings with the coin
incident and his mother's reproach.

SHAME AND FEELINGS OF INARTICULATENESS

Those who were made to feel powerless and incapable of
fair exchanges with significant others tend to perpetuate
these feelings into contemporary relations (Goldberg 1977).
Shame-imbued people are not able to conceive of being part

of relationships, or even interactions, that are characterized by mutual respect, compassion, and decency (Potter-Efron and Potter-Efron 1989).

One's capacity to deal openly and fairly with others is dependent, of course, upon one's awareness and understanding of one's own emotions. Steinberg and Nussbaum, despite their high intelligence and well-rounded education, seem to have been mystified by their own emotions. Brownmiller's (1989) discussion on the backgrounds of Steinberg and Nussbaum suggests that feelings were not openly discussed in their homes when they were growing up. The same was true in Paul's home. As a result, none of these people may have been able to comprehend accurately what they were actually feeling. When they were in pain they were incapable of expressing their needs to someone who could help. Parenthetically, if socially articulate people like Steinberg and Nussbaum cannot express their despair in such a way as to secure caring, imagine how difficult is the plight of children raised in multiple-problem families by physically and emotionally abusing parents. We can be certain of one thing, however. These children share and, undoubtedly, exceed, the frustration, rage, and despair of Steinberg and Nussbaum.

DEBILITATING SHAME AS A FEELING OF LACK OF HUMANNESS

People who are highly prone to pathological shame have grown up believing that they are not fully human. They have been treated by significant people in their lives as if their "true" self and their judgment of what is right and wrong were defective and flawed. This deprives them of feelings of personal power and entitlement to proper treatment from others. Hedda Nussbaum did not feel she had the right to complain or protest Steinberg's treatment of her. People who are shame-debilitated are often overly responsible and feel the need to behave more considerately and more conscientiously toward others than do other people toward them. For example, they become quite anxious if they are not punctually on time for appointments. They keep unrealistic promises at considerable inconvenience to themselves. They believe, without conscious realization, that other people don't genuinely care about them. Consequently, they assume that only by going to a great deal of trouble for others will other people, out of pity or guilt, respond to their needs. If people don't feel fully human, they tend to regard those from whom they desire attention and caring as having more personal resources than they do. This is to say, they assume that other people have more self-esteem, more social skills, and, above all, more interpersonal options than they have. Thus, when questioned about how she felt about Joel Steinberg's mistreatment of her, Hedda Nussbaum initially conveyed the sense that it didn't matter. In Chapter 4, I discuss the conditions in the personal development of people like Hedda Nussbaum, those who have retarded their rightful human legacy for feeling competent and desirable. I have labeled these feelings the concept of "legitimate entitlement."

Hiding from Shame

Shame is one of the most devastating interpersonal weapons a person can use to influence or punish someone else. Consequently, shame is the direct cause, and humiliation the vehicle, of destruction that infuses intimate relationships that become fearful, business transactions that turn contemptuous, and cooperative endeavors that prove unworkable.

Although shame events occur suddenly and are often quickly repressed, the experience can cause long-lasting effects, especially for shame-vulnerable people. Paul has had trouble trusting people all of his adult life. His frequent angry altercations with fellow workers have cost him many jobs. Yet, Paul has not been aware of what makes him so tense and easily annoyed in almost every situation that requires his depending upon and trusting another person. If he were aware of how sensitive he is to being betrayed by people, he would undoubtedly be in a better position to understand and to handle the troublesome feelings that cause him to pick fights and to create distance from people.

Hiding from shame means hiding from one's self. Our Socratic doctrine as therapists tells us that a person cannot be free if he doesn't know himself.

There are serious societal ramifications to the secrecy and cover-ups that result from shame. Recent psychiatric studies have reported some disturbing findings. These pioneering studies have found a surprisingly high rate of emotional illness in young children. In fact, as many as 20 percent of the children studied were afflicted with serious psychiatric problems, sufficient enough to impair the normal course of their lives (Costello et al. 1988).

What is most distressing about these psychiatric findings is the realization that the majority of the parents of the disturbed children were unaware that their child was having serious psychological difficulties. The investigators report that the children who were being studied were not confiding in their parents about the problems that most concerned them.

I will cite a specific example from another source. Consider the John Hinckley family. They were shocked to receive a telephone call some years ago informing them that their son had tried to assassinate President Reagan. They had always believed that their son was afraid of guns. In fact, the sight of a shot and wounded animal had always upset him. The Hinckley family could hardly be called unintelligent, mean, or uncaring. They were well-educated, cultured, affluent, and, reportedly, deeply involved in family life. Yet, what is evident is that they had no grasp of the awful depths of their son's rage and despair. Hinckley's shame withheld his agitated emotions from his parents. Even his psychiatrist was unable to recognize his actual clinical state (Hinckley and Hinckley 1985). It is my impression that clinicians too frequently label as "depression" or "phobia" behaviors that are actually untreated, chronic

feelings of shame and despair. Without more adequately
understanding pathological shame we will fail to properly
fashion appropriate treatment for its symptoms.

Not being able to understand what drives certain people
to violence, we regard them as aberrants. Yet, to claim that
disturbed people like John Hinckley, Jr., Joel Steinberg,
and Roy, the patient I discuss in Chapter 12, are psychological and moral mysteries is an unfortunate clinical cop-out.
They are not mysteries. However, what is true is that most
people, too often, do not know about others' suffering until it
is too late to help.

It should be evident by now that pathological shame is
both a crucial cause of human suffering, and at the same
time, a silencing vehicle that keeps the misery a secret,
unavailable to those who may be in a position to help. The
reasons for this are examined in the chapters to follow. In
this book I discuss the cultural "conspiracy" against recognizing shame. There are numerous, powerful forces in society today that serve to deny us the recognition of what
truly ails us. I will cite four sources now and discuss them
later in the book. Freud and his guilty-conscience theory has
already been mentioned. Second, there are societal agents
in positions of power and affluence who recognize that
people work more productively when they feel guilty. They
use subtle shaming manipulations to induce guilt. Third, we
live in a society that is laden with strong themes of humiliation and shame: from infancy onward, children are pushed
to hone a competitive edge in our highly achievement-
oriented society. They are tutored how to be best suited for
academic, social, and athletic competition. Even those who
succeed may be preoccupied with the fear of being less
competent and achievement-successful than are others.
Toys, educational aids, tutoring, exercises, and parental
exhortation are provided to prevent the child from the
shame of failure.

Television commercials may be the best gauge of our
current social values and attitudes. It would be difficult not
to be aware that television uses persistent "shame persua-

sion" in trying to get viewers to buy their products. The messages that these commercials imply is that the consumer who doesn't use the advertised products is unattractive, ignorant, inadequate, and out of step with the times.

Fourth, modern technology, which has done much to bring relief from physical pain, has, at the same time, hindered time-proven ways of coping with and healing emotional wounds. Chapter 7 examines our cultural taboo against commiseration. The frequent stories we hear of patients who require dialysis or some other expensive medical procedure but are ashamed of being a burden and, instead, take their own lives, are victims of their own shame and society's insensitivity to the devastation of shame on vulnerable people.

In this first chapter I have shown the numerous, subtle, and generally unrecognized ways shame significantly informs daily life. I have related the effects of shame to its manifestations in how people sense their personal identity. As psychotherapists, the influences and vicissitudes of our patients' personal identity are the foci of our daily clinical endeavors.

2

THE CORRIDORS OF CHILDHOOD SHAME

> Malice like lust, when it is at its height, does not know shame.
>
> —Lord Halifax

Unlike Erikson (1950) and the general current of psychoanalytic theory, I do not believe that the crucial conditions for the formation of shame are found in any specific life phase. Shame may and does occur in every stage of human development. Moreover, there appears to be no distinct, common, source for the acquisition of shame.

Shame, as we shall learn in this chapter, has to do with strains in the caring reciprocity of parent and child. The young child is almost entirely dependent upon an exact correspondence of his voracious needs and the attentiveness of a warm, approving, nurturing caretaker twenty-four hours a day. No parent, of course, could fulfill such a demanding obligation. There are reasonable limitations in the capacity to be always there for one's child—even for a dearly loved and cherished little person. Shame, therefore, is an inevitable consequence of having been thrust into the world and suffering disappointments in having needs met. We may refer to this shame as the "normal shame" of living. However, when we speak of "debilitating shame," we are

designating hurts and disappointments—that began in the
required reciprocity of parent and child—that exceed the
reasonable limitations to human responsiveness and caring.

We shall learn in further chapters that what makes
shame in a person debilitating is not that there were faults in
the early caretaking relationship. This is a lead-off condition. It is not a fixed finality for being shame-bound, however. Debilitating shame is the result of shame-sensitive
people colluding with those who humiliate and shame them
on an ongoing and, often, daily basis.

The original sources for the painful hurts and disappointments are numerous.

Many severely shame-prone people emerge from critical
and unresponsive families. Others are marked shamefully
by painful disregard by playmates, classmates, teachers,
and other authority figures outside of the home. Still others
react humiliatingly to the physical and emotional intimida-
tions of lovers and spouses. Some even appear to have a
genetic predisposition to being shy and easily embarrassed.

A Reappraisal of the Occurrence of Shame

Whereas shame may occur at any point in life, because of
its influence on the further development of the self, it is
important to ascertain when it initially occurs for each
person. The earlier that we trace back the presence of shame
in any of our patients, of course, the greater is the period of
time that shame has cast its decisive influence upon the
significant formative periods of personality development of
that person (Natanson 1987b).

Due to disagreements about what shame is, there is still
considerable controversy among psychoanalysts and developmental psychologists about when shame first appears in
human development. In my view, shame responses may be
present in some of the earliest moments of the infant's life.
This view is in sharp contrast to Freud's statements about
the formation of shame symptoms.

In *The Interpretation of Dreams*, Freud (1900) portrays

an unashamed period of childhood bliss that seems like paradise. In this psychic world the infant bounds free and uninhibited. Time stands still in paradise. To the infant and the very young child the "now" is forever. They are aware of only the immediate moment. Having no sense of tomorrow, the unanxious sense of limitless experience conveys an exuberance of ecstasy.

Freud (1905) wrote that the period of uninhibited wonder and delight is not long-lasting, however. The feelings of shyness, inhibition, and embarrassment awaken the child from paradise. These suppressive feelings, we are told, come from the anticipation of loss of love from significant people in the child's life, if phallic and narcissistic exhibitionism aren't curbed. These barriers of shame and disgust are reinforced by the disciplinary actions of those to whom is entrusted the child's education (Straus 1966).

Freud (1930) refers to a second cause of shamefulness in the child. This motive has phylogenetic implications for the survival of the human species. Freud speculated that early in the development of the human race feelings of embarrassment, shyness, and modesty served instinctually to protect the reproductive organs of the species from attack by dangerous strangers. In this sense, being seen nude is risky because it exposes the vulnerable organs of procreation to potential attack. Feelings of embarrassment, shyness, and modesty, therefore, are anxiety signals to alert us to protect the continuity of the human species.

Some psychoanalytic theorists and developmental psychologists have been skeptical as to whether the behavior described by Freud is indeed shame. Shame, they contend, involves a process of the self in danger. This occurs in the transactions of developmental or traumatic instability of the boundaries between self and other. In defending against the threat of invasion of displeased and disapproving others, the self uses a feeling of shame as a vigilant signal (Wurmser 1981). Since Darwin (1872), the negative emotion of shame has been regarded as the consequence of an accentuated awareness of self.

Can there be an experience of shame, critics of Freud's theory of shame question, before a sense of selfhood is clearly differentiated from that of the world of others?

Phylogenetic instincts and defensive reactions in protection of the integrity of the self are two very different responses. One is supposedly built into the human organism, while the other matures over time.

We need to ask, therefore, at what point in human development does self-consciousness distinctly emerge in the child. Research on the mirroring image, such as done by Amsterdam (1972), informs us that self-reflective processes by the infant, as manifested in such behaviors as self-admiration, embarrassment, withdrawal, and so forth, start at about age 14 months and are exhibited by about 75 percent of the infants by the twentieth month of life. This kind of evidence has been taken to mean that shame reactions are scarcely possible in the first year of life.

However, it needs to be pointed out that there is a fundamental epistemological error in assuming that shame doesn't develop before the second year of life because a coherent sense of self has not yet clearly emerged. Broucek (in press) points out that the error results from not clearly differentiating experiences of self-awareness from those of a sense of self-hood.

We now have empirical evidence to support Tompkins' (1962) contention that the young infant has the capacity for organizing its own experiences. Tompkins has put forth the thesis that *affects*, rather than instinctual drives present at birth, are the primary organizing forces in human personality.

Support for Tompkins' view comes from the careful and extensive work of Stern and his associates (1985), who have shown that infants are organizing beings, capable of at least some self-regulatory self-processes from their earliest moment of life (although their capacity for higher forms of self-consciousness may not occur until the second year of life). In other words, infant experiences described by the eminent psychologist/philosopher William James as "the busy, buzzing, booming" of a chaotic world is poetic, but probably misleading.

Just what is the infant's capacity for self-governing behavior, and what are the implications for these processes on the development of shame? Stern and his associates (1985) have found a process occurring between parent and infant, that they call "affect attunement," that allows an infant to take into account how he is perceived by the parent.

From the early months of the infant's life, the compelling attraction of the probe of the mother's face may take on such captivation for the child as to constitute a motivational need state for the child's existence (Stern 1985). It is characterized by "the desire to be known by and to know another, to be understood by and to understand another" (Shane and Shane 1989, p. 63) and in so doing share intimacy and strong feelings with another.

According to Stern's schemata, the parent nonverbally "reflects back" to the infant the child's own gestures and behaviors. The infant uses the parent's face to see himself as perceived by another. Of course, the feedback is never neutral. The parent's face also contains judgments of how the child is being regarded by the parent. The child uses the confounded expressions on the parent's face in order to monitor his own behavior. In turn, the child responds to the reception of his behavior on the parent's face with affect of his own. For example, in scanning the mother's face and finding an affect of displeasure and disapproval, the 3- or 4-month-old may react to the mother's expression and accompanying gestures with shame-affect on his own face.

Tompkins' (1962) work indicates that a very crucial arena for the child's feeling discounted (shamed) comes from finding an incongruence between his own feelings of excitement and joy and what is expressed on the parent's face. The discordance between his own experiences and those of the parent have been found to effect a break in the child's willingness to communicate and interact.

What is the child's shameful withdrawal about? It is probably due to the traumatic impact of loss of emotional attunement between the child and the parent. Ainsworth and Wittig (1969) have described the crying that occurs in infants who are separated from their mothers as "outraged crying." This behavior seems to be an early representation of the "humiliation-rage" syndrome that characterizes adult responses to unrecognized shame (to be discussed in the next chapter).

Bowlby (1969) has shown that the infant's need for the warmth of the mother is of as fundamental importance to the child's well-being as that of food and protection. The loss of contact with the mother results in what Bowlby has described as the infant's "bitter protest."

Losses of any kind seem to evoke shamelike responses in the infant. This is particularly true of *loss of the familiar*. One of the clearest examples of this is what is now called "stranger anxiety." Spitz (1965) describes his observations of 6- to 8-month-old infants as follows:

> If a stranger approaches him, this will release an unmistakable, characteristic and typical behavior in the child; he shows varying intensities of apprehension or anxiety and rejects the stranger. . . . He may lower his eyes "shyly," he may cover them with his hands, lift his dress to cover the face, throw himself prone on his cot and hide his face in the blankets, he may weep or scream. The common denominator is a refusal of contact, a turning away, with a shading, more or less of anxiety. . . . I have called this pattern the *eight-month-anxiety* and consider it the earliest manifestation of *anxiety proper.* [p. 150]

Natanson (1987b) has cogently responded to Spitz's observation and noted:

> Unless one is burdened by a theory that says shame cannot appear for another year or so, it is difficult to conceptualize shyness, lowered eyes and the (pathognomic for shame) action of hiding the face as anything but shame. The eight-month child may

exhibit distress or fear when first placed in contact with a new adult, but only after repeated episodes of the pattern described by Spitz have sensitized the infant to expect a specific type of noxious experience with a stranger. The infant decides to curtail communication because not everyone is mother, the primary mirror and communicant for his or her affective transmission. If we analyze the data without bias, Spitz seems to be describing a primary form of anticipatory shame, incorrectly labelled "anxiety." [p. 7]

Benjamin (1963) has shown that infantile stranger-anxiety has its first clear appearance at ages varying from 5 to 13 months, with a mean of 7 months.

To this coterie of findings, Broucek (1982) has added the fascinating consideration that if strangers can trigger off shame anxiety in the infant, then so too can the mother. If the mother responds in an unfamiliar way to her infant, she undoubtedly will evoke the same signals of danger that a stranger will arouse.

We can summarize the finding on the influence of self-consciousness and shame by indicating that early experiences of shaming in the infant are moments (or just representations) of the loss of the safe-and-certain in the infant. Feelings of shame monitor the infant's relationship with significant, loving, and protective others. The anxiety of shame provides a sense of danger to the infant's physical and emotional safety. In short, the experience of shame comes from a threat to the infant of its loving bonds to its environment, particularly its caretakers.

GINA'S STORY

In the following vignette an examination is given to the role of the absent mother in the reinforcement of debilitating shame that exacerbated faults in the child's early mother–child bonding.

Gina has an enchanting face. Graced with the type of sullen lips and dark, mysterious eyes that inspire flamenco cantatas, her features captivate attention. Despite her ostensible allure, Gina's interest in her appearance ceased abruptly in her adolescence. Frightened by the vacant countenance staring back at her in the glass, Gina never again looked directly and intently into a mirror. She abstains from any activity requiring prolonged attention to her appearance. In locating facial blemishes and other concerns of her external presence, her gaze focuses only on a portion of her image at one time.

Gina, at the time she consulted me for psychoanalysis, was in her early thirties and living with a severely disturbed mother. Without warning, her mother had deserted her when Gina was 5 years of age. She desperately searched for her mother for many years. Only briefly before she began analysis was Gina able to locate her, and to bring her mother into her secluded Greenwich Village apartment. Unfortunately, finding her mother did not put Gina's fears to rest. Gina's desire for human company was considerable, but her mistrust of other people's motives was far more intense.

Gina tried to shield herself from the terror of being taken by surprise by people by continually having her phone answering machine turned on, even when she was at home. In this arrangement, she did not have to speak on the phone to anyone without knowing beforehand who the caller was and the purpose of the phone call.

For troubled people like Gina, the subterfuge of a concealing mirror is required, in order for them to risk contact with other people. Protective mirrors may take various forms (Goldberg 1991a).

Gina's voice on her phone message had become her double, a second self (Simon and Goldberg 1984), which was for many callers the only image of Gina available to them. In a way, the voice on the message was more real than was Gina herself. The message, however, remained constant, unaffected by her feeling states. It was presented to the world of others so that Gina could remain hidden and undisclosed. The cost of her deception was Gina's increasing loss of contact with others and the resultant loneliness and desperation she experienced in her life. Like the earlier vacant expression she found in the mirror, the increasing emptiness of her life frightened Gina and brought her to consult me for analysis.

My own work as an analyst makes abundantly evident that the earliest and most basic aim of social behavior is the striving for intimate relations with a caring other person (Goldberg 1991a). The capacity for intimacy develops in the infant by means of the mother's mirroring function. This is to say, the mother serves as a representative of how other people in subsequent years will respond to the child. However, the mirror between mother and child is a two-way affair. Intimate connectedness is a mechanism of survival for the child. The infant who appropriately responds to what the mother wants and requires of the child is more adaptive in pleasing her and more likely to be rewarded by her caring behavior than is the less responsive child. Reciprocally, the mother's smile evokes pleased responsiveness from the child because her countenance gives the child a sense of being present and cared about. In other words, the child needs to be looked at, smiled at, and approved of by an active, loving, and supportive person. Without this emotional nurturance, people such as Gina experience the world as persecutory and regard parts of themselves as unacceptable. In short, people who are subjected in childhood to an unresponsive or distorted mirroring relationship with significant people in their life will be handicapped to a greater or lesser degree in the capacity to experience their inner being freely, creatively, and courageously.

THE THREE BONDING OPTIONS
THE MOTHER MAY PROVIDE

Let us now examine more closely Gina's mother's role during their bonding in fostering Gina's disturbed sense of self.

I will set the stage for the examination of Gina's relationship with her mother by briefly indicating what we know about the early mother–child bonding relationship. Evidence from developmental studies clearly indicates that the child learns to recognize himself or herself in the eyes and facial expressions of the mother. Prototypically, the mother offers her child one of three very distinct and important options in relatedness. In their early relationship, the child may be given unrestricted *permission* by the mother to look into her depths *through* her eyes and by means of her facial expressions. By so doing, she metaphorically gives access into the mysteries of the mother's psyche. The child's witnessing of the mother's relationship with her own depths allows the child to have a relationship with the mystery of another person.

In sharp contrast with the first option, the child may be provided the opportunity of only looking *at* her eyes and facial expressions and, as a consequence, only be allowed to perceive his or her reflection as the mother's restrictive view of the child. When a mother is troubled, as was Gina's, and she tries to hide her fears and limitations from her child, she is more wont to relate to the child by controlling the child's responsiveness to her. By fearfully withholding her mystery from him or her, she simultaneously discourages her child from trusting his or her own psyche as a place to find beauty and inner contentment. Those inner psychic urges that the child will have access to will be experienced as painful and troublesome.

In the third option, the mother allows her child into her depths. But, in the process, she overwhelms the child with her anxieties and fears. She treats her child as if he or she were her own imaginary parent, there to assuage her loneliness and desperation. Because she does not recognize the child as separate from her, or even as real, she does not allow the child freedom to have his or her own mystery.

I am proposing that open intimacy between mother and child in their early bonding requires the mother's ability to be intimate with her own depths. She must be willing to struggle with, or at least not to deny aspects of her totality as a person. Significant in their relationship, therefore, is the child's witnessing the mother's fortitude in bearing pain and suffering in her caring functions.

Gina's mother, at the time of her disappearance, was pregnant with a second child. The mother was anguished about whether she was capable of giving love and caring to another child. Apparently, she felt that she could not. Without a word of explanation to her husband or to Gina, she left the house one morning to have a secret abortion. Unable to openly face the shame of her furtive deed, she did not return home in Gina's childhood. For many years Gina awoke nightly from perturbing nightmares, replete with self-recriminating scenarios of the possible ways that she was responsible for her mother's disappearance. Only after locating her mother, 25 years later, did Gina learn of the circumstances and reasons for her disappearance.

Children who are denied the open, inner being of their mother for identification of their own psychic experience will be in continual search of external mirrors—other people and "objective" reflections, such as glass mirrors and photographs, in order to find who they are. Of primary concern, they seek experiences that will reflect acceptable parts of themselves, thereby validating and justifying their existence. This relates to the role shame plays in the development of a sense of personal competence.

The great difficulty people like Gina have in concealing troublesome aspects of themselves is what Gina actually fears is not yet apparent in her reflection. Suffering was for Gina seeing her own youthful beauty and simultaneously realizing the impermanence of her outward appearance. The fearful question Gina posed for the mirror before turning away from the reflective glass was whether it could depict what is inside her, but cannot yet be seen by the naked eyes of others. For many of us the reality of our eventual diminution of our vitality and its resultant suffering does not become confirmed until evidence of its symptoms are recognized by other people. Because of the magical belief that mirrors have the propensity to evoke unseen aspects of oneself, the fear one may have of the mirror is the fear of what is yet to be.

Yet, mirrors hold great fascination for most of us. It is essential to our understanding of the role of the mirror in the development of a sense of personal identity that we need to recognize that one of the most important psychological qualities of the mirror for many people is magically assuming that the mirror has the capacity to transcend and even supplant physical veracity. The mirror reflects not only how we appear; we may beg the question of what is or what we fear may be and, in collaboration with the mirror, ask instead how we should appear. Indeed, the phenomenon of the mirror poses the question, "What is real?" The gazer and the mirror may enter into a magical relationship in which aspects or even the whole self are subject to reinvention or change. The hope that we can reverse the natural course of life by means of a special relationship with our mirror comes from the recognition that mirrors, after all, are never absolute. Not only does each mirror have its own peculiar characteristics, but each mirror as well is influenced to some extent by its surroundings. Move a mirror to another room and the light in each place changes what is reflected in the mirror. Each of us has his or her favorite room and own preferred hour to visit the mirror in the hope of finding reflected what each of us wishes to invent of ourselves.

For most people mirrors are an inseparable part of their endeavor to make sense of who they are. For shame-debilitated people like Gina, an inner sense of deficit and worthlessness contaminates the reflective glass. Gina, therefore, was forced to switch from a glass to a recording mirror in order to retain her sense of self-worth.

In order not to become overcome and demoralized by our vulnerability to suffering, we fashion through the years an image of ourselves that conceals our doubts and insecurities. This is the face we present to the world and to ourselves. Like Gina, people avoid gazing into mirrors when they feel most vulnerable to self-doubts. Peering beyond one's ostensible self feels dangerous because probing one's mirror raises disquieting questions in one's self as to who one really is.

What I have stated so far depicts the insidious aspects of the mirror in human experience. Yet, the most remarkable feature of the mirror is its reversibility. Not only can mirrors baldly reveal our flaws; they can also conceal them. Gina utilized her mirror in an attempt to hide her narcissistic vulnerability, this is to say, her realization that her beauty would eventually vanish. She switched from a glass mirror to that of a voice mirror in the magical hope of preserving her presence—her lovely, youthful voice for all time. Gina wished to believe that as long as some aspect of her beauty remained constant, she would not have to examine the troublesome and vulnerable parts of herself. She tried desperately to believe that her beauty justified all efforts to eschew anything about herself that was ugly, untoward, and deficient. Gina's case demonstrates that the price one may pay for being mirrored in any of its manifestations is that, at times, the mirror may reflect an untoward and threatening representation of one's self. These adverse reflections may evoke terror and dread in the person being given his or her similitude. Those like Gina, who prior to and throughout a long period of her analysis, would not or could not share these terrors with others, are forced to suffer their terrors alone (Goldberg 1989a).

BASIC TRUST AND THE DEVELOPMENT OF COMPETENCE

The child is a growing being, capable of complex motivational and creative complexity. Correspondingly, with the need for the safe and the familiar is the child's desire for autonomy and competence. The achievement of maturity, autonomy, and competence in the child is built upon the trust, support, and goodwill of his caretakers in the child's ventures into the world outside the home. A sense of trust needs to be established by the child early in life. Erikson (1950) tells us that this "basic trust" must exceed a sense of mistrust if the child is to enter the larger world with a feeling of confidence and goodwill. When this basic trust is present the child is willing to make bridges of mutuality with others. When mistrust has been a prominent theme in the child's life, the child will not surrender the primary defenses of shame as vigilence to the need for the safe and the familiar.

When Angela was 6 years of age, her "warm, loving" grandfather, a man who chased whatever skirt crossed his path, enticed the trusting young child to his dark basement. First he told her that she was pretty and he loved her. Next, he removed her panties and commented on her immature physical development. Then, he sexually fondled her and left her in the dark. He told her that the family would abandon her if she ever spoke of the incident.

Angela is now an actress who has considerable difficulty developing her artistic talents. She is not able to find acting coaches and drama mentors that she can trust for more than a brief while. Shame has a *sponsorship* with other emotions. This is true even when there is no actual shaming going on. Since Angela was so painfully shamed by the person she had trusted without question, situations that require her reliance on other people for help with important aspects of her personal identity foster intense shame.

Initially, shame-sensitive people experience shame and anxiety only in the presence of specific people with whom they have shaming relationships. However, once a person starts to feel shame on a regular basis in a relationship with a specific person, the likelihood is that he will feel so ashamed of himself that he will lose the ability to command or even to experience respect for almost anyone else.

Child abuse is a crisis in trust between a child and an adult who has violated a caretaking position with the child. The experience is painfully shameful because it violently conveys to the child that his personal power against environmental intrusion is quite limited. He is forced to recognize that his body, mind, and spirit are controlled by others, not himself. And in so doing, it undermines the victim's sense of legitimate entitlement to take proper care of himself.

DISCRETION SHAME

We are valuing, judging, social beings. We require association with people whose sense of pride, commitment, and goodwill correspond with our own if we are to feel that our time spent with others has been meaningfully expended. We feel humiliated and shamed in observing others treated as "replaceable," perhaps, no less, than when we, ourselves, are treated this way.

When Larry was 6 years of age, his stern and exacting European music teacher chased him out of class. Larry was told that he couldn't carry a tune. Larry never sang in public again. As a child in school he lowered his head in embarrassment each morning as he stood with his classmates, who were singing "The Star-Spangled Banner." Obstinately, Larry did not sing a word. Yet, silently he hoped that someone would rescue him by telling him that his voice was not displeasing. Larry did not have the right words to directly request this liberation. Unfortunately, the adults who observed Larry regarded him as shy and felt that they were doing him the best service by letting him alone. They turned to other children who were more joyous and less inhibited than Larry.

Children quite regularly get involved in activities and enterprises that are difficult and humiliating to them. The nature of the activity is rarely the important factor. What is crucial, however, is the caretaker's willingness to respond to the child's upset with caring and concern. Humiliating caretakers behave as if the child's pain is a fault of the child (Edwards 1976). The experience of shame is felt by the child because his needs and feelings are only of resentful concern to his caretakers. The anxiety of shame warns the child to suppress strong feelings and needs because they are dangerous to his harmonious existence with his caretakers. From continual suppression the child loses touch with his own feelings.

Fortunately, this was not true for Larry. As an adult Larry has become a psychotherapist. His work has focused on shy and neglected children. He has become an eloquent advocate on their behalf, teaching them how to gain more effectively the responsiveness they require from their care-takers.

The Inculcation of Shame Experiences

Normal shame experiences of living occur prior to language development. Being preverbal, they become internalized into the self by means of *imagery* rather than by conceptual language. Kaufman and Raphael (1984a) indicate, "Identification is a visual process. What we see and observe transfers inside the self through the medium of visual imagery. These internal images, derived from interpersonal experience, are the basis of the self's developing relationship with the self" (p. 241).

Shame experiences that are incurred after the development of language skills involve both words and pictures. Each shaming experience in the oedipal and post-oedipal periods has an *interpretive script* that attempts to explain the reason for having been shamed.

Tompkins (1978) indicates that the script deals "with the individual's rules for predicting, interpreting, responding to and controlling a magnified set of scenes that comprise the plot of the individual's life" (p. 217).

Interpretive scripts, which translate the scenes and the plot of one's life, demonstrating that one is an incompetent and unworthy person, castigate and devalue the ashamed by means of a contemptuous *negative inner voice* (Firestone 1988). This voice has been scripted and internalized from among the myriad of interactions with parents and significant figures in one's past. When one is shamed as an adult, one is emotionally drawn back into the childhood scenes, imbued with interpretative scripts and a negative inner voice that warns the ashamed that self-respect, competence, and pride are not his lot in life.

Kris (1990) recently has written about the cognitive and defensive mechanisms involved in shame that reflect unconscious self-criticism. "Typically, because of their characteristic all-or-none, black-or-white, either-or attitudes, such patients assume that if they are in any way culpable then they are totally culpable. To avoid this experience, they employ strong defensive mechanisms (repression, denial, and projection)" (p. 620).

BIOCHEMICAL-GENETIC DISPOSITION FOR SHAME

There seems to be some evidence that there are genetic differences in the emotional responsiveness to situations that arouse shame. From its earliest days, the infant has a characteristic temperament (Thomas et al. 1970). Cattell (1965) holds that some forms of shame, such as shyness, are due to biologically determined temperaments, which develop a sympathetic nervous system that is highly responsive to conflict and stress. A sensitivity to shame may begin with a *constitutional* predisposition to overstimulation. The way some infants and children internalize their experience of shame-potential events may differ them from other children. They may be more threatened by separation from parents and feel more inadequate and insufficient in carrying on for themselves autonomously than are other children. This means that they may become more anxious and concerned about the familiar than are others. They might, as a consequence, experience the signal anxiety of shame before other children do.

There are recent studies of importance to the issue of the precursors of shame. Work by LeDoux (1989) suggests the reason for the inarticulateness of shame may be due to its emergence prior to the development of the hypothalamus and hippocampus of the brain. LeDoux's studies suggest that the brain is arranged so that key aspects of emotional life, like primitive fears, can operate largely independent of thought. Accordingly, since certain emotional reactions occur before the brain has even time to fully register what it is that is causing the reaction, emotional input is experienced before cognition. This view is a direct challenge to the prevailing wisdom that emotional reaction follows from thoughts about a situation. A considerable amount of learning apparently takes place during the first two years of life; yet, one has little if any conscious recall from those years. Once the emotional system incorporates an event it may never let go of it. Shame experiences may be such events. As a consequence, shame that is chemically and biologically determined or occurs before cognition may be unresponsive to psychological treatment. Natanson (1987b) is of this view. He believes that affective disorders like shame debilitation are characterized by the striving of normal psychological mechanisms to deal with neurophysiological disorders. He suggests that psychopharmaceutical agents are the treatment of choice for these affective disorders. More empirical investigation is needed to determine the best clinical approach to biologically caused shame sensitivity.

3

SHAME, THE MASTER EMOTION

Guilt lames the human animal; shame stops him
dead.

—Ernest Becker

A young child entered his mother's bathroom and found in
the sink his mother's panties covered with blotches of blood.
The child became upset and frightened. He feared that the
red stains had come from a physical attack on his mother.

An oedipal interpretation of this incident would explain
the child's untoward reaction as his fear of castration punishment for harboring incestuous thoughts about his
mother. In contrast, a clinician who recognized the significance of the role of shame in human conflict might account
for his fearful reaction as the child's shocking realization
that his mother was vulnerable. She was limited in the ways
she could take care of herself, and him as well. As his
mother's child, he feared that he, too, was vulnerable and
incapable of taking care of other people.

The shame that is normally part of one's life usually does
not come from someone's intentional meanness or even
their ill-wishes. Ironically, most of the hurtful shame that we
are usually involved in comes from *our inability to protect
those we care about,* including ourselves. As the anecdote

43

above suggests, individuals harbor feelings of shame when they feel like a helpless observer of a grievous event. The inability to avert illness in one's self or to change the morbid fate of those one cares about leaves a person feeling impotent.

GUILT AND SHAME

Shame is the most complex and least understood emotion that the human race has yet evolved. Darwin (1872) regarded shame as the parent emotion in a cluster of closely related emotions that serve to preserve the human species by responding to potential dangers in the environment with rapid and strong reaction. I agree with the place of centrality that Darwin gave to shame. We will fail to understand the importance of shame if we miss its orchestrational role in the emotional patterns and vicissitudes of both conflictual and healthy functioning.

The logical place to begin to recognize how shame relates to other emotions is by comparing its properties and functions with those of guilt. Theorists have had difficulty in doing this. Shame traditionally has been confusingly interchanged with guilt (Goldberg 1988a). Freud's own writings about shame are not free from contradictions and ambiguities. He often did not clearly distinguish among the affects of shame, disgust, and guilt (Yorke et al. 1990). Therefore, it is important that we clearly distinguish the properties and functions of these emotions from each other in this book.

Spero (1984), in reviewing the psychoanalytic literature on shame, points to five reasons for conceptual problems in differentiating shame and guilt:

1. Guilt and shame are, by their very nature, susceptible to both additive and reversible reactions to one another. This is to say, shame often evokes guilt reactions and vice versa. Moreover, shame may be disguised, denied, or bypassed by a host of subtle psychic mechanisms. For example, some people with a particularly tenuous self-regard cannot tolerate even the slightest sense of shame and,

unwittingly, convert being humiliated into feelings of irrational guilt and self-doubt (Lewis 1971).

2. Phenomenological reports of guilt and shame are highly variable. Many theorists see no advantage in making a distinction between guilt and shame or the other variants of shame, such as chagrin, embarrassment, mortification, and humiliation. Tompkins' (1962) influential theory takes this position.

3. Some theorists have rejected Piers and Singer's (1953) formulation that shame is a product of the tension between the ego and the ego-ideal, while, in contrast, guilt results from conflict between the ego and the superego. The theoretical rejection of Piers and Singer's conceptualization of shame seems to result from the difficulty distinguishing the ego-ideal from that of the superego. Fenichel (1945) indicates that the powers of the ego-ideal and the superego "are as intermingled as were the protecting and threatening powers of the parents" (p. 106). Instead of Piers and Singer's formulation, many theorists continue to regard shame as the superego's condemnation of unbound instinctual strivings.

4. There is considerable controversy as to whether shame is a depressive defense or an affect of signal anxiety. Moreover, there is also theoretical uncertainty whether shame is only an inhibitory emotion, or whether it also functions as an inducement for constructive interpersonal relating.

5. There are disagreements in regard to the relative importance of shame in the various phases of psychosexual development.

The conceptual difficulties noted above could have been more easily resolved had psychoanalysis developed a sound theory of affects (Natanson 1987b). This chapter is an endeavor in this direction by demonstrating the interrelationship of shame and other emotions—both those that are regarded as healthy and creative and those that are defensive and disordered. Table 3–1 provides a summary of the significant differences between guilt and shame that I will examine in the chapters to follow. Helen Block Lewis's

TABLE 3–1.

Salient Characteristics of Shame and Guilt

Central trait	Shame	Guilt
Stimulus	Threat against integrity of self-identity: being treated as inferior, being defeated, feeling disappointed, feeling lack of self-esteem, committing a moral transgression	Committing a moral transgression for which the self feels responsible
Feeling state	Feeling state is strongly aroused, although the affect may not be conscious. The feeling is always self-referential	A corresponding feeling state to the event is not intrinsic to the judgment of guilt. For example, to be guilty is not required to feel guilty; nor is not feeling guilty always due to not being guilty
Primary affect	Inadequacy, deficiency, worthlessness, being exposed, disgusted, disgraced	Feeling bad, evil, wicked, remorseful, responsible
Conscious content of thought	Painful emotion, autonomous responses, rage, blushing, tears, sense of identity threatened, repetitive reviewing and recasting of the event	Not bound to sense of identity, fewer autonomous responses, affect may or may not be present, courses of action to address guilt are rehearsed

Physiology	The body is the central object of the experience; overt manifestations of the affect are difficult to conceal or control	Symptoms can be more easily concealed and controlled than with shame
Facial involvement	Shame expressions apparent: facial blush, eyes cast down, body pulled in and downward	Symptoms may not be apparent
Serious characteristic symptoms	Secretiveness and severe shyness, depression, hysteria, affective lability (such as rage), susceptibility to feelings of guilt	Obsessional problems, paranoia, thought confusion
Onset of the precipitating event	Unexpected, possibly a trivial event	Actual or contemplated violation of code or values
Relation of response to magnitude of offense	A very small offense may produce a marked response	Response usually proportional to the offense
The position of the self in the event	Passive, absorbed in how others see the self	Active, self-absorbed in concern about the effect of self's behavior on the other
Moral sense	"How could *I* have done that?"	"How could I have done *that?*"
Ethical imperative	(+) Pride (−) Contempt	(+) Altruism (−) Humility

(continued)

TABLE 3–1. (Continued)

Central trait	Shame	Guilt
Central fear	Not belonging in human company, being abandoned by others	Fear of punishment for aggressive and sexual impulses
Origins of the basis of concern	Positive identification with parents and/or admired others	Need for protection against injurious parents and/or other authority figures
Myth of the causes of suffering	Having displeased protective figures	Having competed with powerful authority figures
Primary defenses	Desire to hide and withdraw, denying rage	Obsessive thoughts, paranoid thinking, intellectualization, confession and seeking punishment
Effect on activity	Subdues	Increases
Effect on competitiveness	Covers up competition, leads to being a "closet" competitor	Competition is known, direct, and injurious to others
Nature of rage and hostility	Humiliated fury—discharge blocked by guilt or fear of the other; rage self-directed	Righteous indignation—discharge on self and other
Intersubjective process in an interpersonal process	I can "shame" another in order to make the other feel shameful (example, manipulating another's guilt).	I cannot "guilt" another into feeling response, but I can shame another into feeling responsible
Ontological desire	Desire to know intimately	Fear of knowing intimately

	Shame	Guilt
Relationship to society	Shamelessness is not regarded as a virtue; a sense of shame is	Being guiltless is a virtue; being guilty is not
Positive functions	Awareness of self's human limitations, discovery of the conditions of one's self-worth, opportunity to review and modify one's identity, identification and empathic responsiveness to others, awareness of the means for self-mastery, autonomy, and good will	Moral behavior, capacity for reparation and sublimation
Variants	Shyness, humiliation, embarrassment, chagrin, mortification, feeling ridiculous; painful self-consciousness	Sense of responsibility, obligation, loyalty
Form of relief	Acceptance by others, recognition of shame, articulation of feelings, sharing feelings with caring other (particularly in good-natured dialogue and laughter), changing negative inner voice, changing humiliating interpersonal relationships, building relationships based on caring, concern, and goodwill	Forgiveness by others; discharge by confession and reparation

(1971) clinical observations have been particularly helpful to me in formulating this table. Below is an overview of these differences.

The terms *guilt* and *shame* are common descriptions used to characterize how people monitor their sense of their own self-worth, guided by an inculcated code of personal and moral values. Due to their function in drive control (Lewis 1971) and because they are in confluence with each other early in development in our culture (Erikson 1950), guilt and shame generally are viewed together. Many theorists regard shame as the precursor to guilt in the fostering of moral values or, at best, a less vital form of guilt. Accordingly, most people do not readily differentiate the experience of shame from guilt so that it can be distinctly regarded as belonging in one category of moral transgression or the other (Miller 1985).

The designation of "guilt" from the tacit conjunction of guilt and shame experiences has had the unfortunate effect of neglecting shame as an important and distinctive self-function (Lewis 1971). The need to differentiate shame from guilt can be realized by examining how they are experienced phenomenologically.

STUDIES OF GUILT AND SHAME

There now have been about a dozen empirical studies published that compare the phenomenological experience of shame with that of guilt and indicate that subjects regard shame as the more incapacitating and overpowering affect. During guilty states, the experimental subjects were more active and experienced greater control than they did when in conditions in which they were shamed. During states of shame they felt inhibited, inferior, and lacking in power, status, and self-confidence (Wicker et al. 1983).

Lewis's (1987a) clinical studies seem to be in concordance with the research findings reviewed above. She reports that when feeling shame, patients regarded themselves as weak, shy, helpless, and injured in relationship with someone who was powerful, ridiculing, and hurtful.

The self under conditions of shame was experienced as the *object* of ridicule, humiliation, scorn, and contempt. On the other hand, when feeling guilty, the self regarded itself both as the *object* and the *source* of negative judging and valuation. The guilty-feeling person had an image of himself as a powerful and hurtful person in relation to another person, who was weak, vulnerable, injured, dependent, and suffering. Correspondingly, during guilt states the self experienced an omniscient responsibility toward the other and was concerned with self-blame, moral disapproval, and self-criticism. These clinical findings are in keeping with Kohut's (1977) theoretical formulation of guilt and shame. Guilty man, he indicates, is the proscriber of his own destiny, whereas tragic (shame) man is a victim of circumstances.

I examine in the next few pages a number of theoretical considerations about the roles of shame and guilt in human suffering that previous writers on shame have ignored.

The Vital Contrast between Guilt and Shame

We will all, undoubtedly, agree that there are numerous manifestations of human suffering. At various moments of life people suffer anger, jealousy, hate, and fear, as well as guilt and shame. Most human forms of suffering seem to have a loud and insistent voice. However, when we carefully discern the phenomenological components of suffering that we usually find the most perplexing in understanding and clinically treating, we find that these patients often have a great deal of difficulty finding language to communicate their painful experiences. The suffering I am referring to consists of such experiences as the dreaded lost sense of self. This is the feeling that the self is crumbling away, without a new, valued self emerging to replace it. This, in turn, leads to relegating oneself to a restricted life, experiencing social isolation, discrediting oneself and believing oneself to be unwelcome to others. This description is an accurate representation not only of our present-day patients, but also of how Hamlet and Oedipus appear to purport their suffering in the literary texts Freud examined and which I discuss in Chapter 6.

It is important to my thesis that it be recognized that the description of suffering I am referring to is not a guilt reaction, nor can it be adequately explained by the motives of anger, jealousy, or fear. The painful experience to which I am alluding constitutes the distress of shame. The suffering is derived from *our reflection* on our human condition and the realization that we are falling short of some expected desired state of existence. This is to say, organisms experience pain, but pain does not cause suffering until it is translated into a category of meaning (Goldberg 1984). This latter category is derived from assumptions and expectations conveyed to us by others. Often we do not know what we are experiencing until we can see ourselves as others perceive us. Suffering, therefore, is an interpersonal and learned process. Socioemotionally, our state of being is intolerable to the extent that it contradicts how we have been led to believe our existence should be experienced. The realization of our failure to achieve expected and desired goals lies at the core of the experience of shame.

If our suffering emanates from learned experience, then so, too, is the means for denouncing suffering and for experiencing meaningful life events derived from the learned judgments we make about these events. This was as true for Hamlet and Oedipus as it is for our patients. I show in Chapter 6 that shame and its existential implications are more central to Oedipus and Hamlet's tragedies than their sentiment of deserving punishment, as Freud reputes of Hamlet, for past imagined deeds and wishes, or, for Oedipus, for actual forbidden deeds. To understand this we need to examine why shame can be so agonizing to its victims.

There are certain dynamics that crucially differentiate shame from guilt and that help to explain why shame is often the more painful of the two. I am referring to the mechanisms of secret pride and power, psychodynamics that strikingly contrast guilt from shame, but that have been generally overlooked by clinicians.

There is *pride* in guilt even if this attribute is perverse.

So, for example, if every son's deepest desire, as Freud purports, is to bed his mother and to replace his father, we should not fail to wonder whether Oedipus's self-castigation held some perverse satisfaction in attaining "the universal dream," or as Jocasta tells Oedipus, "To lay with her who bore him." This consideration is in accordance with Lacan's (1980) interpretation that despite Hamlet's ostensible loathing of his uncle, he had a perverse admiration for Claudius's skill in captivating his mother with his phallus.

Most importantly, the attribute of guilt implies that one has the *power* to do wrong or even evil. If the person is punished, it is generally because it is recognized that he is a person to be reckoned with and requires restraint. Intrapsychically, in guilt, the self "buys off" the superego by offering it a compromise. It says, in effect, "If you don't destroy or desert me I will redeem myself by agreeing to some form of punishment." In short, one can escape feelings of suffering from guilt by submitting to confession and exculpation.

Doing wrong is but one source of guilt. What of the other type of guilt? In *existential guilt* the person has committed the foible of not living up to some *special* capacity—attributes toward which we might well expect pride to be harbored by the transgressor. Fortunately, for the person this transgression generally can be erased. To the extent one revises his behavior to accord with expectations required of him, a more vibrant life is usually assigned.

There may be some confusion about the difference between existential guilt and transgression against the values that results in the experience of shame. Existential guilt is derived from not being in accordance with what feared introjects want us to be (as opposed to what they don't want us to do or to be, as in transgression guilt). Shame, in contrast, results from failing what is expected of us—which one perceives to be his own values and conditions for self-worth. Existential guilt, therefore, like transgression guilt, has the harbinger of power because both forms of guilt have reference to the person's access to life-sustaining, redemptive strategies.

Of course, if guilt feelings are not adequately addressed

they may, like shame and despair, result in self-destructive behavior. Nevertheless, there is a recognized means for avoiding the destructive implications of guilt reactions. Phenomenologically, there is none for shame. In shame reactions the person experiences the absence of personal power and pride. This is the crux of the problem. One feels transparent, empty, lacking in power and specialness. Erikson's (1950) theorizing makes rather evident that shame results from the experience of having had one's functioning as a potentially autonomous person exposed to others prematurely—before one was prepared to perform adequately. This shameful experience casts self-doubts about one's personal adequacy and evokes feelings that I refer to as "lack of legitimate entitlement" as a person. In short, the earliest experiences of shame are a consequence of the experienced failure to satisfy ego-ideals in the eyes of admired others, which leads the person to believe that he is incapable of achieving the conditions necessary for physical and psychological preservation of the self. Without a firm sense of autonomy and trust in one's ability to handle oneself in the world, the specter of self-doubt haunts each new venture. Therefore, in contrast to guilt, the person in the throes of shame experiences a lack of power and audacity to deal with the devastation of the superego and tries to hide from it. But one cannot hide because the whole self is caught up in the feelings of helplessness. Kingston (1983) cogently indicates that "unlike the guilty act for which one can make confession, expiation, penance, or reparation, the shameful act requires an alteration of the person. The person thinks 'I can not have done this. But I have done it, and I can not undo it because it is I' " (p. 216).

Given the feelings of lack of power and specialness in regard to environmental oppression, the person abnegates his entitlement to prevent or even protest unfair treatment and abuse by others. Instead, the person attempts to hide in order to cover the opprobrium that comes from the disturbed perception that he is disintegrating as a person and that he has not developed the capacity to articulate or to alter the process of loss and dissolution.

In short, in guilt one *did* (translation: it is socially and personally recognized that the person has the power to do) the deed or has the power to withhold his efforts. In contrast, in shame the person experiences the passivity, incapacity, and lack of protectedness from the ravages of hurt and disappointment that come from a lack of legitimate entitlement and result in a state of being, as Hamlet describes his world, "weary, stale, flat and unprofitable" (*Hamlet,* 1.2).

The foregoing helps to explain why during shame, unlike guilt, hostility against the self is tolerated *passively.* As a result, shameful self-aggression may paralyze the self and cause feelings of being overwhelmed and unable to control one's existence.

THE ORIGINS OF GUILT AND SHAME

According to developmental theory, guilt is incurred when a threatening figure from the past operates as an internalized agent of one's value system. In guilt reactions our moral sentiments are the foci of unconscious psychic conflict. In contrast, in the accentuated, disturbed sense of self that we call "shame," it is consciously envisioned, admired figures of our past who are experienced as disappointed by our behavior. In short, the values of guilt are derived from the superego, internalized not from a personal sense of being "right," but from the fear of punishment and abandonment for the violation of moral values. Shame, in contrast, is regarded as a reaction to the subject's failure to live up to those sentiments of people he respects and admires. Shame values are, in short, ego-ideal assignments. The diminution of an idealized self-image results in a reaction of shame. Moreover, unlike guilt experiences, in which specific values and actions are in conflict, shame is often especially painful because frequently the whole self is involved in the opprobrium of such variants as chagrin, embarrassment, mortification, and humiliation (Lewis 1971). This is because shame is more fundamental and occurs earlier in development than does guilt (Gorsuch 1990).

Shame may involve matters in which one intentionally has acted in a way that one later realizes was unworthy of oneself. Shame can also come in a very different way. It may derive from someone else's treatment that causes one to feel humiliated and degraded. But then quite different from each of the other sources of shame, shame is frequently the result of having been in some way associated or identified with someone who has committed a guilt-involving act. This is to say, one can feel ashamed in several different ways. For example, I can feel ashamed that I didn't treat my parents the way they wanted me to, or even the way I would have liked to, but didn't. But it is also possible for me to feel ashamed when I find out that they have done something insensitive or uncaring to someone else. This is inconceivable for guilt! If one doesn't feel responsible for one's actions or those of others, then one doesn't feel guilty. Unlike shame, one does not feel guilty for events and actions (even those involving oneself) which were not in one's control or choosing.

Furthermore, we may not only be ashamed by our mistreatment of others, but also the *inconsiderations others render unto us.* Larry not only felt foolish in returning each time to the store to find the items he wanted still not there, he also felt ashamed that the storekeeper had lied to him and he had believed him. Was Larry responsible for the storekeeper's lying? Yes! Larry could have decided not to believe him, or could have stopped going into his store. But he didn't. Larry wanted to believe him. How responsible we are for our naiveté is a moral/philosophical question. The phenomenology of shame is blind to logical considerations. Consequently, the victim who is helpless to prevent his torture may be no less ashamed than the victim who cooperates. However, the latter may feel guilty in addition to being shamed. In short, one feels shameful when one experiences one's self as abject, degraded, abused, and violated—whether or not one is responsible for that treatment. The sense of shame reveals that we have believed *a lie,* such as that we will be treated properly if we are decent people, for example, or that we live in a safe and predictable world, because only other people, not special people like us, are mistreated and unsafe. Shame comes from finding important beliefs such as these unfounded.

Shame, in this sense, derives from a sense of betrayal—the shocking or startling realization that we are frail, vulnerable, and finite beings, no different than the vulnerable people around us. The function of shame, as a self-process, is to confront us with the impact of our tenuous existence as human beings. We can see from this formulation that feeling ashamed can also evoke feelings of *humility,* as well as curb feelings of *narcissistic entitlement.*

Still further complicating a ready ease in comprehending the intricacies of shame is the manifestation of shame that is derived from one's awareness of one's own collusion with one's victimization because of weakness. In Somerset Maugham's *Of Human Bondage,* the protagonist, Philip, who has a clubfoot, is forced by the bullies in boarding school to show his embarrassing deformity. Maugham tells us that Philip is more angry at himself than at the bullies, because he knows that if he had not given in to the pain inflicted by the bullies he might not have humiliated himself. Here is an incident in which we are given insight into how humiliation differs from embarrassment and its integral relationship to private shame.

First of all, we need, by definition, to distinguish humiliation from embarrassment. Miller's (1985) empirical investigation indicates that *embarrassment* is a sense of one's self "trying to pull inward or to diffuse itself into non-existence in response to a sudden feeling that an aspect of the self has been opened up to view without one's consent or participation" (p. 38). With *humiliation,* Miller (1985) found that the person "is not just undone or rattled, as in embarrassment. One is brought down to an abased or lowly position" (p. 43).

In Maugham's story, humiliation has to do with a secondary reaction—being forced to show others what Phillip already knew about himself, that he was a deprived person. Humiliation is experienced as private shame when "one feels that the public disapproval is in some way in disharmony with one's own feelings of how one would like to perceive oneself" (O'Hear 1976/1977). Like embarrassment, humiliation is a shame about being ashamed. Phillip's shame consisted of his own recognition of his cowardice to pain. His anger and contempt were, therefore, aimed mainly at himself rather than toward his tormentors. Jacobson (1963) was one of the first to indicate that shame is often caused by recognizing infantile tendencies in oneself. At such times, the self, rather than those who have humiliated the self, becomes the object of hostile impulses. Most abused and tortured victims suffer from this unfortunate tendency.

PRIVATE SHAME

Hawthorne, in *The Scarlet Letter*, offers further insight into private shame, recognizing that the deepest shame is not the humiliation reflected in the eyes of others, but weakness in one's own eyes. Although Hester Prynne was openly exposed to public humiliation and ridicule, she suffered far less than the person who caused her ridicule, Roger Chillingworth, whose deed was known to none but Hester and himself. Public exposure of shameful matters, Lynd (1958) suggests, may often be a protection against a more painful inner shame. Freud's greatest discovery was that people erect defenses because of their fear of knowing themselves intimately (Maslow 1963). What he did not seem to realize, however, is that we come to know ourselves, in large part, through the eyes of others. We become anxious about others seeing us too accurately, not so much because they might condemn us, but because we will be forced to see parts of ourselves that others see—parts that, until the public exposure, we have concealed from our own scrutiny. In short, the person who best knows himself should have the least fear of others.

MORAL ASPECTS OF GUILT AND SHAME

Guilt, in contrast to shame, is the violation of a *specific act* or some circumscribed aspect of behavior. Essentially, feeling guilty is a fear of punishment for violating the laws, wishes, and morality of those people one *fears* and believes will cause *abusive* punishment. O'Hear (1976/1977) indicates that "Guilt itself is like a burden or a pollution which can be removed only by undergoing the appropriate punishment or being forgiven by the appropriate authority" (p. 73). This was the basis of Freud's castration-fear metaphor. Unlike guilt, shame is representative of the absence of a legitimate response of the afflicted person toward the cause of suffering. Whereas feeling guilty comes from the recognition that one is at fault, shame is derived from having inhibited a necessary action, preventing one from defining one's personal identity with pride and self-esteem. These constructive self-actions are blocked by a sense of inadequacy from having disappointed those one admires and respects by not living up to their wishes and expectations. The feared punishment for shame, however, is not abuse from others, as in guilt, but the loss of loving connection with significant others, who are, or are believed to be, necessary to one's psychological and physical survival.

The sources of motivation for feeling guilty I have described should suggest that an emphasis on *guilt explanations* for why people behave as they do has the proclivity of erroneously undermining altruism and other positive deeds. It explains away the commendable actions people take as compelled by a guilty conscience, which is defending against irresponsible and destructive urges. This popular notion about guilt being a motivator for enlightened maturity is a misconception. Guilt is experienced as caused by a hurtful invasion from outside of one's self—the demands of authority figures one fears. Contrary to psychoanalytic formulation, guilt, unlike shame, is not internalized. Hateful objects are *introjected,* not internalized. Consequently, a guilty conscience is experienced, at least in part, as *alien*— as a quality of non-self. Actions caused by feeling guilty have a reluctant, compulsive quality to them. They don't have the hallmark of being personal and heartfelt. Behaviors effected by feelings of shame, in contrast, issue from one's sense of who one is—one's personal identity. Therefore, to the extent that one feels goodwill (or that one would like to be a person of goodwill), altruistic actions are congruent with one's ego-ideals (see Table 3–2).

TABLE 3–2.

Defenses against and Responses to Shame and Despair

Degree of functionality and sense of well-being	Interpersonal	Intrapsychic
	Self-esteem enhancers	
High	Intimate identification with desired other	Feelings of competence
	Altruistic deed	At peace with one's self
	Empathy	Courage
	Compassion	Feeling of pride
	Successful open competition	Sense of achievement and self-improvement
	Forgiveness	Humility
		Wonderment
		Optimism
	Adaptive defenses	
Moderate	Heroic action	Superachievement
	Envy	Fortitude
	Pity	Indirect and fantasized competition
	Boastfulness	Repression
	Sympathy	Rationalization
	Patronization	Denial of unfulfilled aspirations
	Adoration	Sadness

Modification of shameful exposure
of self through shyness, embarrassment
and other shame variants
Concealment
Asking forgiveness and acceptance

Regret
Remorse
Disappointment
"As-if" stance

Moderately negative

Secondary Defenses

Jealousy
Shamelessness
Anger
Isolation and withdrawal
Splitting in relationship to others
Projective identification
Manipulation
Identification with the aggressor

Disgust
Introjection
Perfectionism
Bypassing shame and converting
it into other emotions
Mild addictive behavior
Stimulus-seeking behavior
Obsessions
Narcissistic self-regard
Psychosomatic illness
Grief
Bitterness
Boredom
Anguish
Sorrow
Reaction formation
Regression

(continued)

TABLE 3-2. (Continued)

Degree of functionality and sense of well-being	Interpersonal	Intrapsychic
	Contemptuous behavior	
	Humiliating the other	
	Reproach and blaming	
	Lying and deception	
		Catastrophic reactions
Negative	Rage and violence	Acting out
	Physical abuse of others	Panic attacks
		Terror
		Delusional projection
		Depersonalization
		Severe addictive behavior
		Loss of self-control
		Despair
		Suicide

Closely related to the motivational source of these emotive forces is the question of *volition*. There is choice in guilt that is only found in one type of shame, discretionary shame. Therefore, rarely does one choose to engage in a specific shameful act, as one does by virtue of feeling responsible for those things that makes one feel guilty.

In Chapter 6 I discuss Freud's first literary (and most important) case study, *Hamlet*. In the drama, you may remember, Claudius, the King, is unable to pray or repent, although he is guilty of murdering his brother to acquire his crown, joys, and queen. Claudius demonstrates in the text that he will allow himself to be no more guilty than he needs to be in coming to terms with his immoral deeds. Whereas he confesses to himself that he obtained his throne by murder and incest, he rationalizes his sense of guilt by haggling with it. He wishes to believe that his immoral behavior has led to a monarchy of considerable benefit to his people (Barker 1978). The weighing of the pros and cons about one's guilt may be prolonged, as it appeared to be for Claudius, over a period of time. The shameful moment in which one's incompetence is exposed, in sharp contrast, usually takes one by surprise in a sudden flash (Lynd 1958).

THE CONSTRUCTIVE ASPECTS OF SHAME

There is one important form of shame that is less involved with the exposure of incompetence as it is with the recognition that one has a choice, either in acting in a way that is proper or responding in an unfit way. This type of shame, called *discretion shame* (Schneider 1977), has been largely ignored by psychoanalysts and other behavioral scientists. O'Hear (1976/1977) indicates that in some instances the notion that shame only comes from failing to obtain some self-ideal of excellence is too restrictive and leads to misunderstanding the role shame plays in moral sanctioning and to overestimating the importance of guilt in morality. Shame, rather than obedience to a moral order, is the source of *honor*. O'Hear (1976/1977) points out:

[The] sense of self-respect provides the basis for a less
socially dependent concept of honour, in which
shame is not tied to fear of exposure, but to a fuller
view of personal worth, involving ideals such as those
of reliability, fairness, decency and fidelity. [p. 81]

Actualized people develop their own noble vision—a
code of conduct and a world view that transcend those of
their fellow beings' fears and prejudices. Shakespeare's play
shows without question that Hamlet is physically capable of
being a man of action. He does not revenge his father's
assassination because of his incompetence as a man of
arms, but, because he, like Oedipus, has a higher conscience
than those of their fellow sojourners—and this is his dilemma. Hamlet is caught marginally between his loyalty to
his father and his own higher conscience, which morally
and spiritually abhor taking revenge.

The greater vision provided by shameful self-consciousness is also splendidly portrayed in Mark Twain's
Huckleberry Finn. Twain, too, shows the limitation of guilt
as a morality. In one passage, Huck struggles about whether
he should turn in the runaway slave, Jim, to the authorities.
Not to do so would violate the lessons he has been taught
about proper and responsible behavior. Huck feels guilty in
not wanting to turn in his old friend, especially since Jim
has talked about murdering white people. Yet, he realizes
that if he turned in Jim, who escaped to rescue his children,
he would feel worse than if he did what was "proper." He is
uncertain about the basis of his feelings. Neither Huck nor
Twain gives shame a name. But it is shame all the same that
enables Huck to regard Jim as a struggling fellow human
being like himself, rather than a piece of property to be
returned to his owner, as his sense of guilt demands. This
moral sense seems to correspond to stage five of Kohlberg's
system of moral development (Kohlberg 1963).

The shame Huck Finn is impinged with is the same kind
of compassionate sense of humanity with which Sophocles,
Shakespeare, Cervantes, Tolstoy, and Dostoevsky were in
touch. So too, for that matter, did the writers of the Old

Testament share this concern. The Bible viewed the acceptance of shame as the ultimate in commitment. Shakespeare also referred to shame more often than to guilt and associated it with truth and honor rather than inferiority or wrongdoing (Kingston 1983).

Shame has the capacity of spurring on our greatest human achievements by making us self-conscious of the conditions necessary for our self-worth and for the development of a sense of purpose in our lives. Shame provides a *mirror* for reflection of parts of the self that are typically hidden. Shame experiences are vivid and painful because they foster an accentuated and disturbing sense of self-consciousness. These are moments in which we become aware, albeit fleetingly, of aspects of ourselves—our ambitions, longings, and sentiments—that are both valuable to our sense of who we are and, at the same time, prone to misunderstanding and derision.

Shame is constructed out of a judgment of our failure to live up to our own code, honor, values, and standards. On the other hand, guilt is created by a judgment of having transgressed someone else's values—although we generally do not consciously distinguish our own code from those of our superego. Consequently, for shame to occur there has to be some aspiration to live by our own standards. Two great poets, Sophocles and Shakespeare, fashioned in their dramas the message that the suffering of noble protagonists such as Hamlet and Oedipus came about because the codes for living by which they guided their actions, sanctioned by their society, were eventually recognized as thwarting a more noble and courageous view of human conduct. The values of the ego-ideals originally fostered from the sentiments of people Hamlet and Oedipus respected and admired presumably begin to evolve into "conditions of self-worth" formed by their own experiences and noble vision. Developing self-worth requires, of course, self-understanding. The willingness and ability to pursue self-knowledge is generally a more arduous task than simply meeting the expectations of those who have established the basis for our feelings of culpability. In short, because of its central role in the pursuit of self-knowledge, the awareness of shame is crucial to a morality based upon autonomy and responsibility. It is the fine edge of shame as a function interfaced with creative and defensive aims that I am concerned with in this chapter.

In the following pages I will examine the role of shame in affirmative and healthy emotion.

SELF-ESTEEM—ENHANCING BEHAVIOR

Broucek (1982) has indicated that there is a vital correspondence between the feelings of joy, excitement, and efficacy and the development of a positive sense of self, which we call self-esteem. Contrastingly, events, activities, and feelings that interfere with the ability to feel joy, excitement, and efficacy result in feelings of diminished self-esteem. The ability to sustain self-esteem fosters a feeling of pride. An incapacity to achieve joy, excitement, and efficacy results in shame. Pride and shame, as Natanson (1987a) indicates, stand in reciprocal fashion to one another in terms of self-esteem. Because of this interrelationship, when the causes of shame are successfully managed, pride and heightened self-esteem accompany these efforts. The fear of shame, therefore, may serve important social and developmental functions for the individual's sense of personal identity. Morrison (1989) reminds us that "a remarkable result of the Civil Rights Movement was the experience of competence and effectiveness in altering society, transforming shame into pride and a sense of relative well-being for many Blacks in this country (e.g., 'Black is beautiful') as a new rallying cry" (p. 187).

DEFENSES AGAINST SHAME

The *fear* of shame also produces a plethora of rescuing and defensive mechanisms to try to protect one's personal identity, as one of Nietzsche's aphorisms cleverly indicates. Nietzsche tells us: " 'I did this' says my memory. 'I can not have done this' says my pride and remains inexorable. In the end—memory yields" (Yorke et al. 1990, p. 378).

Izard (1977) and other researchers into the psychology of

emotions maintain that shame and shame-anticipation function as regulators of the integrity of personal identity. In this regard, Morrison (1989) makes a useful distinction between the influence of shame in neurotic conflicts as compared to that in narcissistic disorders. This distinction is helpful in understanding the development of specific defenses against despair and the disintegration of personal identity. In neurotic conflicts defenses against shame are more adaptive and specifically related to threats to the sense of well-being involved in relationships that are significant sources of feelings of pride, competence, and mutual caring. In the more narcissistic disorders, on the other hand, the defenses mobilized by the self are more central and total, designed to secure a powerful other to ward off life-threatening feelings of worthlessness and incapacity.

Table 3–2 presents a purview of the levels of healthy response, adaptation, defense, and catastrophic reaction to threats against the self. The conceptual theory behind the organization of the table can be found in Menninger's (1954) paper about the regulatory devices of the ego under stress. Menninger points out that there it may be advantageous in properly understanding human behavior to view it within a continuum between a state of unstressful adjustment and states of disintegration and illness. This being a quite reasonable clinical position, it seems odd that it has not been widely adopted by clinicians. Accordingly, Table 3–2 reveals that pride and other identity-enhancing behaviors may be induced either from the joyful striving of the self, or as a defensive mechanism (Horney 1950), protecting the self from a threat to its personal identity. By emphasizing both sources of endeavor toward pride and other self-enhancing behavior, it can be clearly seen that threats against and stresses within the self lead to increasingly more extreme reactions to ward off the despairing feelings of self-contempt and worthlessness. Bilmes (1967) illustrates this in terms of adolescents:

> Adolescents build their pride and avoid being ashamed of themselves through identification with heroic figures or through the creation of a heroic role

for themselves. When stymied, this effort becomes contaminated . . . with increased aggressiveness, with fantasying oneself to be superior, or with depreciative competition. . . . [A]s Erikson (1950) put it, "he who is ashamed would like to force the world not to look at him, not to notice his exposure. He would like to destroy the eyes of the world." It is striking that criminal and delinquent activities provide a way of doing just this, of obliterating that segment of reality which, if emotionally accepted, means accepting the shame. [pp. 121–122]

In short, when one is ashamed, rescuing attempts by one's desired self may take the form of performing brave and heroic feats in order to restore self-esteem. Counterphobic behavior, called countershame (Levin 1967) frequently occurs with adolescents and young adults, whose personal identity is still highly pliable. For people with less resilient identities, requests for forgiveness and being restored as an acceptable person within one's community and one's significant interpersonal relationship is an adaptive defense against feelings of self-blame and unworthiness. However, when these defenses do not function adequately, more self-absorbing defenses are mobilized, such as obsessive fears about faults and limitations, projection and reproach toward others for one's own unrecognized failings, and the advent of psychosomatic illness. Finally, if all else fails, catastrophic reactions are compelled to try to save one's personal identity from total dissolutionment.

Secondary Reactions to Shame and Despair

Behavioral scientists generally have failed to recognize the role of shame in arousing powerful secondary reactions. In Table 3–2 secondary reactions refer to both secondary defenses and catastrophic reactions. Clinical work evinces that shameful feelings are often times followed by anger, rage, resentment, jealousy, or shamelessness. Because the prolonged feeling of shame is unbearable—perhaps, one of the most painful human emotions—it leaves the victim feeling exposed and utterly helpless. Defenses against shame are fostered to help the victim recover from shame. However, the very defenses mobilized to protect the self often have nasty side effects.

Helpless anger has been noted by many clinicians as an extremely difficult-to-treat clinical problem. Perceptive observers have speculated about the function of helpless anger long before the advent of modern psychotherapy. Nietzsche (1887) remarked on behavior that he called "impotent rage" and regarded as the basis of feelings of resentment. More recently Horowitz (1981) conducted several clinical investigations in which he traced what he calls self-righteous rage to situations in which a subject who is usually calm suddenly becomes intensely hostile and vengeful as a response to a startling insult.

Everyone wishes to be cared about and accepted for who he or she is. Being treated in unreasonable and unkind ways discredits one's identity as a person, arousing resentment and shame. Shame is a signal that the survival of one's personal identity is in jeopardy. Therefore, feeling weak may be "repaired" by arrogance, self-glorification, aggressiveness, and pseudo-masculinity (Bursten 1973).

Instead of being in touch with their feelings of being misunderstood and discredited, our patients, who have not learned how to identify their feelings of helpless shame and express them directly, may be quick to feel annoyance and anger. Shame is the Cinderella of unpleasant emotions (Rycroft 1968). Guilt, anger, envy, resentment, and fear all have articulate voices in the expression of how the afflicted person experiences them—shame rarely does.

Secondary reactions to unrecognized shame, such as anger, are powerful, surging emotions. These explosive responses capture other people's attention. As such, they temporarily overthrow the shamed person's helpless feelings of being disregarded and insignificant. Unfortunately, shame also reproduces itself. The offspring of shame are anger, abuse, and contempt. Therefore, unrecognized shame expressed as anger (especially when it leads to violence and abuse of others) causes painful embarrassment and still further assaults on the shamed person's sense of self-worth—evoking still more shame.

It has been estimated that about one-third to one-half of those people who have been physically abused eventually become abusers themselves (Pianta et al. 1989). The rage and violence that victims of shame display are desperate messages to try to convince themselves, as well as others, that they are not as unprotected and powerless as they experience themselves to be. Consequently, fierce reactions to being shamed and not recognizing its effect can cause a vicious cycle of uncontrollable emotion.

It is noteworthy to mention that recent psychological studies have shown that feelings of not being in control of one's emotions undermine the sense of optimism people require in order to live in a healthy way. As clinicians we recognize that optimism is an indispensable emotional attitude that supports the human immune system against physical and emotional illness (Antoni et al. 1990).

The issue of lack of control over one's life has special significance for addictions. Lawrence Hattener (1971), a psychiatrist with extensive clinical experience with addictions, has estimated that as many as one of every ten Americans has some sort of troublesome addiction. People who have difficulty gaining a sense of being in control over their lives are prime candidates for addiction problems. They are unaware of how shame prevents them from taking a purposive direction in their lives (Pandino 1990). Our daily newspapers show the close link between addictions and violence.

The etiology of explosive and violent behavior was poorly understood until the role of shaming and its secondary reactions were clinically investigated. A key clinical finding about the fate of "helpless anger" has come from Helen Block Lewis's extensive clinical study of feelings of self-contempt generated by either intrapsychic or interpersonal events that are not discharged effectively. Lewis (1987) and her co-workers (Hoblitzelle 1987, Retzinger 1987, Scheff 1987) found three distinctive behavioral patterns in which residual feelings of contempt are unrecognized. Most commonly, shameful feelings are either "bypassed" or experienced as a general mood of uneasiness and agitation.

During bypassed shame, according to Retzinger (1987), "there is *considerable ideation,* but *little or no feeling.* Pain is briefly experienced as a wince or a jolt at the moment of arousal, but it goes by so quickly that there are little or no bodily changes, only, usually, obsessive thoughts or speech" (p. 154). According to Scheff (1987), the second reactive manifestation of shame

> is overt and undifferentiated. In this form, one experiences painful confusion and unwanted physical manifestations: blushing and/or rapid heartbeat, for example. At the same time, one is often at a loss for words and also at a loss for thoughts. One's behavior and thought seem disorganized or disoriented. Embarrassment is one term that is applied to this form.
>
> Many of the vernacular terms for undifferentiated feelings appear to refer to this form of shame, or to combinations of this type of shame with anger: feeling peculiar, shy, bashful, awkward, funny, bothered, miserable. . . . The phrases "I felt like a fool" and "I felt like a perfect idiot" may be prototypic. [pp. 110–111]

The third pattern of secondary reaction to unresolved feelings of self-contempt is referred to by Lewis (1987a) as humiliation-fury. In this behavioral sequence hostility toward the self is experienced passively. The self feels out of control, overwhelmed, and paralyzed by its own self-directed hostility. Lewis (1979) offers a vivid phenomenological description of this tumultuous experience:

> One could "crawl through a hole" or "sink through the floor" or "die" with shame. The self feels small, helpless and childish. When, for example, there is unrequited love, the self feels crushed by the rejection. So long as shame is experienced, it is the "other" who is experienced as the source of hostility. Hostility against the rejecting "other" is almost simulta-

neously evoked. But it is humiliated fury, or shame-rage, and the self is still in part experienced as the object of the "other's" scorn. Hostility against the "other" is trapped in this directional bind. To be furious and enraged with someone because one is unloved by him renders one easily and simultaneously guilty for being furious. Evoked hostility is readily redirected back against the vulnerable self. [p. 386]

Ruth's story is representative of the helpless rage that follows being humiliated. Ruth's mother, a successful businesswoman, is in her senior maturity years. She decided to sell her most valuable commercial property and promised to divide the proceeds evenly between her two daughters. Candice, Ruth's sister, is a narcissistically demanding woman, who lives the lifestyle but eschews the work habits of a painter and artist. She is always in need of money. She convinced her mother that she needed the money more than Ruth, who supports herself. Ruth did not find out about the financial arrangement for several months. She was stunned to find that she had been excluded from a discussion of her mother's financial situation. She found it difficult to concentrate at home and at work. Often, she was awakened by anxiety attacks at night. She feared that she had been neglected because her mother and sister regarded her as a guileless person, who was not worthy of respect. After a few weeks of berating herself, Ruth angrily confronted her sister over a trivial matter while at her mother's house. Candice laughed at Ruth's upset and refused to talk with her for the rest of the evening. Ruth again felt deeply betrayed and ashamed. Yet, she felt compelled to consider that she might have deserved her mistreatment because she didn't have her sister's manipulative wiles and tenacity in getting her needs met.

VARIANTS OF SHAME

Stamm (1978), in his review of the status of the concept of humiliation in the psychoanalytic literature, points out that analysts have made minimum efforts to distinguish humiliation from shame. By and large, he reports, these concepts are employed interchangeably, with patronage usually given to shame. The same can be said of the other variants of shame—shyness, embarrassment, mortification, chagrin, and so forth.

In reviewing the literature on embarrassment, Babcock and Sabini (1990) indicate that it is difficult to distinguish embarrassment from shame. The same holds for the other variants of shame. All are generally characterized by an accentuated self-consciousness, exposure or fear of exposure, a sense of incompetence, stress, and inappropriateness in one's actions (Edelmann 1981, Izard 1977, Lewis 1971, Lynd 1958, Sattler 1965, Wicker et al. 1983). Therefore, most researchers of the psychology of emotions have regarded the experiences of the variants of shame as not significantly distinct from shame itself. Only a few investigators have emphasized differences (e.g., Babcock and Sabini 1990, Mosher and White 1981). These psychologists have claimed that the occurrence of shame appears to be experienced as a more devastating event that holds a greater threat to the person's evaluation of self than do the variants of shame. Babcock and Sabini (1990) maintain

that both embarrassment and shame reflect the individual's concern over violating of his *own* standards, not merely a fear that he has failed or is unworthy in the eyes of another. The difference lies in the exact nature of the standard violated. Briefly, embarrassment is a response to an inconsistency between one's behavior and one's conception of one's persona, a personal, and, perhaps, idiosyncratic standard, whereas shame is a response to an inconsistency between one's behavior and one's ideal, i.e., that which one takes to be a universal standard of what it is to be a worthy individual. . . . As such, embarrassment is best conceptualized as a reaction to perceived discrepancy between one's behavior and one's personal standards, not a reaction to a failure to live up to the expectations of others [as in shame]. [p. 153]

Babcock and Sabini's description of the differences between shame and its variants, while it is definitionally
accurate, may be phenomenologically blurred in our patients' experiences. What each of our patients experiences
in a painful moment—whether it is one of public exposure
about one's self or not—is heavily dependent upon that
person's sense of personal identity. If one has a vibrant and
healthy sense of self, the public display that caused embarrassment will quickly fade when the individual gains a sense
of perspective and can laugh off the social faux pas: for
example, telling oneself "So, I'm not so perfect. Everyone
makes mistakes. Why can't I? No big deal. I don't have to be
perfect." In sharp contrast, the individual whose debilitating experiences with shame have resulted in a negative
personal identity can not easily disregard the embarrassing
moment. It fits congruently with his history of governing
shame scenes and its accompanying interpretative scripts.
He may tell himself: "This always happens to me. I can
never do anything right. Everyone who knows me gets to
find out that I'm incompetent. They told me that I'd never
amount to anything. I'm afraid they're right!"

In short, for some people, embarrassment and other
variants of shame are only isolated experiences of discomfort. But for others, these embarrassing moments readily
meld into their negative identity and are experienced iden-
tically to those of painful private shame itself.

CLINICAL IMPLICATIONS OF HUMILIATION AMALGAMATED WITH GUILT

A colleague, Dr. John O'Leary (personal communication), indicates that he has treated several patients whose
lives are replete with humiliation, who don't correspond to
the clinical picture of shame-debilitated people, who are
passive, humble, undemanding, and self-reproaching.
O'Leary reports that whereas feelings of shame incapacitate
shame-prone people, leading them to social isolation, feelings of humiliation frequently lead his patients to paranoid

delusions and violent action against those who have humiliated them and even against those assumed to harbor hostile and contemptuous feelings toward them.

A purview of Table 3–1 shows that obsessional, paranoid thought, righteous indignation, and high interpersonal activity are salient features of the sense of guilt. O'Leary's patients probably suffer from both guilt and shame. Guilt and shame are susceptible to each other. Guilt fosters shame and vice versa. I believe that Dr. O'Leary is clinically describing patients who have not internalized their humiliation, as shame-sensitive people do with insult. His patients do not internalize their humiliation because they experience it as undeserved. They therefore project it outward, discharging it on other people and property in violent and destructive ways. Quite likely, they are victims of the humiliation-fury cycle, which serves to augment both their shame and their guilt. Table 3–2 suggests that these patients have lost the ability to use adaptive and secondary defenses and feel no recourse but to react in a catastrophic way.

In this book I will not endeavor to make fine distinctions in the manifestation of shame and its variants, unless such a distinction is of crucial importance to the understanding of the material in that specific discussion or clinical vignette.

The Variants of Shame as Adaptive Defenses

There is one important aspect of shame variants that deserves special attention. This manifestation concerns variants of shame as adaptive defenses against private shame and despair.

The variants of shame represent a sense of being ashamed for being shamed. As such, these secondary emotions are heightened and accentuated signals of shame anxiety, alerting the self to hide that which is shameful from the self. For example, all shame-prone people are, I believe, "closet competitors." Shyness, therefore, is a punishment, in the sense of an adaptive reaction, for feeling inferior; yet, at the same time, daring to put one's self at risk in public places in which direct comparisons and open competition with other people may take place. In short, the painful feelings of shyness is a reminder to the self of the imprudence of going public. The interpretive script that accompanies "shyness scenes" says something to this effect: "Only inferior people, who are stupid, expose themselves and their ambitions, appearance, and performance to more powerful people. You deserve the painful feelings of shrinking from the critical eyes of others. Maybe now you will be more careful!"

There usually are "characterological reminder rituals" that accompany the shaming scenes of shame-prone people. For example, people who are easily embarrassed by rejection regularly pinch or poke their own bodies in a painful way, to distract themselves from fantasies that harbor the desire to ask other people to respond to their needs. The pinching behavior, then, is an adaptive reaction to the fear of being devastatingly shamed.

CULTURAL MANIFESTATIONS OF SHAME

Shame is experienced differently across cultures. A number of prominent anthropologists have contended that shame and guilt induce opposite behavior and moral values from each other in certain societies. The prevailing criterion for distinguishing between shame and guilt cultures has been the discrimination between *external* and *internal* *sanctions* applied to normative behavior. If a society primarily depends on criticism, ridicule, and contempt of other people to insure moral behavior, these cultures are termed *shame*-oriented. On the other hand, if a culture relies upon an internalized conscience for conformity to moral behavior, it is designated as a *guilt*-oriented society. This doesn't necessarily imply that shame is the only form of external sanction, or guilt the only type of internal sanction in these cultures, but the assumption is made that shame and guilt are respectively the principle representatives of external and internal proscriptions.

An early and highly influential version of the external–internal classification of the moral values of different cultures is found in Margaret Mead's work *Cooperation and*

Competition Among Primitive Peoples (1937). Mead regarded *sanctions* as those "mechanisms by which conformity is obtained, by which desired behavior is induced and
undesired behavior prevented" (p. 493). The person who
"so internalizes the standards that he obeys them in the
absence of force exerted from the outside" (p. 493) is said to
be responding to internal sanctions. Mead refers to ab-
staining from forbidden sexual activity for fear of punishment by ghosts and obeying tribal taboos about eating
rituals for fear of incurring disease or death from the curses
of tribal predecessors as typical examples of internal sanctions. In contrast, Mead defines external sanctions as being
the social force for moral compliance with societal norms for
the individual who has not internalized his tribe's standards
and, therefore, only heeds "forces which must be set in
motion by others" (p. 493), such as ridicule, abuse, and the
awareness of royal decree.

Piers and Singer (1953) were the first theorists to revise
classical psychoanalytic and anthropological views about
shame and guilt. They concluded their extensive examination of the theory of guilt and shame cultures as follows:

> There are sufficient reasons for doubting the prevail-
> ing assumption that most cultures of the world are
> shame cultures, and that Western culture is one of the
> rare guilt cultures, to warrant a careful reconsidera-
> tion of the distinction between shame and guilt cul-
> tures and of the presumed correlation between guilt
> cultures and moral and technical progress. [p. 96]

One of the most important criticisms against the internal–external distinction between guilt and shame is the
erroneous assumption of Mead that shame requires an
audience who knows about the misdeed, whereas guilt
operates in the psyche without an audience. In fact, there
appear to be "inner" forms of compelling shame that correspond almost exactly to those of guilt-directed sanctions.
Nor can one save the distinction by saying that guilt involves a reenactment of childhood experience, whereas

during shame there is only the perception of the immediate social event. This criteria merely serves to differentiate among the different forms of guilt and shame, but does not validly differentiate between them (Ausubel 1955).

The differential cultural approach to morality in terms of guilt and shame, however, does have some usefulness. In comparing cultures, anthropologists have consistently found that each group of people is shamed by different conditions (Riezler 1942). Pertinent to our own culture, men and women differ in regard to what is shameful. These patterns of shame values appear to remain constant throughout a historical period (Kaufman and Rafael 1984b). In the United States today we can accurately describe the "male culture" as being "shame phobic." Values are placed on pride and love of self. Negative values are attributed to an emphasis on caring and concern for others. This cultural value system emphasizes achievement, competition, power, and dominance. These values become integral to the sense of personal identity of many men growing up in this culture. Not being willing or able to achieve as well as others leaves many men with a sense of dissonance, depression, and despair. The "female culture" prioritizes values in ways that appear to be in sharp contrast with the male culture (Wright 1987). Males expecting females to conform to their value orientations and vice versa become obvious sources of sex-oriented shaming.

Other psychocultural studies suggest that it is not only the specific values that differentiate what is shameful and what is not among cultures, but it also is the precise ways that cultures respond to violations of their norms that distinguish among societies. Marsella and his associates (1974) empirically found that Caucasian-Americans rated shame as phenomenologically experienced as "lower," "weaker," and "duller" than did two Oriental groups. They also regarded shame as more "passive," "hazy," "bad," and "serious" than Japanese-Americans and more "rounded," "relaxed," and "stale" than did the Chinese-Americans. The Japanese-Americans rated shame as significantly more "low," "rounded," "sharp," and "serious" than the Chinese-Americans. It was concluded that shame is less clearly identifiable (or, perhaps, less understood) for the Caucasian group than with Orientals. Benedict (1946) has indicated that for the Japanese

> shame is pervasive partly because the Japanese, unlike culturally and ethnically diverse societies such as the United States, have their cultural norms well defined so that their violations are readily recognized, and partly because the Japanese individual is more surrounded by significant audiences to whom his action is exposed. So when everyone is playing by the same rules and mutually supporting each other, the Japanese can be light-hearted and easy (p. 224).

Benedict's statement can be interpreted to mean that shame, because it is used more explicitly in Oriental cultures than in the West, enables Easterners to more correctly read the disapproval of others for shame values and respond to these situational cues more accurately and with less conflict about how to correct behaviors that are regarded by others as shameful and dishonorable.

4

Shameful Secrets

Shame catches the self at the quick.
                                    —Helen M. Lynd

Intimacy plays a central role in enriching our lives. Unfortunately, many of our patients are unable to obtain the trusted companionship that they desire. Yet, few of them are aware that destructive shame repeatedly is blocking their attempts at intimacy.

Richard and Jennifer's Story

There was a soft knock on Richard's apartment door at 8:10 that Tuesday morning. Richard was startled. It was too early for visitors. So he assumed it must be Jennifer, his fiancée. She had stayed over and had left just fifteen minutes earlier on her way to work. Jennifer had probably forgotten a manuscript she needed for her editorial work.

Richard cautiously opened the front door. It was Jennifer, a small, slim woman, with dark, alluring Mediterranean features and long, soft hair. She was standing there with her eyes downcast and her slight shoulders

81

rounded. An uneasiness quickly swept over Richard, an advertising executive, a man of imposing height and presence. He knew her posture so well. Something terrible had obviously happened.

"What is it, honey? What happened?" he asked. "Someone took my money, stole my whole wallet," she bitterly replied and began to sob.

Richard's emotions reeled. His thoughts raced back over the five years he had known Jennifer. His recollections took a mood of agitated insistence, finally arriving at the angry sentiments, which he only barely managed to keep to himself:

"Jennifer, when will you ever learn to take care of yourself! Why don't you just hand over your hard-earned money to anyone you find in the street? At least then you won't have to worry about being robbed!"

Richard's scornful inner monologue dislodged and ejected a feeling of contempt for Jennifer. He looked straight at her standing in the doorway, and with considerable disgust, disregarding the consequences of his words, baldly told her that he felt sorry for her. He added that if he had ever loved her, then it was truly a sick love and was of no consequence to him any longer.

Richard's statement had the ring of condemnation for Jennifer. Without a word of protest, she turned around and fled down the hall corridor, blindly making her way down the many flights of stairs into the lobby of the apartment building. Sobbing, she bolted into the street, running wildly until her embarrassment, evoked from the stares of the passing pedestrians, forced her to try to conceal the agitation of her flight. Jennifer then slowly made her way home to her lonely studio apartment, accompanied by considerable self-pity and contempt. Why does Richard hate and resent me so much that he would treat me so cruelly? she implored herself. She regarded the unkind behavior and scornful words of the man she had hoped to marry as the inscription of her own epitaph. To Jennifer, it signified the end of all her hopes and dreams of living a happy and meaningful life with another person. Now she was certain that she faced a lifetime of solitude and intense loneliness.

For Jennifer, being regarded as incompetent was her shame button. Sadly, she regarded Richard's opinion of her worth as a human being as having more merit than her own unsure judgments about herself. A lifelong mistrust of her own common sense made Jennifer dependent upon others' opinions. Consequently, Jennifer experienced Richard's statement that he felt sorry for her as an ordaining message that served to validate her own innermost, fearful beliefs about herself. As a clear-thinking and knowledgeable man of the world, Richard was perceived by Jennifer as mirroring reality. If he regarded her as an inadequate, incomplete, and inferior person, then Richard was only finally confirming her own continual nightmare of being helpless in protecting herself from the abuses of living.

People like Jennifer, who are easily humiliated, are likely to become upset by interactions and events that other people let go unnoticed, or regard as so inconsequential as not to warrant their emotional involvement.

For example, Jennifer has become badly thrown on more than one occasion by a store clerk who looked at her sternly and didn't thank her for making a purchase. After those incidents Jennifer felt compelled to show Richard what she had bought and inquire: "Richard, do you really think I need this item?"

Her dependency on Richard causes her to be ashamed of herself. She cannot imagine ever being part of a relationship that enjoys mutual respect, dignity, and pride. She is too embarrassed by her displays of incompetence to ask Richard or anyone else for help with the way she feels about herself. The hopelessness of her situation produces a desire to flee. Yet she cannot break free. Jennifer experiences no realistic escape because she can sense no moment in the future in which she expects to go beyond the present painful moment. She is too entrenched in her way of being to see a way out.

Consequently, Jennifer's humiliating moment with

Richard is not an isolated moment in her life. Jennifer's feeling of intense shame is not something that she will get over and forget, even if Richard were to apologize for his wretched behavior and wish to resume his relationship with her. Jennifer's self-condemnation is part and parcel of a pervasive, persistent, and destructive set of emotions that grips her whole existence with a crippling sense of terror and pessimism. Jennifer's fright has resulted in a lifetime of cover-ups and secrecy. Her inability to share her feelings with anyone else has made her misery especially painful.

What Jennifer suffers from, yet can do nothing about because she is not even aware of its presence, is the devastating, helpless, self-blaming feelings of shame.

You may assume that Jennifer can be simply written off as a sadly high-strung and unstable woman. Therefore, let me hasten to add that despite how Jennifer comes across in my description of her dreadful encounter with Richard, she is not seen as an emotional cripple to her professional colleagues. Jennifer is a highly regarded book editor, who is not hesitant to offer her knowledgeable opinions on literary matters.

If we consider Jennifer capable of superior intellectual functioning, then we are puzzled why Jennifer cannot effectively use her intelligence to find out what is actually bothering her and to do something constructive to alleviate her disturbed feelings about herself. To help us better understand this apparent absurdity let me point out how facilely and unwittingly many of us as clinicians have assumed the readily available psychological explanations offered by psychiatry in our endeavor to try to understand our patients.

Since the time of Sigmund Freud, psychiatric theories have fostered a guilty-conscience explanation to account for human misery. These theories tell us that someone like Jennifer or Hedda Nussbaum sets herself up to being humiliated by a Richard or a Joel Steinberg because she feels that she deserves punishment for morally unacceptable thoughts and/or deeds in her past. She unconsciously believes that by being mistreated she will be cleansed of her sins. In counterpoint to psychiatric theory, common decency tells us categorically that blaming the victim for her suffering is deplorable.

Excessive emphasis on guilt, masochism, and sadism ignores the existence of more constructive explanations for understanding and doing something helpful about human unhappiness.

This certainly seems true of Jennifer's situation. If we consider the fugitive way she fled from Richard's apartment we might readily assume that Jennifer believed that she had committed some wrongful act. But what is she actually guilty of having done? In Richard's mind, of course, Jennifer is culpable of being incompetent. Many of us, reluctant as we may be to admit it, might agree with Richard. But is guilt really the correct explanation for Jennifer's behavior? Guilt is derived from the violation of a moral code, such as acting in a way to harm or violate another person intentionally. But wasn't it Jennifer herself who was the victim, not the perpetrator of a wrongful act—being robbed? We can see from Jennifer's situation, then, how shame and guilt get confused and how this results in the victim's being punished for her victimization—often, over and over again.

Too frequently, we unthinkingly attribute the causes of our patients' unhappiness to their being guilty of some unknown wrongful act rather than carefully examining their situation and realizing that they are harboring a feeling of shame in experiencing themselves as the helpless victim or powerless observer of some grievous event.

A common illustration should help make my point more clear. Our inability to avert illness in ourselves, or to change the morbid fate of those we care about leaves us feeling helpless. For example, a powerful barrier against responding to the care needed by victims of AIDS, by family and friends, is an anger the potential caregiver experiences toward the victim for rendering the caregiver unable to change the ultimate course of the victim's illness. The feeling of helplessness is a shame reaction. Unlike guilt, which usually has an articulate voice, shame generally is experienced as an unfathomable uneasiness about one's life and is expressed, as in Jennifer's sobs, as a muffled cry. Too often, when we are shamed we are unable to articulate the precise cause of our grief to other people. Indeed, I would go so far as to describe shame as an *ironic* emotion. Often, the stronger the emotion, the less is the sufferer aware of its presence. The more intensely Jennifer was being hurt by Richard's behavior, the less she was able to do anything constructive about her unhappiness, because the heightened shaming that pervaded the interaction at Richard's door made it increasingly more difficult for her to understand and to express what she was actually feeling at the moment.

On the other hand, had Jennifer been guilty of some wrongful act, she undoubtedly would have experienced less pain and misery than she did with Richard. If, let's say, Jennifer had admitted to Richard that she had, as Richard might accuse her, encouraged a co-worker's romantic attention at a party they both attended, a solution for Richard's jealousy is readily available. There are words and agreed-upon actions to express guilt that enable wrongdoers to confess their misdeeds and to redeem themselves. In this instance, Jennifer could confess that she enjoys other men's attraction toward her, but promises that she will never again encourage it. She then could ask Richard for his forgiveness, because he is the only man she loves.

But Jennifer could not confess. Quite frankly, she simply has no idea about what happens within her psyche that prevents her from taking proper care of herself.

Fortunately, we do not need to be as mystified by Jennifer's helpless despair as she is. The agitation of helplessness that victims of shame demonstrate are continually being fueled by "the feeling of lack of legitimate entitlement" to those aspects of life necessary for a happy and fulfilling existence. What do I mean by the term "legitimate entitlement"? Our patients can answer this for us by remembering back to innumerable everyday situations and recognizing how they responded to potentially exciting interpersonal opportunities. When their eyes encountered someone they found very appealing—whether walking down the street, shopping in a market, sitting across from that person in a train or bus or even in a crowded restaurant—what did they do? Did they smile and encourage the other person's attention? Or did they try to look nonchalant and unaware of the attractive person? Or, even more sadly, did they feel embarrassed and quickly look away?

Jennifer almost always averts her eyes from someone to whom she warmly inwardly responds, a common sign of shame. In contrast, if we experience ourselves as legitimately entitled as a person, then we experience ourselves as deserving to find and secure for ourselves the most interesting, attractive, and worthwhile people available for friendship. Correspondingly, we feel confident that the people we are drawn to will find us of interest to them. Jennifer never feels that she deserves the best.

Not surprisingly, the most powerful adult experiences of being shamed are based upon the types of painful humiliation that people suffered during their tender developmental years. Feelings of lack of legitimate entitlement replay the shameful and humiliating events of one's past.

We tend to see in another's response to our overtures for intimacy and friendship reflections of how we have been led to regard ourselves from early in life. Crippling feelings of shame and pessimism come from the limited ways we were permitted to be useful and attractive in our own families and in the countless other significant growing-up experiences we have had.

In many families one or two members become targets of blame for the problems that the family is experiencing. Jennifer served this role in her family. Repeatedly, throughout her growing-up years, various people in her family said and did hurtful things to her, while at the same time ignoring her emotional needs. Jennifer was made to feel surplus, a burden, and an unwanted younger child in her large family. Her immigrant parents had trouble making ends meet. When she was young, Jennifer wanted the same privileges that her American-born classmates regarded as their birthright—higher education, ballet and piano lessons. Her unsympathetic, hardworking mother said to Jennifer more than once: "You ask too much. Sometimes I wish you were never born." While in college after having made an expensive purchase of clothes, her father angrily indicted her with the judgment: "The more education you get, the dumber you are."

As our patients move away from their families, many of them, like Jennifer, tend to perpetuate the limited ways of expressing themselves they have derived from their families. If they dislike their appearance, the way they speak or walk, or if they feel they are not as intellectual, skilled, or admired as some other person, then they are victims of the shaming and self-contempt taught to them in the bowels of their families. The result of continual self-contempt, as Jennifer demonstrates, is helpless unhappiness.

From my description of Jennifer's shameful self-regard and her callous treatment by Richard, you reasonably may assume that Jennifer is the victim of this story. However, if we reexamine the situation between Richard and Jennifer you may be startled to learn that Jennifer and Richard are *both* victims of shame. Unless we appreciate the precise way Richard is also a victim, we will fail to grasp the complexity of shame.

In the remainder of this chapter I will seek to show you that the shaming that is normally part of one's daily life usually does not come from someone's intentional meanness, or even their ill-wishes. I will demonstrate the very important consideration made in the last chapter: that much of the hurtful shame that we are usually involved in— both as the shamer and the ashamed—comes from our inability to protect those we care about.

After I provide you with the groundwork for understanding the reciprocity of being both shamer and ashamed in humiliating events, I will turn to Richard's side of the story to demonstrate my contention that shaming events leave few participants unscarred.

INTERSUBJECTIVE SHAME

One of the best definitions to help us understand the decisive factors involved in shame was offered by the famous German philosopher, Georg Hegel. Hegel (1892) tells us that shame is an anger about what *ought not to be.*

Applied to everyday life, Hegel's definition seems exceedingly accurate. We all know of the notorious father who viciously slapped his young daughter who had tearfully returned home from having fallen from a tree she was climbing, badly abrasing her knees. His angry words and actions imply that she was being punished for having done something wrong. Viewed from the outside, the father as a representative of society was attempting to discipline his daughter into taking proper care of herself. The father's anger and the daughter's guilt seem to be the major emotional players in this allegorical drama.

However, quite a different psychology ensues from viewing the drama from the psyche of the father. The father is the caretaker of his child. He loves her and cares deeply about her. Not surprisingly, then, he became frightened and upset from seeing how vulnerable his child is to injury. Moreover, he not only fears for her, he is ashamed that he has failed her as her protector. His fleeting awareness of his inability to shelter his child sufficiently stirs his anger and resentment against what ought not to be. In other words, the father feels self-recrimination that he is not an adequate father at such times when he is forced to realize that he can do little to protect his beloved child from being vulnerable to life's hurts. To divest himself of his painful impotence, which he doesn't understand, and does not know how to deal with, the father strikes out at his daughter. By blaming her for his uncomfortable feelings (of helplessness) he unconsciously has transposed his daughter from being a victim of injury to that of a perpetrator of a wrongful act— being an irresponsible child. Moreover, by becoming angry at her, the father self-protectively insulates himself from his daughter's hurt. Unfortunately, in the transformation of feeling helpless to blaming the person who arouses feelings of inadequacy, a destructive interpersonal pattern is established. Emotionally separating himself from people who awaken his sense of vulnerability makes it difficult for the father to be empathically in touch with his daughter's needs, or any one else's, for that matter.

With these considerations in mind, let us return to Richard. When Richard stood in his doorway early that Tuesday morning he had flashbacks to events he had experienced with Jennifer in the past. The first of his remembrances was of an incident that had occurred six months before. In this previous event Richard had opened his door early one evening to find Jennifer mournfully upset. She told him that she had been mugged and robbed two hours before as she entered a subway station on her way to his house from her job. She was too embarrassed to call the police. She was afraid that they might ask her if she had been robbed before. It was too humiliating, she said, to tell them that this had happened several times before. She just left the train station and wandered through the streets for more than an hour.

Richard had responded very differently on that earlier occasion than in the situation described in the beginning of this chapter. He drew Jennifer gently into the apartment. He took off her carrying case and her heavy winter coat. He guided her to the sofa, putting his arms around her. He held her close to him for a long while without speaking.

And when she began to stir, he told her how susceptible he was to her feelings. Her hurts, fears, and sorrows struck him, he told her with tears in his eyes, as if he himself was being jabbed by something sharp. He could always sense in a split-second when something was wrong with her—whether he saw her in person, or if they were speaking on the telephone. He admitted that his sensitivity to her did not come from his trying to be empathic and understanding. His attunement with her feelings just happened spontaneously when she was in some sort of distress.

Richard felt that being emotionally sensitive to Jennifer wasn't enough. He knew that he needed to help her become more resourceful. Later that evening he carefully described to Jennifer a number of effective ways that she could protect herself and her valuables from the predators of the city. To his dismay, however, Jennifer became bored and annoyed with the details of Richard's strategies for taking care of herself. Like most shame-sensitive people, Jennifer specializes in attending only those activities in which she excels, avoiding situations that make her anxious and uncomfortable. Consequently, Jennifer dismissed Richard's concern for her safety. She claimed that it was too much trouble to have to think about these things constantly. She expressed indignation that she had to concern herself with the psychopaths of the city. With resignation, Richard let the matter drop.

Standing in the doorway that fateful Tuesday morning, Richard also remembered a second incident about a month earlier. Jennifer had opened her purse to pay the driver of the taxi that brought them home after going to see a Broadway play. She had placed her purse on the seat as she paid the driver. As the cab was pulling around the corner, after they had stepped out into the street, Jennifer realized that she had not retrieved her purse. She yelled after the driver, but he didn't stop.

Arriving inside Richard's apartment she sobbed, "I'm worthless! I'm a loser! Everything I do is wrong! I can't do anything right!"

At first, Richard felt unusually cold-hearted toward Jennifer. He realized that he was annoyed not only at her carelessness, but also angry that the loss wouldn't have happened if she hadn't refused his advice on how to protect her valuables.

Gradually, Jennifer's desperate self-punitive mood overcame his displeasure toward her. He recognized that the most important consideration at that moment was not the lost money, nor her carelessness. He should be more concerned, he told himself, about the depth of her self-dejection. She was a valuable person and he truly loved her. He urgently wanted her to know that and to firmly believe it. So Richard put aside his anger and his uneasy feelings about how vulnerable he was to her inability to protect herself. He held her closely and spoke softly to Jennifer about her many admirable attributes.

You might well ask that if Richard had really cared about Jennifer how could he have treated her so shabbily—telling her that his love for her was sick and allowing her to flee in an emotional panic?

Standing in his doorway that last morning with Jennifer,

Richard realized, remorsefully, that his close identification with her portended continuous hurt and rage for himself. His close bonding with Jennifer, which once had been the sanctuary of intimacy, had now become little more than a crucible of self-hatred and hopeless anguish. To his dismay, Richard realized that Jennifer's despair was unbearable for him. He was becoming violently oscillated by the precariousness of her life. Insofar as she saw herself flawed and degraded as a person, he was aware that she would continually depend upon him for reassurance that her life was worth continuing. He was no longer willing, perhaps even unable, to assuage her misery and reassure her. Intuitively, he sensed that telling her that he felt sorry for her would distance her from him. Yet he experienced no other means of escaping from his unbearable feelings of helplessness in taking care of her. So he dolefully suppressed his tender feelings for Jennifer and acted and sounded as if he no longer cared about her.

Why was Richard, who appears highly competent and self-confident, so sensitive and vulnerable to Jennifer's shame?

Richard's sensitivity to shame had grown out of a series of events that completely eroded his trust in his father. Until he was 5 years of age he had unquestioningly believed that his father understood and loved him. He had always felt safer with his father than with his mother, who continually criticized him and made incessant demands on him for attention.

To Richard's dismay, his father left him quite mysteriously some months before his fifth birthday. His endless questions to his mother and to his relatives only brought the spare, and what he later realized was an embarrassed, reassurance that his father was away working and would be home soon.

A few weeks before his birthday, a letter finally arrived from his father. He remembers his mother reading to him that his father would be home for his birthday. He also wrote that he would bring with him a wonderful gift for Richard.

The waiting for his father seemed endless. Richard's

friends would ask him, "Where is your father? Don't you have a father?" He did not know what to tell them.

But, worst of all, his father failed to appear for the party. This was the first time Richard had known his father to lie to him. So confused was Richard by what had happened to his father that Richard assumed that he had done something awful to make his father angry at him. Similar to Gina discussed in Chapter 2, Richard awoke nightly from perturbing nightmares, replete with self-recriminating scenarios of the possible ways that he was responsible for his father's disappearance.

A week or so later, without further notice, Richard's father appeared at their home. He didn't tell Richard where he had been, or even why he had not shown up for his birthday party. He just smiled and said, "Happy Birthday, son!" and handed Richard a wrapped gift.

At that moment Richard saw the man he had known as his father as a stranger—a person he didn't recognize and didn't trust—but who acted as if he knew Richard intimately. In retrospect, Richard realized that this man did not know him, because if he did he would have understood that no gift at that moment could erase Richard's deep disappointment in his father for having deserted him, leaving him with his bitter mother.

Richard did not remember what the present was that he had been given. He was certain, however, that whatever it was, he hurled it onto the floor. He distinctly recalls his father's reaction. It began with a look of surprise. Next, his father's usually piercing gray eyes turned away from Richard, as if his father was uncontrollably angry at Richard and was trying to compose himself.

From that day onward, Richard continued to perceive his father's attitude toward him in all matters, except athletics and scholarship, as bitter disappointment and displeasure.

Richard had viewed his father as a man of strong character and high moral values. He had always feared that if he ever did something wrong his father would somehow know about it and would again desert him, as he did when Richard was 5.

It was a startling surprise to learn from his mother, at the time he had started dating Jennifer, that his father had gone away from home when Richard was a child because he had been caught by Richard's mother in an affair with one of her friends. She banished Richard's father from the house.

Richard's father was a man I knew well. What young Richard saw in his father's eyes was not rancor and disapproval at Richard, but his father's own diminished self-regard. His father's gray eyes were stung with the hurt and shame from a shattered belief. He had assumed up until his son's angry rejection of his gift that he had been a reliable father, whose love Richard would never question. But his son's bitter reaction revealed the fictitiousness of this pretense. Feelings of shame come not only from revealing our frailties to others but, perhaps more importantly, from being forced to face aspects of one's own vulnerabilities in one's self, which, up until that moment, have not been recognized. Shame, in this sense, comes from the realization of how one's life has been duplicitous. To reiterate, shame is closely associated with the bitterness and animosity directed toward oneself, which comes from the realization of having lived a lie.

For people like Richard's father, shameful experience is regarded as impossible to communicate and to share with another human being. No one needs persuasion that our most terrifying moments are those that cannot be shared with others. They cause flight and secrecy, leaving us isolated and frightened.

As disturbing as his father's shame might have been for him, it had a no less devastating effect on Richard. His father's continual sense of inadequacy about how his life had been lived fostered a destructive bond between him and his son.

Shame is highly contagious. It can be discharged in such a subtle and indirect way that the person who is inflicted with the painful feelings of humiliation and shame is unaware of the reception of unwanted feelings.

The process of a sensitive and vulnerable person assuming someone else's shameful feelings is called "borrowing their shame." Very few people go through life without acquiring, at some time or other, this unfair burden. We are especially susceptible to borrowed shame when we care about and are closely identified with a person harboring painful self-punitive feelings. Richard cared about his father. But he was too young to understand and to help him with his hurt feelings. Understandably, it left young Richard feeling helpless and upset in his father's presence. He felt he had done something wrong because he did not realize that his bad feelings came from taking on his father's sense of failure and dishonor.

We can see from Richard and Jennifer's backgrounds how shame contaminates the language and the transactions of caring and concern in an intimate relationship, transposing them to those of angry and hurtful expression in their current lives.

We shall see in Chapter 15 how their unrecognized shame was treated.

PART II

UNDERSTANDING SHAME

5

USES OF THE CONCEPT OF SHAME

I am ashamed of what I *am*. Shame therefore
realizes an intimate relation of myself to myself.
Through shame I have discovered an aspect of
my being.

—Jean-Paul Sartre

This chapter serves as a brief account of the traverse of ideas
concerning the nature of shame in the history of Western
thought. This survey will include an examination of the
meanings of the concept contained in the old and new
Scriptures, as well as in the works of influential philosophers and men of letters.

To date, there has been no review of shame that inte-
grates psychoanalytic and psychological views with the
philosophical development of ideas, except for Thrane's
(1979) article. Generally, when clinicians write they tend to
ignore the important insights made by philosophers and
writers.

In tracing the history of ideas we find that the notion of
shame was not a very significant concern early in Western
thought. It served only to differentiate among the diverse
manifestations of disapprobation and guilt. The perspective
of the Old Testament Scripture focused on the Hebrew

99

people's relationship with their God. The primary concern was one's appearance in the eyes of God rather than with one's fellow beings. Moreover, the classical Greek idea of a personal conscience, as self-reflection on one's own behavior, receives little emphasis in the Old Testament (Achtemeier 1985).

The Hebrew words *bos* and *kalain* are used most often to indicate shame in the Old Testament. They convey the notion of disgrace attending any event that causes public humiliation because one has done something unfitting God's decrees (Richards 1985). The shameful situation may involve action physically injurious to another person, but more often it conveys a disobedience to God or a loss of pride and confidence in one's relationship to the Lord.

The prophets were often depicted as scolding the Hebrews for trusting foreign alliances rather than their covenant with God. They warned that the shame of defeat by one's enemies would result from the Hebrews' disobedience to God. For example, Isaiah cries out to his flock, "Pharaoh's protection will be your shame. Egypt's shade will bring you disgrace."

The word generally used in the New Testament for shame was the Greek verb *aischyno*. A survey of the New Testament suggests that shame takes on a new meaning there (Richards 1985). No longer is the objective situation that evokes shame emphasized, as in the Old Testament; instead, the ashamed's subjective reaction to the ridicule of other people for acts dishonorable to the decrees of the Lord is stressed (Achtemeier 1985).

What other people think of one is portrayed in the New Testament as the primary source of shame. While this distinction is shared with classical Greek culture, an important exception should be noted. Far less frequently in Greek writings than in the New Testament do the words that refer to shame have a positive tone—such as in commending an unassuming or obedient attitude. The Greeks saw man as the measure of all things. Consequently, to be low on the social scale, to know poverty, or to be socially powerless was regarded as dishonorable. The New Testament, on the other hand, viewed human action and proper attitude as measurable only in regard to God Himself. Compared to Him, humans are righteously viewed as humble (Richards 1985). For example, Peter the Apostle wrote: "If you suffer as a Christian, do not be ashamed, but praise God that you bear that name."

In summary, then, shame is an evolving notion in the Scriptures. In the Old Testament shame emphasizes the objective aspects of the situation—be it a national disaster or a personal one—that humbles people before their God. In the New Testament shame is conveyed by public ridicule and represents a powerful fear compelling adherence to the Scriptures (Richards 1985).

The classical Greeks had a notion of personal conscience that differentiates them from the peoples of the Scriptures. The double meaning of shame connotes this state as both disgrace and as respect of reverence. Riezler (1942) points out the importance of this compounded meaning of shame:

> The Greek distinction between *Aidos* and *Aischyne* does not correspond to the French between *Pudeur* and *honte* [*Pudeur* means a kind of shame that tends to keep you from an act, whereas you feel *honte* after an act]; nor has it anything to do with a distinction between sexual and non-sexual matters. . . . The origin of *Aischyne* is dishonor, of *Aidos,* awe. Dishonor puts the emphasis on man-made codes. If you are ashamed of violating or having violated such codes, the Greeks use the verb that corresponds to the noun *Aischyne. Aidos* is not concerned merely with man-made codes. You feel *Aidos* when confronted with things nature tells you to revere and not to violate. Shame in sexual matters is *Aidos*, not *Aischyne.* In the *Odyssey,* Hephaistos catches his wife, Aphrodite, with her lover, Ares, in nets he spread around Aphrodite's bed. He calls all the gods and goddesses to look at the adulterous couple. The gods hurry to the place, but the goddesses stay at home out of shame. Homer calls this shame *Aidos.* [pp. 402–403]

The sanctioning emotion that instills shame, according to Plato, was fear. Plato writes in his epic, *Laws:*

Do we not distinguish two kinds of fear which are opposite . . . On the one side we are afraid of some evil that we anticipate might happen—and on the other side we are often afraid of opinion, namely, that we believe to be judged evil because we do or say something that is not honorable. We call, and I believe everyone else calls, this fear shame—*Aischyne*—This fear now is opposed to all other fears and pain as well as it is opposed to most and the greatest pleasures. . . . And isn't it so that both the legislator, and everyone else who is worth anything, respects this fear and holds it in the greatest honor, calling it *Aidos*—shame or reverence or awe—and the audacity opposed to it he dubs *shamelessness, anaideia,* and he holds it the greatest evil to everyone privately or publicly. . . . And isn't it further so that this fear saves us in many important ways. . . . There are two things which give victory—courage before enemies and fear of cowardly disgrace with friends. . . . Hence it is necessary for each one of us to be both fearless and fearful. [Wurmser 1987, pp. 65–66]

Aristotle also emphasized the element of fear as key to the arousal of shame. Introducing the dimension of time to his discussion, Aristotle contended that "the impression of dishonor" is a manifestation of self-awareness that enables the person to *anticipate* that his misdeeds will cause him future dishonor. The sense of the future is shame's instrument for effecting courageous and moral action and avoiding pain and uneasiness.

Thomas Aquinas, in reworking Aristotle's ethical system, took up the significance of the *character* of the actor, a consideration Aristotle ignored. Shame he regarded as awareness of evil. Aquinas claimed that the more the ignominy of an act of sin is felt, as opposed to the fear of future dishonor, the more virtuous is the sense of morality (Rotenstreich 1965).

Spinoza put a greater emphasis on the precise emotion governing shame than did his predecessors. "Shame," he wrote, "is pain accompanied by the idea of some action of our own, which we believe to be blamed by others." A close examination of Spinoza's text shows that the pain to which he is referring is not (as with Plato, Aristotle, and Aquinas) fear. Spinoza uses the word *Tristitia* to note the feeling of sadness that accompanies dishonor and sin (Rotenstreich 1965).

Spinoza's stress on sadness, rather than fear, is a significant insight into the nature of shame. It captures the vital contrast between shame and guilt (discussed in Chapter 3). Guilt is *bodily* oriented. It is concerned with the anticipation of corporeal punishment for acts and thoughts abhorrent to feared, powerful, authority figures. Shame, in contrast, as Spinoza intuitively recognized, contains an emotional substratum that guilt does not—the *regret* at being lesser in virtue than one aspires to be.

Baruch Spinoza, the excommunicated and exiled Jewish philosopher of the seventeenth century, in noting the sadness that accompanies dishonor, brought the sense of shame into its appropriate place as a monitor of personal identity. The shame experienced as sadness expresses the tension between what "is" in one's current condition and the "ought" of one's sense of who one is or should be.

Goethe's *Faust* can be interpreted as powerfully depicting the sadness of shame that appears to be a prominent theme in modern Western culture. Goethe suggests that our culture strongly exhorts us to have boundless aspirations and pride built upon personal achievement. But, at the same time, we are left with a haunting doubt whether the fragile, vulnerable beings we regard ourselves to be have the vibrance to live our lives well.

Rarely has the unbearable sadness of our sense of who we are been more harrowingly described than by the seventeenth-century French philosopher Blaise Pascal. He portrays man as the feeblest reed in nature such that:

> When I consider the brief span of my life, swallowed up in eternity before and behind it, the small space that I fill, or even see, engulfed in the infinite immensity of space which I know not, and which know not me, I am afraid, and wonder to see myself here rather

than there; for there is no reason why I should be here rather than there, now rather than then. . . .[p. 35]

The eighteenth-century philosophers decisively tied shame to personal identity. Beginning with Kant's claim that shame, not guilt, was the only reliable motivator for moral behavior, shame came to be regarded as reflecting the good feelings that would come from living virtuously and eschewing disgraceful behavior (Thrane 1979).

In his precritical period Kant wrote:

The law of duty, through the positive worth which obedience to it makes us feel, finds easier access through the respect for ourselves in the consciousness of our freedom. It is well-established, so that a man fears nothing more than to find himself on self-examination to be worthless and contemptible in his own eyes, every good moral disposition can be grafted on to this self-respect, for the consciousness of freedom is the best, indeed the only, guard that can keep ignoble and corrupting influences from bursting in upon the mind. [p. 167]

Hegel pursued the Kantian imperative of shame as a means of transcending the less-developed sense of consciousness of self. A vital concern in Hegel's transcendental ethics is that of other-directed love. He writes that shame does not mean to be ashamed of loving, say on account of exposing or surrendering the body—but to be ashamed that love is not complete, that there still be something inimical in oneself which keeps love from reaching completion and perfection (Wurmser 1981).

Hegel's concern with the sense of shame as an *incongruity* in man's reflection upon himself is found prominently in the work of the modern German philosopher Max Scheler.

According to Scheler, the human organism is bound to a state of shame because of the discord he suffers from a lack of equilibrium, the disharmony between the demands of his animal, carnal appetites, on the one hand, and the meaning and intentionality of his spiritual being on the other. Only because he experiences his corporeal being reaching for a spiritual fulfillment is he capable of being able to feel ashamed (Rotenstreich 1965).

Scheler's work makes evident the *dual* nature of shame. The sense of shame acts as a constraint against bodily impulses, while at the same time carries an accentuated acuity as to who one can be. In this regard, it should be noted that psychoanalytic views on the human condition suffer from the erroneous assumption that the basic cause of any psychic phenomenon can be found only in some part of the person's physical condition (Hazard 1969). This point of view negates the *ontological insecurity* that is exigent from one's first moments of self-consciousness. As the developmental evidence presented in Chapter 1 shows, shame comes from not only feelings about how one's body is regarded, but, even more significantly, the identity and intention of that body. The insecurity of "who one is" is a vital source of human conflict ignored by the mainstream of psychoanalytic theory.

A close purview of psychoanalytic writings on shame reveals that theorists have followed Freud in regarding shame as being little more than a *defensive* mechanism to conceal concerns about bodily vulnerabilities and deficiencies. Miller (1989) in her review of Freud's writings on shame concludes:

In almost every instance in which he undertook a formal, focused analysis of the shame experience, he elaborated a reaction-formation concept of shame as a defense against the sexual-exhibitionistic drive. The following passage is characteristic of Freud's comments on shame as reaction-formation:

"During the period in life which may be called the period of 'sexual latency'—i.e., from the completion of the fifth year to the first manifestation of puberty (round about the eleventh year)—reaction-formations, or counter-forces, such as shame, disgust and

morality, are created in the mind. They are actually
formed at the expense of the excitations proceeding
from the erotogenic zones, and they rise like dams to
oppose the later activity of the sexual instincts." [p.
231]

Alfred Adler (1933) supported Freud's views about
shame, although he never used the term itself, when he
emphasized that "organ inferiority" and the "inferiority
complex" were the causes of neurotic suffering. Fenichel's
(1945) highly influential textbook on psychoanalytic theory
was also a key factor in confirming for the clinician Freud's
preliminary views about shame. Fenichel contended that
there is a direct correlation between shame and the need for
a defense against exhibitionism and scoptophilia. He used
as a clinical example shame as a specific force directed
against urethral erotic urges.
    As with most psychoanalytic perspectives in regard to
the purpose of a psychological function, there has been a
diverse opinion among theorists about the precise intent of
shame as a defensive mechanism. A major position, popularized by Freud, Jacobson, Nunberg, and Wurmser, view
shame primarily as a defensive strategy in the service of
morality. According to this view, shame is a reaction formation that intends the converse to what is phenomenologically experienced by the subject. As such, shame inhibits
exhibitionistic impulses by disguising forbidden wishes
from conscious awareness. This type of psychic vigilance
renders superego-disapproved wishes an inaccessibility to
action (Miller 1985). This position is the classical conflict–
drive theory of psychological functioning of shame.
    The second influential analytic position, includes the
more recent theories of Kohut, Knapp, Lewis, and Morrison.
These theorists agree with the first group that the experience of shame serves as an inhibitor of exhibitionistic
excitement. However, this theoretical position does not
regard morality as the primary impetus in the monitoring
process involved in shame. These analytic theorists contend
that the major intent of shame is to retain or restore a

cohesive self from overstimulation of self-expansive striv-ings (Miller 1985). The mechanisms the self uses in this regard take the form of humiliation and embarrassed inhi-bition of self. This theoretical contention is based on the rationale that the adaptive attention to the whole self is more vital than is the prohibition of specific acts injurious to morality. This is the self-psychology theory of psychological functioning of shame.

Is shame better understood in self psychology than it was in classical conflict theory? No, not really! Kohut and his followers still tie shame closely to the drives. Unfortu-nately, both positions are bound to bodily representations and defenses against sexuality and aggression. Psychoana-lytic theory, even self psychology, has evolved into a dy-namic account of emotional effervescence and turbulence (Goldberg 1989c). Sadly, it lacks a delineation of positive affects. The threads of analytic explanation of sensual and sexual pleasure, taken collectively, report these experiences as little more than the hydraulic release of tension. Freud's beliefs about love still hold forth.

According to psychoanalytic theory, inhibitions in expe-riencing passion egresses from the person's unconscious realization of wishing to seduce or be seduced by the parent of the opposite sex and to prevent one's rival, the parent of the same sex, from possessing the desired parental object. Anxiety from the incomplete repression of these desires carries the harbinger of abandonment, the ultimate punish-ment. To defend against punishing parental introjects, which are awakened by experiencing new objects in a sexually similar way to parental introjects from the past, the person develops one or the other of two specific self-protective defenses. The first of these is an ascetic attitude toward objects in which the mechanisms of humiliation and disgust are subliminally employed to thwart self-expansive, romantic impulses. The second psychological defense is a moral masochistic (guilt) reaction in the face of the desire. The person unwittingly assumes that yearning for new objects of desire is an act of disloyalty to parental introjects. The person, without awareness, induces hurtful and rejecting responses from the desired object. These interpersonal punishments disrupt the new object relationship, preventing the person from the threat of continued reawakening of incestuous impulses transferred from parental objects onto the new object. In defending the subject from additional narcissistic hurt and abandonment, asceticism and guilt work together, alternating in dominance.

What is the compelling force driving these defenses? Frankly, Freud (1905) mistrusted passionate love as a binding force in a mature relationship. He viewed the desire for intimacy as a seductive and repressive magical wish, which inflicts everyone. Freud believed that emotional attachments were the rediscovery of the lost object. This is to say, the experience of love repeats infantile patterns. Predicated upon the mother–child bonding, disappointments in our adult attempts at intimacy result in inevitable narcissistic hurt and depression. Weiner and White (1982) aptly describe the Freudian phenomenological experience of renewed disappointments in love as: "I am so unworthy that no one can love me in a reliable way and nothing I can do will insure that I will be permanently loved so there is no point in doing anything at all" (p. 492).

Freud, unlike Shakespeare, contrasts love not so much with fear as with hate. Shakespeare believed that love could cast out fear. In so doing, he used the term shame nine times more than guilt (Lynd 1958). In this regard, Gilligan (1976) points out that to the extent that Freud overestimated the degree to which aggression was instinctual, he failed to recognize how often shame was employed as a defense against passive and dependent libidinal needs to be taken care of and loved. Shame reminds us of the deep mutual involvement we have with others. Our discomfort with shame reflects our lack of comfort with the reality of our interdependence.

With psychoanalytic theory not offering us a fruitful understanding about the role of shame in the development of personal identity we need to find another direction in the history of ideas.

It is from the phenomenological accounts of playwrights,

poets, and novelists that we can at this moment in time receive the most illuminating descriptions of how shame struggles with personal identity.

An account of writers who, from their literary descriptions, have helped my own understanding of shame includes: Sophocles, Shakespeare, Tolstoy, Dostoevsky, Cervantes, Hawthorne, Melville, Conrad, Kafka, Faulkner, Hemingway, Maugham, Eliot, and Sartre.

I will here briefly discuss the writings of Jean-Paul Sartre, a philosopher, novelist, and playwright, with an interest—although a critical one—in psychoanalysis. Sartre (1956), when he indicates that the structure of shame is intentional, draws upon Nietzsche's observation that shame occurs when a person feels that he is nothing but a tool in the hands of a will infinitely greater than his own. Shame results from the apprehension of a thing; that thing is *me*. It is through the eyes of the other that I *am* ashamed that I *am*. Sartre (1956) writes:

> I see *myself* because *somebody* sees me—I am for myself only as I am a pure reference to the other—shame—is the *recognition* of the fact that I *am* indeed that object which the other is looking at and judging. I can be ashamed only as my freedom escapes me in order to become a *given* object. . . . My original fall is the existence of the other. . . . I grasp the other's look at the very center of my *act* as the solidification and alienation of my own possibilities. [pp. 349–352]

Sartre is telling us that *the look* of the other overthrows our omniscient belief in our autonomous independence and personal sovereignty. Sartre's examination of shame makes evident that our sense of who we are cannot be separate from those who see us. We can note the close parallels of Sartre's ideas and those of modern developmental psychology (discussed in Chapter 2).

Sartre's perspective on the importance of shame in personal identity should not be taken without some critical revision, however. He views the individual as thrown into the world of others without recourse to how he is seen. In so doing, he presents the individual as a *passive* object, powerfully assaulted by the critical eyes of the other. This point of view fails to recognize human *intersubjectivity*. What I mean by this is that not only are we looked upon by the other; in turn, we are observers and critics of others. Indeed, how we regard the other is integrally tied into how we are viewed, communicated with, and treated by the other. In our daily human scenarios, we simultaneously humiliate and shame our humiliators as they shame us. The need to recognize the healthy and constructive implications of shame (Schneider 1977) is accentuated by the critique on Sartre's one-sided view of shame. This is to say we must take responsibility for the humiliation and shame that are a daily part of our world.

Erik Erikson (1950) was, I believe, the first psychoanalytic theorist of prominence to recognize that psychological development was concerned more with issues of identity than with the vicissitudes of libido. However, although he had some insightful ideas regarding the identity issues in shame, he also had a number of misconceptions—especially about when shame occurs in personality development.

Helen M. Lynd, a sociologist interested in psychoanalytic theory, drew upon Erikson's ideas about identity to write a fascinating account of shame. Her erudite book, *On Shame and the Search for Identity* (1958), contains ideas, reflections, and passages from literature, philosophy, and social science. Her book has been my most valuable compendium in examining the unrecognized issues of shame in my patients. There also have been a few recent books written by clinicians who have made some inroads in how to treat shame-sensitive people. Their ideas will be contained in the clinical section of this book. These writers are: Lewis (1987c), Natanson (1987c), Morrison (1989), and Kaufman (1989).

6

A REEXAMINATION OF THE OEDIPAL MYTH AND MORAL MASOCHISM

O Shame! Where is thy blush?
                        —William Shakespeare

Modern psychotherapy, based upon psychoanalytic examination of the human condition, has fostered a moral masochism (guilt) model to explain monocausally the experiences of suffering. In this schema the sufferer has set himself up to be punished because of an internalized sense of deserving retribution.

Whether moral masochism or some other explanation is regarded as the central motif in the psychoanalytic explanation of suffering does not rest on idle curiosity. The ontology of psychoanalysis is not simply descriptive. It is intended to provide a powerful and veracious system of therapeutics.

In this chapter I explore how the moral masochism model evolved in psychoanalytic theory. I discuss Freud's rationale in choosing the Oedipus myth as the cornerstone of psychoanalytic theory. I show that Freud's interpretation of the Oedipus complex in Sophocles' *Oedipus Rex* is based upon a limited selection of the components of the story. I also contend that vital features of the myth, necessary to a proper understanding of human suffering were excluded from Freud's purview (Goldberg 1989b). To demonstrate my thesis that shame and its existential consequences, rather than moral masochism, lies at the heart of our difficulty in understanding complex manifestations of human suffering far more often than the psychoanalytic literature suggests, I reexamine the same "case study"—Shakespeare's *Hamlet*—that Freud did in purporting to evince that oedipal conflict is a universal, biological condition that is the essential source of psychopathology.

The drama Freud chose as his cause célèbre has an intriguing history (Goldberg 1991).

Four centuries of review and commentary have not sullied the marvel of Shakespeare's *Hamlet*. The play continues to be regarded as depicting universal human dilemmas in an unusually compelling manner. Today, however, few readers and playgoers approach the character of Hamlet without firm, prior beliefs about the precise psychological basis for Hamlet's mystery. According to Freud (1900), the conflict in *Hamlet* is of such perplexing concealment that the reader can *only* discover the cause of Hamlet's puzzling malady by the guidance of the oedipal metaphor. As every analyst well knows, the answer Freud provides, the question of Hamlet's procrastination in taking blood revenge against the murder of his father, established the foundation of psychoanalytic character analysis.

Should we be satisfied with Freud's explanation? I don't believe so. Despite the poetic facility of Freud's response to Hamlet's mystery, Freud's account is quite misleading. The use of an oedipal-conflict explanation actually offers us no real understanding of the unique character of Hamlet. If Hamlet's oedipal complex is the source of our fascination with the play, as Freud claims, then all other works of art with a strong oedipal theme also would raptly hold our attention. However, Western literature is replete with novels, short stories, and plays in which the characters are caught up in oedipal struggles. Most of these works have long been forgotten (Slochower 1971).

The central fascination of the drama is not due to the presence of an oedipal theme, but to Shakespeare's genius in presenting to us the intriguing personification of Hamlet—his values, ambitions, and the conditions that tempered the manner in which Hamlet presents himself to us (Mairet 1969).

THE OEDIPUS MYTH

To understand properly how Freud came to interpret Shakespeare's drama in such a way that enabled him to lay down the building blocks of psychoanalytic understanding, we must begin with how he personally identified with an even older universal drama, *Oedipus Rex.*

Freud regarded his own self-analysis as his most powerful and trustworthy investigative tool. He reported his introspective realizations in a series of letters over many years to an internist friend, Wilhelm Fliess. Because he highly valued Fliess's intuition he utilized the internist's comments for critically reviewing his own speculative findings (Goldberg 1989b).

On October 15, 1897, Freud reported to Fliess that he had discovered in his own self-analysis all the symptoms displayed by Oedipus in the drama *Oedipus Rex,* which Sophocles transformed from two early Greek myths. From 1897 on Freud utilized the concept of *oedipal conflict* as the explanatory metaphor of his metapsychology, contending that the desire for the mother and rivalry with the father is a universal characteristic of the early childhood of the male gender. Unsuccessful resolution of the oedipal conflict, Freud indicated, results in neurotic suffering. For the neurotic, all experiences, including interpersonal events, are little more than the subject's repetitive fantasies, ushering from origins of an oedipal nature. Freud (1928) points out: "Every punishment is at bottom castration and, as such, a fulfillment of the old passive attitude to the father. Even fate is ultimately only a father projection" (p. 25).

Freud further indicates that his oedipal interpretation of human experience that all ills that befall a person are experienced unconsciously as deserved is contained in every work of literature that is generally regarded as holding universal truths. A beautifully worded statement of the universal importance of the oedipal dilemma was written in 1900 in Freud's monumental work, *Interpretation of Dreams:*

> [T]he compelling force of destiny [in Sophocles' *Oedipus Rex*] moves us only because it might have been ours—because the oracle laid the same curse upon us before our birth as upon him. It is the fate of all of us, perhaps, to direct our first sexual impulses towards our mother and our first hatred and our first murderous wish against our father. Our dreams convince us that that is so . . .while the poet, as he unravels the past, brings to light the guilt of Oedipus, he is at the same time compelling us to recognize our own inner minds, in which those same impulses, though suppressed, are still to be found. . . . Like Oedipus, we live in ignorance of these wishes, repugnant to morality, which have been forced upon us by Nature, and after their revelation we may all of us well seek to close our eyes to the scenes of our childhood. [pp. 296–297]

Forbidden Wishes, the Harbingers of Guilt

To effectively demonstrate that his oedipal explanation of tragedy was contained in other great works of literature besides *Oedipus Rex,* Freud chose as his next "case study" Shakespeare's *Hamlet.*

Since the inception of the play, critics have been intrigued with the question of Hamlet's hesitation in carrying out his revenge against Claudius. Revenge, the critics have contended, would have been reflexively expected of a person of Hamlet's position in his era. For Hamlet it clearly was not.

Freud tells us that Hamlet is suffering from a guilty conscience of oedipal origins. Hamlet unconsciously senses that he had desired to do precisely what his uncle, Claudius, has consummated—doing away with Hamlet's father and seducing Hamlet's mother. Consequently, were Hamlet to carry out his revenge against the man who fulfilled the repressed wishes of Hamlet's own childhood, then Hamlet would, according to Freud's interpretation of the oedipal metaphor, also have had, like Oedipus, to castigate himself. Hamlet's self-abnegation egresses from his unconscious realization that he is no better than is his uncle.

Freud's interpretation of Hamlet's guilty conscience should not be taken without some questions about the logistics of his deductions. In examining Freud's analysis of Hamlet we are struck by an apparent lapse in reasoning caused by what seems to be an equivocation in existential logic. We cannot fail to notice that in explaining a guilty conscience in the person of Hamlet, Freud offers an unprecedented interpretation of human motivation—a line of reasoning that parts company with common wisdom.

I am referring to the material in the drama that shows that although Claudius admits his guilt for murder and adultery in the prayer scene (3.3),* he expresses only a modicum of emotional distress about his deeds. This is to say, Claudius indicates absolutely no concern about the effect of his crime on other people; nor does he mention the immorality of his actions, except for a passing concern that his soul might be punished for his acts. I assume that some readers might not accept these contentions about Claudius as substantial without additional evidence. Therefore, I will point out that Claudius has ample opportunity to repent, but he does not. He tells us (3.3) that he would commit these crimes *again* because he would *not* want to relinquish his desire for "My crown, mine own ambition and my Queen."

In fact, Claudius becomes agitated only when he senses that Hamlet is planning to dispatch him in a manner similar to the way in which he murdered his brother. In short, throughout the drama Claudius is far less upset by his *committed deeds* than Hamlet is for his reputed *forbidden wishes*.

We are moved to inquire that if guilt is so powerful a

---

*References are to act and scene.

motivator, why is Claudius not highly distressed by his villainous acts? Our clinical experience might suggest that the reason for this is that Claudius is a psychopath, whereas Hamlet is a civilized neurotic. Freud, however, offers no such facile diagnostic explanation. Freud, instead, provides a powerful paradoxical explanation in which he reverses and radically reconstitutes the dynamic import of *thought* and *deed.* We should notice that this explanation, if invalid, would unravel the entire fabric of moral masochism as a viable understanding of most types of human suffering. But first, let us look at the etiology of Freud's rationale before we judge the validity of moral masochism.

Freud explains Hamlet's agitation and Claudius's lack of emotional distress by contending that psychical reality, not objective reality, is the basis of psychological conflict. Presumably, the dreams and fantasies of Hamlet were of such illicit tenor that they even exceeded the villainous nature of Claudius's actual deeds. From this perspective, Freud can be seen to be contending that a forbidden wish might on occasion, as with Hamlet, be a more potent wellspring of guilt than is the actual commission of the act itself. In so doing, Freud (1900), cleverly links Hamlet's fate to that of Oedipus. He indicates that

> [T]he changed treatment of the same material reveals the whole difference in the mental life of these two widely separate epochs of civilization: the secular advance of repression in the emotional life of man-kind. In the *Oedipus* the child's wishful phantasy that underlies it is brought into the open and realized as it would be in a dream. In *Hamlet* it remains repressed—as in the case of a neurosis. [p. 298]

Did Freud have clinical evidence for assuming that re-pressed desires are often equally dynamically charged ex-periences of guilt as are the actual criminal acts? He claims he does. It is important, however, to be aware of the context in which Freud gathered the clinical data upon which he formulated repression theory.

These findings came at a time when Freud was attempting to resolve one of the most serious dilemmas that has ever threatened the acceptance of psychoanalysis as a legitimate scientific method. In his autobiography, Freud (1935) tells of the uneasiness he was undergoing prior to his observation that repressed wishes were the cause of neurosis.

> I must mention an error into which I fell for a while and which might well have had fatal consequences for the whole of my work. Under the pressure of the technical procedure which I used at that time, the majority of my patients reproduced from their childhood scenes in which they were sexually seduced by some grown-up person. I believed these stories, and consequently supposed that I had discovered the roots of the subsequent neurosis in these experiences. However, I was at last obliged to recognize that these scenes of seduction had never taken place, and that they were only phantasies which my patients made up or which I myself had perhaps forced upon them, I was for some time completely at a loss. When I pulled myself together, I was able to draw the right conclusions from my discovery; namely, that the neurotic symptoms were not related directly to actual events but to phantasies embodying wishes, and that as far as the neurosis was concerned psychical reality was of more importance than material reality. [pp. 62–63]

"Psychical reality," as a force of suppression of material, is isomorphic with the physics of Freud's day. In psychological language this position posited that the repression of a motive renders that motive a more powerful force than the aftermath of a spent, expressed motive (regardless of the actual content of the motive). The physical theories of Freud's day have been radically transformed—so should repression theory.

CRITICISM OF REPRESSION THEORY

We can still marvel at Freud's brilliant tour de force in cleverly modifying a clinical theory whose "invalidity" threatened to nullify years of arduous clinical investigation. Nonetheless, Freud's contention that repressed wishes are more powerful wellsprings of human suffering than are actual events is a mistaken invention. Indeed, it is one of the most serious pitfalls of Freud's theorizing and is partially responsible for psychoanalytic misunderstanding of the importance of shame in human experience.

Rarely can repressed motives be empirically demonstrated. At best they can be inferred and be deductively evinced. Psychoanalytic investigators too often have not been content with deductive reasoning. In many instances in which the evidence for a theoretical hypothesis is not apparent or even when contradictory evidence is found, a reaction-formation explanation is enjoined to confirm the hypothesis. The concept says, in effect, if evidence is not present to verify the analytic hypothesis it is because the (reputed) dynamic at work is so powerful that it had to be repressed. The lack of evidence, ironically, becomes a proof of the theory being tested and an especially strong corroboration at that.

Freud has been accused of using literary material as proofs of cherished ideas rather than open-minded tests of his inferences. Therefore, we must take more heed than Freud seems to have when he mentions only in passing in the above quotation from his autobiography that he may have forced his own beliefs (derived, we assume, from his own self-analysis) onto his patients.

Reaction-formation explanations by psychoanalytic investigators are especially troubling to those practitioners and other behavioral scientists who believe that psychoanalytic theory contains premises that are capable of scientific verification. Semantic sciences, such as psychoanalysis, are properly judged not by the substantive truth of their premises, but whether or not there is a *methodology* that is logically capable of assessing the credibility of its hypotheses (Edelson 1984). Reaction-formation formulation makes hypothesis-verification impossible. By employing theoretical premises that prevent the opportunity for accepting alternatives to its hypotheses, psychoanalysis operates as a nonscientific discipline (regardless of the degree of veracity of the clinical observations it offers).

I have stressed the self-defeating imposition of reaction-formation strategies in psychoanalytic explanation because, as I will shortly demonstrate, reaction-formation theory was ubiquitously employed by Ernest Jones to avert the deficiencies in Freud's theoretical contention that moral masochism was the cause of Hamlet's suffering.

Hamlet's Reputed Oedipal Complex

Let us look at the literary evidence Freud claims to be sufficient to support his contention that a guilty conscience caused Hamlet's suffering.

What we find in examining Freud's claim is that evidence for Hamlet's oedipal conflict fueled by pangs of guilt is strangely lacking in the play, no matter how persistently the reader searches for it. In fact, rather than finding supportive data for Freud's guilty-conscience notion, there is ample *negative* evidence in the play of Freud's contentions. In short, the reader comes away from examining Shakespeare's masterpiece and assuming that Hamlet's suffering is due to oedipal guilt only by disregarding several essential components of the drama. I will discuss briefly five of these considerations.

First, it is highly questionable that Hamlet's attachment to his mother was either prolonged or unusually strong. Evidence of intermeshed bonding is a primary necessity for verification of oedipal conflict. Goddard (1960) and others have indicated that Hamlet's vibrant male friendships, especially with Horatio, and his falling in love with Ophelia, a girl rather different in temperament and personality from Gertrude, seems to have occurred at phase-appropriate times in Hamlet's development. Moreover, Gertrude appears to encourage her son's union with Ophelia. This evidence serves as negative validation that Hamlet was suffering from an intense, pathological oedipal conflict.

Second, another primary consideration in validating oedipal-conflict evidence is the presence of destructive impulses toward the father. Nowhere in the play is there any suggestion that Hamlet desired his father's death. Indeed, Hamlet throughout the drama describes his father in exultant terms, such as, "So excellent a King," a man "for all in all, I shall not look upon his like again" (1.2).

Jones (1976) tries to rescue Freud's oedipal explanation by employing the discreditable reaction-formation strategy to account for Hamlet's apparent lack of oedipal rage at his father. Jones indicates that

> If . . . the "repression" is considerable, then the hostility towards the father will be correspondingly concealed from consciousness; this is often accompanied by the development of the opposite sentiment, namely of an exaggerated regard and respect for him, and a morbid solicitude for his welfare, which completely cover the underlying relationship. [p. 79]

Rank (1964) warns us of the invalidity of reverse explanations of oedipal conflict. He indicates from his own clinical observation that the oedipal complex

> is not to be found in practice so clearly as mythology represents it and as Freud first believed. This purely biological scheme may indeed exist in the child to a certain extent, but it is permeated, indeed, even sometimes completely dominated, by other tendencies emerging from the unfolding ego, so that it was difficult even for psychoanalysts to maintain the original Oedipus complex. The Freudians speak of a reversed Oedipus relationship, of a rudimentary, even negative one, which at least devaluates, not to say, contradicts, the purely biological viewpoint. [p. 297]

Rank's warning compels us, from a rational point of view, to insist that if Jones's explanation is to be accepted as plausible, it has to be on the basis that we are offered evidence that we readily recognize from our clinical experience to be valid. But we are given no actual clinical evidence of Hamlet's oedipal conflict with his father. Freud, who was remarkably astute in detecting slips of the tongue in literary work, does not assign a single slip, or any type of displacement or condensation of affect to indicate that oedipal rage is being indirectly expressed by Hamlet toward or about his father.

In contrast, there is sufficient evidence to share Wertheim's (1941) contention that Hamlet's considerable rage and resentment are evoked by his mother. The text of the drama bears out the thesis that Hamlet's primary emotional struggle is to take revenge on and to punish his mother. Only his father's repeated admonition (as a ghost) appears to be what stops him from physically attacking her. In this regard, we cannot easily ignore Hamlet's rageful description of his mother, whom he refers to as, "O most pernicious woman!" This hateful invective Hamlet melds, without pause or distinction, to his reaction to his murderous uncle, saying, apparently in the same breath as his previous epithet, "O villain, villain, smiling, damned villain!" (1.5).

Still again, Jones (1976) erects a reaction-formation ploy to try to turn Hamlet's potent rage toward his mother on its head and to transform it into evidence for confirming the existence of Hamlet's oedipal conflict. Jones tells us that an unduly sensuous mother, such as Gertrude, commits symbolic seduction with her son. He will, as a consequence, develop disgust, prefer emotional distance from her, and even act toward her with overt hostility. Correspondingly, he will have difficulty acquiring appropriate social skills. As simplistic as these manifestations appear to be as indications of oedipal seduction, they are, nonetheless, used by Jones as diagnostic confirmation.

In the case of Hamlet, Jones's thesis finds no confirmation. Hamlet was when he wished to be, as the play amply shows, a consummate social person. Moreover, Hamlet's disgust and anger toward his mother was not a constant factor from his tender years. Apparently, it emerged silently with his puzzlement over his mother's hasty marriage. It ebulliently erupted only *after* being told the circumstances of his father's betrayal and murder. We have no indication, moreover, that prior to his father's demise Hamlet's relationship was either overly involved or strained with his mother. Nor, for that matter, are we given evidence of any discernible psychopathology prior to the opening of the drama. Would not guilt over oedipal strivings have been manifested in Hamlet's relationship with his mother if he suffered from intense oedipal guilt?

Third, we need to return to the Oedipus myth to help us see how little attention Freud generally gave to the whole fabric of a literary work in purviewing the material in support of his theories. We find that Freud has done only a perfunctory job of examining the Oedipus story. His interpretation has totally ignored the first half of the myth (Bloch 1966). For reasons that his own self-analysis may not have permitted him access, Freud disregards the importance of Oedipus's parents' fear and hatred of their child. He makes no mention that they actually attempted to murder their helpless infant.

This consideration suggests that Freud misinterpreted the source of Oedipus's suffering when he contended that it was derived from Oedipus's *guilty recognition of who he was* (namely, the slayer of his father and seducer of his mother). An examination of the components of the Oedipus myth that Freud ignored would suggest instead that Oedipus's tragedy emanated from the *shameful realization of who he is* (namely, a frail and vulnerable mortal, who has been resented and unwanted by his own parents). Shame, as I have indicated earlier, is derived not only from revealing our frailties to others, but perhaps more importantly, being forced to face aspects of our vulnerabilities to ourselves that have heretofore not been recognized. Shame, in this sense, comes with the realization of how we have lied to ourselves about the meaning of our lives. Uncovering the lie exposes us to our alienated relationship to others. From this vantage, we cannot fail to educe that Oedipus is an estranged man. But so, too, is Hamlet, for similar reasons. Why has Freud failed to notice their shame and despair while, at the same time, emphasizing their moral guilt?

SIGMUND FREUD'S OWN SHAME

One of the most remarkable qualities of Sigmund Freud was his inconsistency in regard to himself. He was a person who could be so refreshingly candid about certain aspects of our personal feelings, such as his devotion and disappointment toward his father. On the other hand, it would seem that he was self-guarded and secretive about other feelings—such as how he regarded his relationship with his mother.

Ruth Abraham has written that Freud's inability to analyze and come to terms with his extremely complex and ambivalent relationship with his own mother was the major source of his misconceived ideas about the oedipal situation (Abraham 1982/1983). According to Abraham, Amelie Freud was the most influential person, by far, in her son's life. Yet, repeatedly in his writings and in Jones's three-volume biography of Freud, it is his father rather than she with whom Sigmund Freud struggles to come to terms.

Abraham claims that it was Amelie Freud, rather than Sigmund Freud's father, who is the primal figure that Freud described as the universal father in his theoretical formulation of the Oedipus complex. Abraham states:

The jealousy, sexual possessive [sic] and awe-inspiring Oedipal figure whom Freud claims every little boy fears and admires, is widely assumed to be grounded in Freud's experience with his own father. But in fact the Oedipal father bears little resemblance to Freud's father. The construct does, however, closely fit the character of his mother and describes with unusual accuracy some important aspects of his relationship to her. [p. 441]

Sigmund Freud, as he was growing up, seemed to have regarded his mother in some ways as a fountain of unceasing love and caring, and in still others, to be exceedingly powerful, sexual, demanding, and possessive. Abraham tells us that Freud "adored and depended on his mother and yearned to approach her for the satisfactions of his needs, but he could not help fearing, avoiding . . . her. He was torn by his love and hatred of her" (p. 441).

It can be reasonably assumed that his difficulty tolerating the anxiety aroused by his vulnerability to his mother may have prevented Freud from clearly identifying and understanding his relationship with her. He conceivably felt ashamed of his inability to come to terms with his mother's influence in his life. In a letter to Karl Abraham, Freud wrote: "So I have really reached the age of sixty-two, still unable to achieve that quiet firm resignation . . . my prevailing mood is powerless embitterment or embitterment at my powerlessness" (Freud and Abraham 1965, p. 275). Abraham (1982–83) points out that this statement was made in regard to his mother's controlling presence in his life. Sensitive to shame and unable to properly recognize its impact, Freud emphasized in most instances of human conflict an emotion with which he was more comfortable— guilt.

We should realize from his account of Hamlet's guilty conscience that Freud has reductionistically explained Hamlet's suffering. Germane to an understanding of Freud's account of Hamlet is an unyielding belief that sexual guilt, due to forbidden wishes and to acts of masturbation, is a sufficient explanation of suffering. Freud's theorizing totally ignores the threats to the individual's sense of well-being, which are derived from experiencing the terror of formulating the conditions of self-worth in face of the realization that beloved and admired figures—our parents—have misled us in what we can expect from life. Jones (1976) articulates Freud's arrant "nothing but" thesis in indicating that by various defensive mechanisms, such as despair, doubt, and depression, Hamlet has translated his conflictual sexual problems, namely, his desire for his mother, into anxiety about mortality, the salvation of the soul, the value of life, and so forth.

In a letter to Marie Bonaparte, August 13, 1937, Sigmund Freud (1960) wrote: "The moment a man questions the meaning and value of life he is sick, since objectively neither has any existence; by asking this question one is merely admitting to a store of unsatisfied libido to which something else must have happened, a kind of fermentation leading to sadness and depression" (p. 436).

Such a reductionistic view of self-examination disregards the fact that Hamlet was struggling with important and valid issues about his human condition. Lynd (1958) shows us that Hamlet was faced with a host of difficult questions. At the inception of the play Hamlet could not be certain of the identity of the ghost. Was the apparition the personification of his father or a clever interloper? Hamlet was appalled by the haste and disregard for proper ritual (the lack of a period of mourning) after his father's death. Nevertheless, what evidence had he of Claudius or his mother being implicated in the crime? And when Hamlet did realize that they were guilty he needed to resolve for himself how justice would be best served. As a man of apparently equal parts poet, warrior, and metaphysician, Hamlet could not tacitly accept the code of justice of his day—a life for a life. He was concerned about a world beyond his own. He struggled, therefore, with the question of whether murdering Claudius at prayer would only serve to reward Claudius's soul with salvation rather than to punish him with damnation.

Our own clinical experiences should offer further corroboration that, for many people, including those who are not sexually repressed, sexual issues are not the most vital concern of their existence.

Fourth, Freud's view of oedipal rivalry in *Hamlet* and *Oedipus Rex* seems to regard the child's experience of the father as inordinately negative, namely, a powerful barrier in the way of the child's libidinous reunion with the mother. This may be due to Freud's attempt to explain what he regarded as the universality of oedipal conflict, even in cases in which the behavior of the father was above reproach, as due to a phylogenetic factor of human nature (Kardiner et al. 1966). This view seems unnecessarily pessimistic. Surely, the child's growing identification with his father is much more than a defense against paternal punishment. Recent work by Blos (1985) indicates that Freud's interpretation of the oedipal situation inaccurately overemphasizes "the child's desire to take the place of the same-gender parent in relation to the opposite-gender parent" (p. 4). Freud's oedipal thesis is opposed to the realization that the father establishes a sense of trust and safety in the pre-oedipal child. This early bond of love between father and son, Blos indicates, frequently continues despite the conflicts of the oedipal period. Accordingly, the affectionate bond of the father–son relationship, as it would seem in the case of Hamlet and his father, serves to engender caring and respect for the father, not hostility.

Shakespearean scholars, such as Ehrlich (1977), have in recent years reversed the inordinate emphasis that Freud, Jones, and other psychoanalytically oriented commentators have given to the maternal issues in *Hamlet.* They have convincingly demonstrated the importance of the paternal themes in the drama. According to Ehrlich (1977), the King of Denmark is the character central to understanding young Hamlet's psychological condition in the drama.

In this context, Osherson (1986) has pointed out that to understand a man's attempts at love we have to understand his unfinished business with his own father. Throughout the play, Hamlet appears to be in search of a masculine model from which to fashion his sense of self. Yet it is his father's public persona that he is given to emulate. The press to identify with the father, Osherson (1986) indicates, poses a difficult dilemma for the son. Boys are supposed to relinquish their close identification with their mothers in order to bond with the father. Yet who is this man to whom he must turn in separating from his mother? For Hamlet, like most sons, the father is a shadowy figure, a person difficult to know. Hamlet implores his father to allow him to know his sire. He wishes to share his inner being, such as how he views himself as a man, and the questions with which he struggles in his role as a husband, a father, and an adult.

In the following discussion I will examine the role of intersubjective shame in the context of Hamlet's attempts to know his father, and in so doing, respond caringly to the person who he believes his father to be. In Chapter 10 I will further extend an examination of the father–son relationship in the fostering of shame.

THE SHAME OF BETRAYAL

In examining the father–son relationship in Hamlet, Freud seems to have neglected two of the most obvious and important functions of the father toward his child—role modeling and protection against external intrusion. This consideration is especially vital in regard to the father shielding his child from "the other side," so to speak, of the oedipal situation—the excessive demands of a mature woman toward her unprepared child. The father has the capacity of forcing the child out of what is regarded, phenomenologically, as the timeless space of intense bonding with the mother (Goldberg 1991a). The failure to fulfill this paternal function carries the threat to the child of unabated maternal demand.

I contend that if Hamlet, the King, had been a more attentive husband, who spent less time at war, the prince might have been better protected from what Ernest Jones regarded as the excessive oedipal demands upon him by Gertrude. Indeed, had Hamlet's father been more attentive to Gertrude, she might not have been easily seduced by Claudius. Without Claudius's bond with Gertrude, Hamlet may have been saved from his uncle's murderous plans for him. I say this because it can be reasonably inferred that Gertrude, as well as Jocasta, was freed from a loveless marriage. We should note how quickly and easily they were seduced and wed. Many a child who has lost a father has been forced to deal with a "Jocasta mother," a frustrated woman who has felt unfulfilled in a loveless marriage.

Rank (1964) tells us that Laius, in fear of seeding a child of his own destruction, forbade himself the marriage bed, except for a night in which his vigilance was clouded by drunkenness (during which Oedipus was conceived). Laius's behavior must have left Jocasta a frustrated woman with strong desires.

We get a sense of this frustration in Gertrude's displeased attitude toward Hamlet. Literary critics have failed to take note that she is vexingly disappointed by Hamlet. She seems to be in agreement with Claudius, who, ironically, considering my point of view about loveless marriage, tells Hamlet in her presence (1.1) that because of his "unmanly grief," Hamlet is not the man his father had been. Parenthetically, believing oneself a lesser person than an admired parent carries the threat of shame. Unable or unwilling to meet the demands of a once-admired and loved parent (Gertrude) would effect still more shame.

I am suggesting that *the loss of protection* by the father and its transmutation into homicidal impulses toward the child by the father (in the case of Oedipus) and by the stepfather (in the case of Hamlet) is the central theme of both *Hamlet* and *Oedipus Rex.* In the following pages I will pursue this line of inquiry and I will contend that the psychological dilemma that most significantly involves the protagonists of these dramas concerns the question of what happens to exceptional humans, men of nobility and a high sense of honor, who are suddenly forced to live without protection and without illusion. Material for pursuing this thesis can be discerned by examining the clinical picture of Hamlet provided by Jones (1976). Jones indicates that Hamlet has a

> deep depression, the hopeless note in his attitude toward the world and towards the value of life, his dread of death, his repeated reference to bad dreams, his self-accusations, his desperate efforts to get away from the thoughts of his duty, and his vain attempts to find an excuse for procrastination. [p. 57]

This clinical description may be indicative of a "tortured conscience," as Jones infers, and/or symptoms of deep mourning. In that we have found no evidence of repressed guilt in the play, let us examine the possibility of Hamlet's malady being perpetuated by mourning. If Hamlet is lamenting, what is it that he has lost? Ostensibly, of course, both Hamlet and Oedipus can readily be seen as grieving the loss of their fathers. More importantly for each, I would submit, is the grief from the loss of innocence. Each has been shaken from a tacit trust in their parents' ability to assure them a safe, predictable, and just world. Trust in oneself and in one's physical and social worlds develop together (Lynd 1958). Our inability to perceive correctly and to predict the events of the external world disturbs, often with lasting impact, our trust in ourselves. Thus, for example, the uncovering of cowardice and other moral ineptitude in ourselves is disturbing, but it is less devastating to our integrity of self-worth than is the realization that we have had misplaced confidence in the qualities of love, trust, happiness, or a desired response from a beloved person. The more fervently we believed in the benevolent qualities of life and the more our expectations were not substantiated, the more exacting are our pangs of shame and despair (Lynd 1958). In short, our suffering comes from the realization that we are living a futile and fictional existence.

The futility of our lives is experienced as betrayal. Clearly, both Hamlet and Oedipus have been betrayed. Oedipus was abandoned by his parents to die at the hands of their hirelings. Hamlet's conjuring comes from his father's death and his mother's infidelity. The shame of betrayal, as Erikson (1950) has shown, has to do with a *crisis in trust*, particularly, those feelings involved in a mother–child relationship. Hamlet, we should notice, has complained not only that his mother is unfaithful as his father's wife, but more importantly, that her motherly affection can not be depended upon either. False to the love and trust he held for her, Hamlet's "[F]aith in all womanhood has vanished; his own sense of moral health too—for is he not her son, her very flesh and blood? That side of life has been poisoned for him; the taint is betrayed in his treatment of Ophelia" (Barker 1978, p. 235).

Consequently, in Hamlet we find a young man who

suddenly finds that his parents are imbued with frailty. As such, he sorrowfully realizes that fatherly protection and motherly care must come to an end. The manifestation of loss of innocence and the feelings of betrayal characterized in Hamlet and Oedipus, are felt in others as well—those who experience profoundly disturbing feelings of shame by a diminished sense of self (after the initial shock of self-consciousness and embarrassment) and the feeling that the self is transparent, fragile, and in the process of dissolution.

What may have been frightening for Hamlet in his father's death was not his own "murderous" wishes, but the fact of his father's weakness. If his tall and mighty warrior father, presented when a ghost—as a man of steel—can be easily felled by his weak brother, then we all are unprotected, vulnerable mortals! These emotions lead to the wish to restrict one's life. They also result in confused identifications and vacillations in the presence of people who were once objects of supreme exaltation, as Ophelia was for Hamlet and Jocasta for Oedipus (Lacan 1980).

Fifth, Freud's exclusive intrapsychic concentration does not take into consideration in examining Hamlet's condition that Denmark is a rotten state psychologically and politically. All of the characters in the universe of the drama (including the ghost) are involved in perfidy. The climate of the court makes impossible an environment in which honest regard, mutual trust, and open caring (especially between parent and child) can take place (Friedman and Jones 1965).

The political implications of Shakespearian characters are vital to an understanding of his dramas. The political metaphors in Shakespearian tragedy are concerned with the conditions that temper character. In this regard, there are remarkable similarities between Oedipus and Hamlet, not so much in their transgressions as in the nobility of their characters. Each far exceeds those around them in intellect, articulateness, moral sensitivity, and emotional responsiveness. Ophelia refers to Hamlet: "O! what a noble mind is here o'erthrown! The courtier's, soldier's, scholar's, eye, tongue, sword: The expectancy and rose of the fair state"

(3.1). Yet, despite their superior personal gifts, the efforts of their lives are all to no avail. At the conclusion of the play each is lonely and destitute, sexually unresponsive, and resentful in the belief that he is powerless to avert his morbid fate.

Hamlet represents an older time—an age of integrity and honor. He is worn down through the drama by the welter of intrigue and mistrust he finds all around him. His responsibilities as heir to the Danish throne appear to be duties he would gladly eschew. He goes on with his mission only out of obligation to his father's honor and to avoid the shame of shirking his responsibilities.

Oedipus, too, is a man of probity, whose misfortune is to be cast unwittingly in a position of dishonor. Suffering, from the moral and political perspectives, come for both Hamlet and Oedipus from their inability to reconcile their condition with a view of a just and equitable universe. Each experiences an abrupt rupture with the values, expectations, and certainties of their world. Consequently, whereas Oedipus attributes his troubled state to his guilty deeds, the discerning clinician nevertheless cannot fail to recognize that existential anxiety underlines his guilt. Oedipus's dark feelings are due to the sudden and violent discovery that there is a sharp discrepancy between how he has been seen by himself and others and what he has now found out about himself. Oedipus can thus be seen as suffering more from shame than guilt in his self-perceived inability to live up to his own code of values. We find this in Oedipus's own words: "You could discover no blame of willful wrong doing in me; unwilling have I acted. . . . Why have I been born so that I do things and am so that the gods and mankind have to extrude me as unacceptable and unloveable and treat me as a monstrous aberration? Why must I walk through the world all alone?" (Wurmser 1981, pp. 292–293).

Oedipus's painful outcry is shared by Hamlet. For Hamlet the values and mores of his society that he was expected to live by, blood revenge for example, could no longer be accepted. In his anguish in trying to carry out his father's revenge, Hamlet presumably became aware of his own human potential and destiny; which abiding with what was expected of him by others would serve only to deny. Hamlet seems especially sensitive and reactive to injustice and hypocrisy—more so than the average person. If this is valid, then, Hamlet would have been caught between two contradictory expectations—carrying out revenge in restoring his father's honor and the realization of a higher morality in eschewing the primitive revenge of his day. Accordingly, these divergent expectations may cancel each other out, effecting a sense of a meaningless universe. This interpretation seems to accord with the tenor of the play. Hamlet is a marginal man. Not only does he have trouble with the situational morality of his day, but also he has been unable to fashion a morality acceptable to himself in order to anchor him to the world in which he lives. Lacan (1980) has pointed out that because Hamlet does not seem to know what he wants he is unable to set goals for himself. Instead of acting on his own initiative he is always waiting for others to act in their time, not in his own.

The individual forced into moral ambivalence over time because of loyalties to membership groups of strongly contradictory values may be expected to experience denigrative self-worth. Such a person may seek to restore the conditions for renewed self-worth by embracing any predictable code of morality that specifies the conditions for redemption. Lynd (1958) insightfully points out:

> Experiences of shame may call into question, not only one's adequacy and the validity of the codes of one's immediate society, but the meaning of the universe itself. Acknowledgement of personal sin or confession of guilt may sometimes be a defense against the possibility that there may be no meaning in the world. After some experience of shame and fear of emptiness we may welcome guilt as a freedom. Sin, guilt, punishment—each is, in one sense, an affirmation of order and significance. Shame questions the reality of any significance. Guilt in oneself is easier to face than lacking of meaning in life. [pp. 57–58]

Presumably, Hamlet and Oedipus preferred confession and punishment to living in a world that had lost meaning for them.

What can we now say about the questions of guilt and shame in the myth and drama Freud used to support his moral-masochism theory? I believe that I have sufficiently demonstrated that both Hamlet and Oedipus have experienced a pervasive and disabling sense of shame, which comes from being exposed as frail, vulnerable, and unable to control the events of their lives. Each is plagued less by guilt than by the fear and trembling of the human condition.

Let me speak more specifically of the fear to which I am referring. Impeding our attempts at personal identity, significance, and unification is the realization that we are essentially frail, limited, vulnerable, and finite beings. The recognition of our vulnerability may be assuaged somewhat by the busywork of our daily endeavors. There are moments, however, such as the experience of serious illness in ourselves or those we care about, that baldly force us to face the impermanence of our existence (Goldberg 1986). For Hamlet it was the murder of his father and the betrayal by his mother. For Oedipus it resulted from the loss of favor with the gods. Such moments evoke more than just anxiety. They often unleash sheer *terror.*

Some mortals experience this terror more acutely than do others. For Oedipus the effacement of all his achievements was a disgrace from which he could never recover. As guilty as he may have felt because of his deeds, the disgrace of being a broken man, a man despised, must have been far more devastating. Similarly for Hamlet, his loss of innocence and the realization of betrayal so overcame his being that he no longer preferred to live. Thus, for example, the motives for Hamlet's suicidal preoccupation does not seem to be guilt, but the trembling—the powerlessness and uselessness, as he experiences it, of human life. Does not Hamlet allude to this in his two famous soliloquies (1.2 and 3.1)?

Hamlet, therefore, can not constructively confess his guilt because there is really nothing to confess. If Hamlet is guilty it is only in that he has become humiliatingly aware of the temptations, the sins and errors of the flesh. If Hamlet identifies with his uncle, as Freud and Jones have contended, it is not because he feels guilty in thought for what his uncle performed in deed, but because he realizes, that, like Claudius, he is vulnerable, frail, and subject to fears of erasure and nonbeing. In his speech to Ophelia (3.1), Hamlet repines that it would have been better had he not been born than to fail and suffer as any common man. Similarly, Oedipus laments that although he was a favorite of the gods, sufficient to vanquish the supernatural sphinx, he can no longer look anyone in the eye, because he is unable to alter his dishonor.

What makes Hamlet and Oedipus noble characters is not that they suffered, but how they responded to their suffering. Their responses offer an important lesson about the interface of the proactive and the painful aspects of shame. This insight concerns the interrelated role of shame and knowing one's self intimately. It is a message also contained in the warning Oedipus's sage, Tiresias, gave to another fateful mythical Greek, Narcissus. When Narcissus's mother implored Tiresias to tell her whether her son would enjoy a normal life, Tiresias cautioned, "Only if he never comes to know himself" (Ovid, p. 95).

Jocasta similarly warned Oedipus to accept things as they are. She pleaded with him to enjoy the ignorance of his origins, cajoling him with the caution, "In God's name, if you place any value on your life, don't pursue the search" (Sophocles, p. 77).

But Oedipus would not be stilled. He insisted, "Nothing will move me. I *will* find out the whole truth" (Sophocles, p. 77).

As surely as Oedipus sought the humiliating truth beneath his guilt, Hamlet's dilemma ushered from his refusal to accept the perfidy of his uncle's court. He seemed by nature compelled to question himself and others, resolving to be his own counsel. Shakespeare's intuitive genius helps us realize that conscience for Hamlet, as we are forced to realize in our own experience, makes cowards of us all. This notion of conscience, however, appears not to be the kind that represents guilt, but, as Barker (1978) makes a convincing case for, was intended by Shakespeare to represent a person's ambivalent struggle for the pursuit of intimate self-knowledge. The issues of self-awareness and melancholy are confluenced.

Shakespeare was undaunted in his dramatic examination of melancholy in his tragedies. He probingly sought its causes and the reasons it took the forms it did in people's lives. Goddard (1960) indicates that Shakespeare came to the conclusion that melancholy, as I have described shame and its existential implications, signifies that a person "is living or trying to live a miscast, partial or obstructed life— is functioning far under his capacity or against the grain of his nature" (p. 354).

7

THE ROLE OF SHAME
IN THERAPEUTIC MISALLIANCE

> We seek to turn shame into nobility. What is
> hidden is revealed.
>
> —Euripides

There is no more constant, faithful companion to human striving than suffering. Suffering is a concern that pervades the thoughts and conversations of everyone. Yet, other than Albert Camus, Søren Kierkegaard and some theologians, few modern scholars and behavioral scientists have attempted a penetrating examination into the etiology and meaning of suffering (Goldberg 1986). The seminal philosopher of science, Georg Simmel, reportedly remarked that suffering is not what philosophy is about, as if there is something tainted or unclean about the subject matter (Natanson 1983). Psychologists have not been much more diligent about suffering. We are expected to be concerned with human suffering as part and parcel of our daily endeavors. But we have done little more than treat the symptoms of suffering.

The reason for behavioral scientists' lack of understanding of suffering, I submit, resides to a significant extent

137

in our theory. By necessity, theory guides our clinical work. Inexperienced practitioners rely on the authority of theory. These theories can cause considerable harm to patients by saddling practitioners with mistaken concepts, which must be adapted to the vicissitudes of clinical practice, as I shall demonstrate shortly. Dogmatic theory perpetuates itself. Years of clinical experience impresses upon most seasoned practitioners the necessity of blending analytic theoretical notions with liberal doses of compassion and common sense. Without this clinical amalgamation a constructive alliance between practitioner and analysand is rarely attainable. However, to the extent that analytic practitioners rely more on the nonspecific factors in the healing process (such as compassion) than they do to the tenets of analytic theory (because they are found inapplicable), the practitioner is likely to feel that he is not practicing psychoanalysis. Shamefully reluctant to disclose to colleagues how he actually practices, he may pass on mistaken theory from one generation of practitioners to the next, without the critical discernment and clinical reservations that these concepts require.

In translating psychological theory to clinical practice, the most vital dimension of the theory is the *attitudinal* stance required of the practitioner by the theory. In this regard, I recognized for some time the need to replace moral masochism with a more viable explanation for elucidating clinical practice. Several years ago I viewed a documentary film showing mental health professionals interviewing survivors of the Nazi Holocaust and their children. What was so striking about the survivors was not the trauma of their horrible experience, as terrible as the experience had been. What impressed me most was the humiliation and disgrace that these people appeared to evince without being able to articulate their feelings—as having been the subjects of these ignoble events. Yet, the suffering they seem to be expressing in the film appeared to derive not only from their having humiliating aspects of their personal lives talked about freely and in considerable detail by the interviewers and by their own children. What seemed most disconcerting

for these people was the interviewers' probing of the subjects about possible *untoward feelings* they had harbored
against friends and relatives who had not survived the
Holocaust. They were told by the interviewers that they
were suffering from "survivor's guilt." Guilt, as we have
already discussed, is an emotion of moral intent. To feel
guilty one needs to act in a way injurious to others. The
interviewers' questions implied that the subjects may have
unconsciously desired the deaths of those who had not
survived. How valid is such a contention? Wasn't it rather
than feeling responsible for having chosen in some way to
contribute to others' mistreatment, the survivors felt "survivor's shame" at their powerlessness and incompetence to
change their own fate and that of those who didn't survive?
In brief, in utilizing moral masochism as the cornerstone of
their understanding of the survivors' distress they were
"blaming" the victims for their suffering.

The documentary film alerted me in a way of which I had
not been aware before of the crucial impact that feelings of
shame and humiliation have on our experiences of pain and
suffering. Of course, people often are guilty of some
wrongful action and suffer terribly because of it. It is also
obviously true that many of us believe (at least we did as
children) that our thoughts and wishes are powerful enough
to cause real tragedies. However, it is simply a misconception, as antagonistic to careful clinical investigation as it is
to common sense, that we all suffer from the guilty feelings
of our oedipal desires.

My intent in this chapter is to examine a crucial problem
in clinical practice that results from a misunderstanding of
the role of shame in human suffering. This clinical problem
has two major contributors. First, therapeutic misalliance
may be due to the clinician being supine in recognizing that
his patient's suffering is derived from shame (as I pointed
out in earlier chapters), and, second, therapeutic attitudes
based upon the explanation of psychopathology as due to
moral masochism may, in fact, shame the patient into
therapeutically stultifying, pseudoguilty confession.

The following clinical vignette should give us some

pause in order to reconsider the role a moral masochistic explanation of psychopathology plays in therapeutic relationships.

A number of years ago I was invited to observe a group therapy marathon session held for analysands of a psychiatrist I knew, a graduate of a well-known psychoanalytic training institute (Goldberg 1988b). The session was conducted by the analyst in conjunction with half a dozen of his clinical staff who were in training with him. During the first hour of the marathon one of the patients reacted with intense anger at several of the analyst's rather impolite (in my view, base) responses to the patient's attempts to initiate a dialogue with him. The analyst, rather than dealing with the ostensible source of his patient's anger, insisted that the analysand was actually upset at a nongroup-related issue. The matter that was unconsciously troubling the analysand, the analyst told the group, was resentment and guilt that the patient harbored toward a significant person in his past. Because of his internalized guilt, the analyst indicated, the patient continually evoked disrespectful responses from other people. Indeed, the therapist concluded, the patient seemed even to derive perverse pleasure in being mistreated.

I was taken aback by the analyst's unwillingness to accept the common wisdom that being treated uncivilly is sufficient reason to be upset. In the discussion with the analyst and his staff after the session, I indicated that I believed that the analyst should acknowledge his own behavior before or, at least, along with the probe for the unconscious reasons for the patient's anger. One of the analyst's staff members told me that in the orientation in which they worked, objective reality was regarded as misleading. Only dealing with unconscious motivation was clinically productive. To corroborate their contentions they invited the patient involved in the incident back into the postgroup discussion. To my dismay the "offended" subject told me that he now realized that the analyst's acknowledgement of his impolite behavior would not really be necessary. He could see that the analyst's behavior during the group session was not that important. He knew that there must be deeper reasons for his reaction than what happened in the session. The problem, he said, was that he did not know what these reasons were. However, he added, he had full confidence that with his analyst's and the staff's help, he would eventually get at the bottom of the problem.

The work of Seligman (1972) has convincingly shown that people who feel disapproved of because of their lack of confidence and ability to deal with oppression are burdened with additional sources of guilt and shame. Low self-esteem subjects especially are not helped by attempts to expiate their unconscious guilt (Goldberg 1988b). It was evident to me that the marathon had been a setting in which a patient had been shamed into feeling guilty and acting compliant. Erikson (1950) has written that each culture has its own way of encouraging or breaking down the human will. Therapeutic misalliances are fostered in treatment cultures in which self-estrangement is a dominant theme. The reason for this, as I've stated earlier, resides to a significant extent in clinical theory. Without an accurate account of the etiology of suffering we can not efficaciously treat the symptoms of suffering, much less address its sources in human development. I found that analyst's behavior during the session was not only unkind and indecent, but was also theoretically unjustifiable.

The analyst's response to the patient discussed above fostered a misalliance, not only because the patient could hardly deny his own analyst's contempt for him, but just as importantly, it reinforced *the lie* that shame uncovers.

IMPLICATIONS OF SUFFERING FOR PURPOSIVE EXISTENCE

To help the person suffering from shame, we need to examine more closely the avoidance and objectifying responses in people that tend to isolate the sufferer from positive human validation. Perhaps no more excruciating articulation of this tendency is found than in the writings of the great Russian novelist, Leo Tolstoy. In his short story, *The Death of Ivan Illyich,* Tolstoy writes of the tragedy of living and dying without being understood and personally cared for by those closest to oneself.

Ivan Illyich was a man who, while progressively deteriorating in health, found his entire family proceeding to deny his condition. What tormented Illyich the most was that his wife and children were annoyed at him for being downcast. His confession of his suffering only met with censure and denial. Tolstoy, aware of the solitude that develops from not being accepted after confessing to others, writes, "And he has to go living like this, on the brink of doom, all by himself, without a single person to understand or pity him" (p. 69). However, Tolstoy tells us that Illyich suffered most of all from *the lie:* ". . . the lie adapted by everyone for some reason, which said that he was only ill and not dying . . ." (p. 179).

This is the *vital lie,* which hides the terror of our own vulnerability and creates the attempt to redo our projected image in the mirror (discussed in Chapter 2).

To confront this lie constructively we need to realize that human purpose is only meaningful to an existent—someone who is finite and will someday cease to be. Our creativity and our imagination are dependent upon our frailty and our vulnerability. An individual gains purpose by seriously grappling with his finiteness and mortality. The passion that comes from this struggle enables us to create a better world and a more developed self. It enables us to transcend suffering or, at least, to use what we are confronted with constructively. The function of suffering is to confront the self with the reality of its tenuous existence. Without this tragic sense we might mistakenly assume that we are fully taken care of. Under this illusion we need not seek to better ourselves or improve our world (Goldberg 1980b).

This should suggest that an overemphasis on guilt in psychoanalysis compels the analysand to discuss more superficial and often irrelevant material rather than the profound concerns we harbor about our vulnerability in trying to foster the conditions of our self-worth. In contrast, practitioners who acknowledge their analysand's shame open up a vital avenue of existential concern, as I show in the next section of this book. It takes a responsive other to dialogue with in order to touch the deeper sources of our existence. It is from contact with the deeper recess of his being that the analyst is able to respond to the profound protest his analysands feel about their lack of control and significance in the face of their destiny. However, to the extent that shame is not liberated and worked through, painful feelings about betrayal of trust are experienced. They are accompanied by the beleaguering conviction that dealing with the misplaced confidence in the caring and compassion of figures upon whom one has looked up to and depended upon will cause the person to be viciously exposed as unable physically and psychologically to care for himself. These feelings are fostered and strongly reinforced in contemporary society.

ATTITUDES TOWARD SUFFERING IN THE MODERN WORLD

Modern technology, which has done so much to bring relief from pain, has frequently become instrumental in some of the most insidious and horrible kinds of suffering in history. Moreover, modern scientific technology, trying to supersede and replace traditional ways of addressing suffering, has actually prevented time-proven ways of coping and healing from occurring.

The persistent problem of modern human suffering derives from an apparent "taboo" against commiseration. There appears to be a silent conspiracy about sharing of suffering, as if suffering should be kept a private matter. This conspiracy has come about from a radical shift in the role of the healer in relation to the sufferer (McGill 1982).

Traditionally, the mandate for understanding the sufferer's problems came from the healer's insight into his or her own suffering. From earliest times healing practitioners have created systems for those they treated in terms of the meaning they have made of their own suffering and life crises. Healers could be of assistance to others only to the extent that they were fellow sufferers. In the oldest myths of healing it is precisely because the healer was vulnerable to psychic wounds and suffering that he had the power to heal. The psychological implications of the "Myth of Aesculapius" is that the sufferer has a healer within himself and the healer a sufferer within himself. Each agent in the healing encounter must accommodate the needs of the other if meaningful healing is to take place. To do this, the practitioner needs to be prepared to have his own psychic wounds activated by the healing process (Goldberg 1991).

This traditional belief system has eroded and been replaced by another rationale. According to the Harvard University theologian, Arthur McGill (1982), contemporary attitudes toward human suffering reveal the pernicious

> [C]onviction that suffering is somehow utterly incompatible with being genuinely human . . . To many suffering has become the most dreaded and most overwhelming form of evil . . . since suffering effectively destroys our humanity, those who exercise their humanity to help the sufferers can only do so from a vantage point apart from suffering. Only because they stand outside of suffering are they able to work humanely and creatively, and thereby deliver others from suffering.
>
> In the prevailing view, then, there are two domains . . . the domain of successful humanity, characterized by people who are healthy, confident, outgoing and capable of serving others . . . [and] the contrasting domain of suffering, where the humanity in us is so thoroughly twisted and shattered that nothing very human is expected of us . . .
>
> Thus, in the prevailing attitude there is working a thorough-going dualism, with humanity in secure well-being on the one side and dehumanized wrecks ravaged by suffering on the other. We can see a vivid example of this dualism in our hospitals. The staff who work there helping others do so in such a way that traces of their fragility and suffering are carefully hidden. The mask of "expertness" identifies each worker with a successful effectiveness that allows no room for his or her victimized agonies. There is an

incredible pretense involved in this stance, but it is believed to be essential, so that physicians hardly ever present themselves as sharing in the same misery as their patients. [pp. 165–167]

A feature article in *The New York Times* some years ago by Susan Jacoby (1983) rhetorically asked, since grief is a universal human experience, why do "so many people find themselves unable to offer the right sort of consolation even when they desperately wish to do so?" To offer true consolation, Jacoby answers, is to "share something of the taste of grief."

An incident I was involved in several years ago showed me that even those who are supposedly the best informed on the subject of suffering and are involved in treating its maladies may show considerable discomfort in the presence of those who suffer. Late one afternoon, while attending a psychiatric conference, a colleague and I observed a crowd gathering in the lobby of the hotel in which the conference was being held. There were fifteen or twenty poorly attired, sad-looking men and women linking arms and silently sitting on the floor of the lobby. Some even looked frightened. A few held poster cards protesting against electroconvulsive therapy and excessive psychopharmaceutical treatment. Among the bystanders we recognized a number of physicians from the conference. We were told that the protestors had been sitting there for a few hours. During the time we stood there these people expressed neither hostility nor provocative action toward anyone. In fact, they neither spoke nor moved from where they sat. After we were there about an hour, six policemen appeared on the scene and began to disrupt the calm. First, a police sergeant and a plainclothes officer spoke with each of the protestors. After a while, police reinforcements arrived. They began pulling each of the people from the circle. Since they had joined arms in an attempt to maintain their position within the circle, they had to be separated forcibly. Nonetheless, the resistance was quite passive. Two officers were assigned to each protestor; one by one they were dragged on their backs through the long and crowded lobby of the hotel and taken who knows where. By this time, we developed strong feelings that these people, who were causing no apparent harm to anyone, were being abused. My colleague and I went to investigate the cause for their removal. The hotel management had no grievance with the protestors. The request for their removal was in response to a number of doctors from our conference who had sternly reproached the hotel management for not having the protestors removed from private property. Clearly, the hotel management did not want to antagonize its clients. What we found most disconcerting was the response of the physicians who requested or demanded the removal of the silent objectors. That some of us, as professionals of the healing professions, could not tolerate the manifestations of some silent controversy of people who appeared to be suffering did not say much for the courage or caring of our colleagues. Their actions did more to confirm the validity of the protestors' accusations than all the placards in the world.

In her thoughtful article in *The New York Times,* Susan Jacoby indicated that our contemporary society contains social forces that encourage us to ignore the suffering of others. Americans, she points out, "tend to become impatient with those who do not make haste to 'get on' with their lives." Therefore, "we tend to ignore grief that is somewhat removed from the predictable social order." Perhaps the physicians who opposed the presence of the protestors could assume concern and involvement with their suffering patients in the clearly defined role of "doctor," in a setting in which the sufferer is clearly defined as a "patient." On the other hand, removed from the confines of these allocated roles of doctor and patient, they could or would do no more than express their inhumanity.

8

THE SHAME OF A TRAGIC PSYCHOTHERAPY

Oh, damned despair, to shun the living light, and
plunge thy shameful soul in endless night!
—Lucretius

As a psychoanalyst, it is a great privilege being a member of
a small, select enclave of people who study the individual
psyche in the only way that it can be explored in depth
(Spruiell 1984). At the same time, being an analyst is a
difficult and sometimes devastating responsibility. Unlike
most other professionals, practitioners of analysis can not
readily retreat from the world when they are ill, depressed,
or feeling particularly stressed. The issue of the analyst's
vulnerability is a rather cogent theme in analytic work as
the vignette in this chapter demonstrates. As long as practitioners feel responsible to and for their patients they
remain under their critical scrutiny, regardless of the degree
of the precariousness of the practitioner's feeling state. In
the next vignette we will see what happens when an analyst
is not able to retreat into privacy about an unfortunate event
in his practice, so that his clinical tragedy becomes known
to his patients.

147

The phone rang midway into a busy day of practice. "I am Mr. Strauss, Julie Strauss' husband" (Julie, an analysand of mine, had missed her appointment that morning, which was unusual for her). "I think you ought to know that Julie is dead. She killed herself last night with pills. You probably know she has tried this before. This time she succeeded."

I reeled, as my feelings were turned inside out. In subsequent moments, I became numb with disbelief.

The psychoanalyst is involved in high drama. However, unlike literary or theater drama the story frequently remains incomplete. Analysts often are not permitted to see the drama to its successful finale. These circumstances are especially disturbing to the practitioner when a tragic plot is involved. One of the most frightening threats to the analyst is the prospect of a patient's suicide. Unlike the surgeon who learns early in his career that it is imprudent to allow himself to be deeply affected by patients who have a high probability of not successfully pulling through the operation procedure, the analyst can not work effectively from a strictly scientific or impersonal methodology. He must allow his sensibilities, even his most vulnerable feelings, to usher forth in order to be maximally responsive to his analysands. Consequently, losing a patient for a surgeon may be regrettable, but it is often assumed to be inevitable, just as we expect our parents and relatives of their generation to pass away before us. In sharp contrast, the suicide of a patient is not inevitable for the analyst. Indeed, there is something morbidly strange and unnatural about it, like the demise of a child before that of his parent.

It was not as if Julie's prognosis had not been guarded. Nor was her suicide attempt unpredictable from her psychiatric history. Actually, Julie had made numerous suicide attempts before. She had had two psychiatric hospitalizations and had been given electroconvulsive treatment. Moreover, despite the considerable progress she had made in her life during her analysis, I knew from my clinical experience that people suffering from devastating feelings of lack of self-worth, as was Julie, no matter how well they might appear to be doing with their psychological issues, are never safely past a self-destructive fall of the curtain. All that is required for them to end their life is a single event in which they feel emotionally abused or misunderstood. Indeed, even months or years of hard work in analysis may be undone by a lingering and desperate thought that the future is a place where they will continue to suffer.

Such psychiatric awareness did not lessen the pain of the suicide of my patient for me. I had come to like and respect Julie. She had been a highly intelligent, vital, and competitive person, despite her considerable emotional problems. Julie and I had developed a warm and caring therapeutic alliance. Many times, often late at night, in the throes of her despair, we spoke for hours over the phone. No matter how hurt and angry Julie had felt toward her husband or someone else in her life, my reassuring voice and my encouraging words, she told me, eventually reached her and she felt understood. Consequently, then, I believed that no matter how desperate Julie might become, that if I could speak with her, we would be able to deal with the troubling issue together.

Our working alliance rested upon a pact of trust. When Julie first came to consult with me, she told me that she never would allow herself to be hospitalized and be given shock treatment again. She was wringing her hands when she said that she would rather be dead than undergo the ordeal of being hospitalized again. She had asked me firmly to promise that I would never try to have her involuntarily committed, no matter how depressed she became. I regarded her statements about how she intended her life to go at that moment—a period in which she was making life changes but was not particularly desperate or despondent, as a psychological will. This is to say, I believed that Julie had the right to decide for herself what were those conditions of existence beyond which life was intolerable.

It is safe to assume that my philosophical belief about Julie's freedom was buttressed by my confidence in my clinical skills. In the ten years I had then practiced, working with numerous highly disturbed and suicidal patients, I had not lost a single patient, having to hospitalize only one patient for a drug-related problem. I believed that if Julie could completely trust me and I was careful not to be put off by her angry and hurtful demands, her life could be made less painful and her self-destructive behavior could be averted.

My clinical reasoning was predicated upon the realization that no patient can be therapeutically reached by a practitioner in whose hands the patient feels unsafe. My clinical experience indicated that Julie would feel terrified by a therapist who refused her "no hospitalization" condition. In such a case, Julie would go to a doctor only when she was severely depressed and desperate. She undoubtedly would spend the rest of her life subjected to heavy doses of mood-controlling drugs and be shuttled between involuntary hospitalization and her home. Besides, would her family and doctors be able to prevent her suicide if she was firmly bent on doing so? A resourceful person like Julie could always find a means of gaining an exit to an intolerable life.

I also believed that Julie's previous doctors had focused too exclusively on her psychopathology, rather than on her considerable strengths. This striking woman had never accepted her own high intellect. She had been pampered and protected as a child by her adoring parents and, as an adult, by her less-adroit, businessman husband. She had rebelled, finishing college while raising four children. Afterward, she tenaciously developed a business in a highly competitive field and was more successful at it than her husband was in his own business. I believed that her high drive and tenacity, if sufficiently encouraged, could pull her through her periods of despondency and irrational rage. Consequently, I agreed never to hospitalize her.

Unfortunately, I did not get the opportunity to pull her through her desperation and rage the fateful night of her suicide because my wife had been on the phone much of the night. I will never know for certain whether I could have saved her if Julie and I had spoken together.

Although Julie's suicide was not an altogether intentional act—she had tried unsuccessfully to reach some friends and did speak to an emergency psychiatric service counselor on the phone—the result was the same as if she deliberately sought her end. I had lost someone I felt close to, as I might the passing of a family member or a friend. Yet the difference was that I was somehow implicated in her demise. I was forced to question how I had handled Julie. Had I been too self-confident of my skills and of Julie's capacity for healing herself? I then questioned my ability to treat other patients in distress, asking myself whether I should ever again allow myself to be put in a situation in which I was responsible for the life of another person. I seriously considered ending my analytic career.

The analyst uses himself as a mirror to help the analysand see himself. However, the mirror is reversible. The analyst in holding up the analytic mirror must witness unbearable aspects of himself in the faces of his patients. As I put the phone down I felt in a vicious trap. I felt responsible to my patients. I did not feel permitted to cancel my remaining sessions, despite how miserable and ineffectual I felt. Yet, next to the loss of a person I cared for, the most agonizing feature of the aftermath of the tragedy was the shame I felt imagining colleagues and my own analysands finding out about Julie. I was certain also that my patients would lose confidence in me and leave my practice, once they knew.

My worst fear came to pass. A member of my analytic therapy group that evening had spoken to a person affiliated with the emergency service that Julie had called and told that I was her doctor. The emergency service had sent out an ambulance, which arrived at Julie's house too late.

Sitting in the group, I felt devastated by embarrassment. I felt exposed and inadequate—unable to find any means of hiding.

Most practitioners experience their reputations, self-esteem, and sense of adequacy in some way linked to their effectiveness in preventing suicide among their patients. I certainly did. Suicide is clearly different from most other behaviors by patients. Patient actions, except serious violence, may be explained away by the practitioner as an intermediary and necessary step in the patient's recovery—such as encouraging the passive and dependent patient to express his repressed anger. In sharp contrast, suicide is clearly not intermediary. It is final and, therefore, difficult to rationalize as a successful therapeutic outcome. The patient can never recover from suicide. The therapist is left alone to try to understand and come to terms with the reasons for this tragic outcome.

What I experienced from my one-and-only patient suicide has had a deep cast on how I have practiced and have come to understand shame in my subsequent clinical work. This understanding will be examined in the case study section.

9

HEALTHY AND CONSTRUCTIVE SHAME

The cruelest lies are often told in silence.
—Robert Louis Stevenson

Most of our patients share a secret. Conscious realization of the secret is sensed to be so humiliating that they won't allow themselves to discover how pervasively their uneasiness influences their lives.

Daily and in large numbers, people consult therapists with a slew of complaints, such as depression, addictions, marital conflicts, and so forth. Few realize that it is boredom and loneliness, the consequences of unrecognized shame, for which they are actually seeking help.

All doctors soon learn that patients consult them far less often for specific illnesses than they do because they are unhappy and seek relief from their loneliness and despair. Countless numbers of people find themselves entrenched in lives that are barren of intimate and trusting companionship. Each of our patients bears witness to the consequences of the absence of satisfying friendship in marriage, family, collegial, and peer relationships in the contemporary world. For many of them the search for a wise and caring friend to inspire and support them has been long and futile. Few suffer well an inability to secure intimate fulfillment. Self-esteem and a sense of living well is dependent upon being

1

desired, understood, and appreciated by other people. Moreover, a sense of security is bolstered by the awareness of people to whom one can turn who care about that person. Repeated rejection and failure to foster caring from others leads directly to feelings of inadequacy, depression, and intense loneliness.

Behavioral scientists have offered numerous reasons for the failure of friendship in contemporary society. These explanations include: the highly mobile nature of society, militating against holding and maintaining long-term relationships; the loss of extended family and the absence of ready access to effective role models for transacting friendship; and today's highly competitive society, fostering narcissistic self-interest.

Each of the above-mentioned factors, of course, plays a role in militating against close companionship. Yet, while each of these explanations is valid it is not sufficient psychological cause to explain the failure of friendship.

Failure of friendship seems in a more profound sense than the causes suggested by sociologists to precipitate from an alienation from one's self. People have become increasingly more alienated from their own selves, as well, as from others. The alienation and suffering I encounter daily in analysands seems to derive from their difficulty in responding with emotional touch and close personal regard to significant others (or, at least, to those who are potentially significant people in their lives).

The vignette I will discuss in this chapter has as its scenario a distant land. The specific location should not divert our attention from the realization that the requirement of the situations I will be describing are similar to those many of us are confronted with daily. Certainly, there is considerable similitude with the contents of this story and the conditions found in large, urban centers in the United States today.

PEDRO'S STORY

He was a slight lad of 9 or 10 years of age. His tan, rough, hemp shirt was tattered and his trousers, a couple of sizes too large, were held by a length of cord. He may have been wearing shoes, although the impression I have of him was barefoot. What I remember best was his immutable, sad mien and his tightly clutching in his left hand of a picture postcard and a small box of plastic matches. The tenacity with which he held these meager items suggested that his postcard and matches were all he possessed.

The photo on the postcard was that of the city plaza of Cuzco—once the sacred city of the Incas—now a shabby Peruvian metropolis, visited by tourists for its historical sites and awe-inspiring churches, filled with priceless religious artifacts. The picture card was carefully wrapped in a piece of clear plastic paper. The matches were the kind manufactured throughout South America and purchased in shops for the equivalent of a North American nickel.

The child had approached my table as a female friend and I were having dinner in a popular Cuzco restaurant late one summer night. Three musicians, young men of Cacharpayan Indian descent from the Andes mountains, were playing haunting ancient tunes on a small stage in the front of the restaurant. Throughout the evening small children, in groups of twos and threes, slipped into the restaurant and approached the patrons' tables. They were acrimoniously ousted from the establishment by waiters who wore both white smocks around their dark suits and no-nonsense grimaces. A few of these poorly dressed children furtively returned. Making their way to where the patron families sat, they looked up with their sad child faces at the customers consuming their food with apparent gusto and abandon.

The boy who approached our table stood mute. His large brown eyes seemed filled with tears. Or were they my eyes that countenanced despair? By what quirk of fate was I, a North American, well educated and financially successful enough to travel regularly to Latin America, while, at the same time, this small child stood before me impoverished and uneducated. I had no doubt

that by his socioeconomic circumstances he was destined to a life of hardship, perhaps not a very long life at
that. Were he to live long enough to have children of his
own in this land of disadvantage and violent political
strife, his unhappy legacy to his offspring would be to
have no real hope for the better things in life, perhaps not
even the necessities. The pack of cigarettes my friend
smoked each day was undoubtedly more costly than the
price of food his family, if indeed he had one, could afford
him.

We spoke to him in Spanish. He told us that his name
was Pedro. It was difficult to comprehend where he lived.
It wasn't so much that our Spanish was faulty as that
Pedro was quite inarticulate in his own native tongue.
But conversation was not Pedro's immediate interest. He
thrust his left hand toward us, without a single word,
revealing his postcard and matchbox. We tried to help
him express his intention by inquiring if he was selling
these items. He nodded slowly.

Because he didn't speak, he didn't state a price. He
seemed to want us to exact the value of his items. We felt
reluctant to purchase what Pedro was holding. If he sold
them to us, what besides his shabby clothes would he
have left?

Not surprisingly, he looked malnourished. The food
on our plates was simple but plentiful and savory. We
realized that it would make more sense to feed the child
than to purchase his only salable holdings.

We invited Pedro to sit at our table. He fretfully
looked around at the other tables and refused. In re-
tracing the sweep of his glance it was evident that
Pedro's sitting at our table would be a breach of local
mores. The other waifs were standing by the customers'
tables and, at the same time, rapidly eating leftovers
from the patrons' dinner plates with their bare fingers.

My companion and I felt too uncomfortable with the
idea of Pedro standing by our table and eating the scraps
from our plates to respect local custom. I cringed embar-
rassedly from the mental image of myself as a feudal lord

throwing unwanted food from my table to begging peasants.

I more emphatically repeated my invitation to Pedro to sit down at our table, pulling out a chair next to me for the boy. He reluctantly sat down. We ordered from a disapproving waiter a glass of milk and a plate of food for Pedro. He consumed the food rapidly. Oddly, as hungry as he appeared, he did not touch the potatoes on his plate. Throughout the meal he used only his right hand to eat. His left hand held fast his two possessions, as if someone might grab them away from him if he lost sight of them.

When he had finished eating he looked up at us and then turned away, staring ahead with the same unhappy expression as when he had first appeared at our table. I sensed that this inarticulate child was feeling embarrassed sitting at our table, not knowing how to thank us or what he should say or do in taking leave of us.

In realizing Pedro's awkwardness I became aware of my own uneasiness. To ease my shamefulness in having affluence in the face of the dire impoverishment this child represented I needed some way of bridging the vast socioeconomic gap between this child and myself. I felt pressed to find a way of indicating to this inarticulate, intellectually limited, and depressed child, that our brief encounter together was mutually gratifying. Do I mean satisfying? No, I am speaking of a sense of being emotionally moved by another person's pathos. This moment of shared pathos revealed something of my own inner being in such a way that I was in closer touch with my inner sensibilities and convictions than I had been prior to the encounter. I suspected that this was as true for my friend as for myself. Consequently, I felt the desire to inform Pedro that he wasn't being given food sheerly because of our pity for him, but that all three of us had gained something from our shared moment. But how, I wondered, could I convey this to Pedro?

My eye again caught the scenario of Pedro clutching his postcard and matchbox and my friend's pack of

cigarettes on the table before me. She routinely lit up a
cigarette after a meal. The solution suddenly struck me.
I asked Pedro if he would allow me to examine his
matchbox. He readily handed the box over to me. The
cardboard container had a pretty design on it, but the
matches themselves were worthless, except for their
intrinsic value. I said to Pedro in carefully chosen
Spanish idiom that my friend, as he could see, smoked
cigarettes and she needed matches. I suggested to Pedro
that we exchange the food we had bought for him for his
matchbox. He instantly nodded in agreement. It also
appeared as if his facial expression had changed following my suggestion. For a brief moment it seemed as if
he were faintly smiling. But I cannot be certain. In an
instant after my offer, still gripping his postcard, Pedro
had bolted up out of his chair and was through the door
of the restaurant into the night. The agreement of a swap
of goods had freed Pedro and my companion and me
from an embarrassing moment.

The Role of Shame in the Desire to Know

It is the experience of many of the unhappy people I work
with as a psychoanalyst that their inability to express their
humiliation in the nexus of their repeated attempts at
intimate relating leads them to enforced solitary and lonely
lives. Experiences of shame generally are vivid and painful
because they foster an accentuated and disturbing sense of
self-consciousness. These are moments in which we become
aware, albeit fleetingly, of aspects of ourselves—our ambitions, sentiments, and longings—that are central to who we
are and at the same time prone to misunderstanding and
derision. During moments of shame we become acutely
aware of how fragile are the conditions upon which our
hopes and aspirations depend. At these moments we realize
how easily and quickly our desires may be taken from us.
We may even painfully recognize that our wants will be
empty, even if they are satisfied. The customary response to
heightened self-consciousness is that of trying to hide our
valued and vulnerable self from everyone, including our-

selves. The experience of shame I felt with Pedro interrupted the placid and unprobed satisfaction with myself I was feeling the moment prior to meeting him. I realized that I was still struggling with the need to justify what I am and what I have learned as a person and as a practitioner of psychotherapy. These were issues I subsequently pursued in my own personal therapy.

Do such struggles disqualify me from helping my analysands? No! We, as psychotherapists, are not paragons of self-actualization. I do not think that we could help our patients if we were. We are human and subject to the common foibles of being human. However, I believe what is required of us, if we are to abet our patients in their struggles with their own humanity, is that we be scrupulously honest with ourselves and with our patients. We need to be uncompromising in our willingness to examine our behavior and actions, especially those that involve struggles with compassion and caring. It is in this way that we realize and utilize the healthy aspects of shame.

Learning has its roots in shame (Shane 1980). The desire to know begins with the recognition of what one does not know. The constructive intent of shame is the realization that one does *not* know, and that which one does not know is knowable and *should* be known.

Shame is not a disease when we recognize its constructive intent. Shame may serve admirably as a mark of our humanity. We are valuing beings. Shame plays an important constructive role in our system of values (Schneider 1977).

PART III
SHAME IN CLINICAL PRACTICE

10

THE SHAMEFUL SECRET

Nothing is so oppressive as a secret.
—La Fontaine

The early winter rain descended upon my consulting room with a rhapsodic resounding. At the same time, the intense resentment I was experiencing toward Vincent, my analysand lying on the analytic couch, was more than a match for the cascades of rain. My fitful mood was alarming to me. The prolonged downpour had been predictable. The weather reports had forecast that we would be bound by several days of showers. My inner displeasure with Vincent, on the other hand, was unexpected, unsettling, and unfathomable. I was a psychoanalyst, then beginning my career. I was well trained and clinically experienced. I was not supposed to lose composure with patients. Yet I realized with concern that wintry day with Vincent that I was barely managing to keep my resentment to myself.

Because of a strong, unusual reaction to a patient I assume that my patient and I share a secret. Our mutual concealment may lie at the heart of my understanding him.

I will start at the beginning. Something curious was happening in Vincent's session that morning. But I was not aware of how remarkable this session would prove to be

until moments before the analytic hour was to end. At the
outset I was aware that Vincent, a fluent speaker, was taking
longer than usual to begin. Vincent was a handsome man of
tall, slender stature. His wavy gray hair, wire-framed glasses
and neatly groomed beard gave him a distinguished presence. On the other hand, his typical attire of ascots and
ill-fitting, casual suit vests and slacks presented Vincent
with the admixed sartorial presence of the man of a past
world, unsure of the present. Actually, he was quite mindful
of how people perceived him. He was often, however, uncertain about how to influence their positive regard.

I constructed a synopsis of Vincent's history to refamil-
iarize myself with the troubling person lying on the couch
only a foot from my chair:

Vincent's father scorned humanitarian pursuits. He was
a free-spending, dashing character. He lived as a compulsive gambler and womanizer, deserting Vincent and
his mother when Vincent was 9. Vincent saw his father
only occasionally. Unexpectedly, he would ring the bell
and lead Vincent to an expensive imported roadster.
Vincent never saw the same car twice. Sitting in the
backseat, enrobed in furs, was a smiling, overdressed
woman. The same woman never reappeared. The day
they spent together was magical. They went to lavish
restaurants and sat in a private box at the racetrack in
the afternoon. Young Vincent was introduced to an array
of men with long cigars and expensive suits. His father
would whisper to him that one of these men and he were
on the verge of finalizing an important deal, which would
make him financially secure and enable his father to take
Vincent to live with him.

During the time Vincent spent with his father, Vincent felt it necessary to conceal his fears and insecurities.
He sensed that it was unsafe to put any demands on his
father. He later realized that he had never been free to be
close to him.

The big business deal apparently never came off.
Vincent's mother tried to hearten him by telling Vincent

that his father really loved him and would be very proud of him when he became a famous person. Hope had been Vincent's innocence. As long as he believed his mother's words about his father's intentions, he was inspired and self-confident. When his father died he felt deserted, left to the mercies of an angry and embittered mother, who continually blamed his father for her miserable life. We had reconstructed in our analytic work together that Vincent's refusal to give in to pain and illness during the earlier part of his life was an unconscious attempt to impress his father. Vincent had always tried to be as different as he could from the mother, to whom his father had referred as a hypochondriac.

I found in my sessions with him that when Vincent began to converse, he did so with an almost inaudible cough, revealing his shyness. His persistent lack of self-assuredness seemed ironic. Vincent once had been a world-famous radio commentator and an international correspondent, who had covered, among other international events, the Spanish Civil War and the Second World War. His lack of good taste in his choice of clothes was offset by the natural grace and simple dignity of his speech. He spoke in a deep, musical voice, trained by the love of operatic harmony. It was, of course, the warm, reassuring baritone of his talks, rather than his appearance, by which he was known to countless listeners of my parents' generation, as they waited anxiously at home for good news about their beleaguered sons and husbands serving in war across the sea.

In the session this chapter describes, Vincent finally began to speak by relating a memory from long past. He spoke of sitting in the living room of his mother's home. It was only hours before he was to catch a Pan American clipper flight with a select cadre of correspondents to report the battles of North Africa. His mother was at the time of life at which Vincent realized that he might never see her again. The room in which they sat had been Vincent's childhood bedroom. It was filled with the relics of seven thousand nights of uneasiness and insecurity. They were listening to a recording of Puccini's *La Boheme.* Vincent had heard this particular rendition in his childhood many times before. Yet, once more he was flooded with bittersweet feelings. His first thought was that if anyone could compose music of such beauty then there must be some reason to live. His second thought was to recall the many evenings while listening to opera, he was simultaneously casting his plans for the future, which almost always involved a reunion with his father. His mother, he recalled, was showing him a tattered album of cracked, old photos. One of the pictures was of a striking, joyful looking young woman. He was told that she was his father's sister. Although his father had been the eldest, she had been the light and hope of the family. His aunt had been on the onset of a promising concert and theatrical career. Vincent's grandmother would not allow her carefree, young daughter to be out alone at night, going to and from the theater and to parties she was expected to attend. Vincent's father had been her constant escort. He had not been able to keep her from harm. Due to a failed love affair a few years before Vincent was born, his aunt had committed suicide. His father had never spoken to his son of his beloved sister. Indeed, until being shown the album and having his mother speak of her, Vincent had not known of her existence.

Tears filled Vincent's eyes and slid down his cheeks, as he said that he knew at that moment in his mother's home that his life ambitions would never be realized.

I inquired about his tears. He did not respond. He had yet to turn his head in my direction in the session. I have learned that when I interrupt an analysand early in a session and receive no direct reply it usually is a signal to me that it is still too soon to involve myself in the patient's narrative. I must, for at least the time being, allow the analysand to tell his story in his own way.

Vincent moved restlessly on the couch. He said in a low voice that before he left his mother's house for his flight to North Africa he learned that with his aunt's death the sense of well-being left his father's family. His grandfather stopped working. He remained in idle seclusion until his death, when he was well past 90. His father's brothers and sisters had to drop out of school to support the family by finding whatever jobs they could. A shared depression settled over the family. It lasted the lifetime of all its members. Each of Vincent's aunts and uncles died tragically young. In our session Vincent raised his voice a bit to say that the sense of the tragic is a legacy that he also bears.

His mother's family had not offered him much solace, either. They were not very successful in hiding their fears. From an early age Vincent had been aware of the tense, hushed conversations of his mother's relatives. The worst moments for Vincent in his mother's house was when the telephone rang. She acted as if each incoming call was a harbinger of another family misfortune.

His father, in contrast, kept his feelings private. He cloaked his sadness with merriment and good cheer.

Family secrets are frightening for children. This is not simply due to the actual information one fears that secrets hold. Often, more devastating to one's developing sense of self are the reasons one has imagined for the secrecy. Vincent's father's unwillingness to share his pain with him indicated to Vincent that he was regarded as incapable of handling painful emotions. Vincent, in turn, came to view himself as weak and fearful.

There is a close relationship between family dynamics and vocational pursuit. Vincent's choice of a career as an investigative reporter was related to his being excluded as a child from family secrets. As a friend and, frequently, a confidante to presidents, prime ministers, and premiers, Vincent was the person who frequently broke important news stories. Throughout his career Vincent was bound by his word to some powerful authority figure not to reveal a vital secret of international importance. For Vincent there always was a measure of discomfort in keeping these secrets. He could never set aside his dreadful fear that some day he would mishandle vital information and cause misfortune to many others.

By any fair measure, Vincent would have been regarded by most people as brave. He had been imprisoned and tortured by more than one political regime. This had not deterred Vincent from taking on still other dangerous assignments. Yet Vincent's self-deprecation proved resistant to disconfirmation. Once after he had told an audience of businessmen of a hair-raising mission, one member of the audience stood up and commented to Vincent, "With all the exciting intrigues you have been caught up in, haven't you sometimes felt like James Bond?" Vincent told me that he had fixed his gaze on the questioner and quietly replied, "Hardly, sir. I would be hard put to recall any such incident during which I was not badly frightened."

As Vincent spoke of his cowardice I was aware that the room in which we were meeting had become less comfortable than before Vincent's session started. Unexplainably, his clothes looked more threadbare than usual. I wondered if it was the lighting in the room. It seemed darker than I remembered it. I was not even certain what the colors in the room were. The various hues were verging into a somber gray. My attention to the depressing climate in the room alerted me to some danger imminent, but yet unspoken. Some vulnerable part of my psyche was keeping me from following my intuitions. I was still not aware of why I was fearful.

I returned my attention to Vincent for further clues. I had watched him closely for the past twelve months, aware of particular patterns in his reactions. Vincent was a person who was from the very beginning of our work together desperately seeking my approval. His not trying to draw me into his monologue was at odds with his usual style of relating with me. It seemed this morning he needed my presence, but, at the same time, required that I not enter into his narrative. The position I felt I was being placed in had an alarming knell. He was relating to me like a guilty parishoner to his priest to hear a shameful secret that he was compelled to confess. As a priest, the listener was being required to participate ritualistically, but without personal feelings or subjective judgment.

The concept of secrets, as I have already suggested, has special relevance to the analytic situation. Behind every disturbed life resides a painful mystery. The victim intuitively knows that unless his secret is revealed and understood by someone caring and wise, his life will be lived out in constriction and despair. Ironically, though, as desirous as he is to confess and rid himself of his painful burden, no less urgent is his need to retain his shameful secret. There are inordinately powerful agents requiring his silence. These forces consist of loyalties to people from the past to protect them from disclosure of their shameful and incriminating involvements in his life.

Although I adhere to the same requirement of confidentiality as do priests, I cannot of course give absolution. Instead, my task is to enable the victim of the painful secret to question his loyalties to people who the victim feels require him to suffer his mystery alone. What I mean by this is that the patient's narrative, containing hidden guilts and shames, is an unfinished story. I must help him rewrite his narrative, and in the process find a more viable and hopeful way to live. And as important as are the contents of the secret, no less vital is the climate of the encounters in which powerful and painful secrets are probed in analysis. The fostering of new and healthier loyalties and relationships can only take place in an atmosphere of caring and trust. Most analysts, therefore, would take cautious note of an analysand, such as Vincent, keeping them at bay. Psychoanalysis, in principle, is a mutual dialogue in which the innermost thoughts and feelings of the analysand are examined freely. The more disturbed the patient's willingness to relate, the more difficult will be the disclosure of secrets. Consequently, Vincent's efforts to exclude me from dialogue with him required my drawing his attention to his lack of involvement with me. I asked him if he had any awareness of my presence.

Vincent turned in my direction for the first time. He spoke as if from a disturbing dream, saying, "It is odd that I, who have known all the vanities of the world, am asked this question!"

Vincent's statement was a strange response. Nevertheless, I had realized from the beginning of our work together that Vincent had long suffered from a periodic thought disorder. When severely stressed, he became momentarily confused and unable to judge appropriately what was happening to him. For example, Vincent was unaware that he was angry at times, whereas anyone in his presence could clearly observe his rage. Vincent's statements were, because he was not readily in touch with his feelings, sometimes difficult to comprehend. However, to understand a person analytically means, in an important sense, that I am able to explain the patient's behavior and motives as these agencies defy common sense. This is to say, my clinical formulations need to account for why people like Vincent act in ways that seem pernicious to their best interests. Consequently, I find it necessary to assume that all communication, no matter how egregious, contains within it understandable statements about what is going on in the heart and mind of that person.

As an analyst it is of considerable help to have a serious and continuing interest in history, philosophy, and the arts. I recognized the words Vincent had used in his strange statement as taken from an Italian opera, *Don Carlo.* I did not remember much of the story line. But, then, it matters little to my analytic inquiry what the story is actually about. What is more significant was Vincent's conception of the story. I asked, "Would you tell me what the story of *Don Carlo* is about?" He told me: "It is about a mad king, who kills his son and is condemned to live forever as his own son might have lived. But since he had never given himself the opportunity to know his son he finds the requirement impossible. He is unable to find out who he, himself, is and might have become."

Upon hearing Vincent's words I became aware that my usual analytic curiosity was being impeded by soft tremors of anxiety. At moments like this in analysis I intuitively know that a secret will follow that involves me in some uncomfortable way. I turned away from my own subjective reactions and to the material Vincent was presenting. Clues to the mystery were, undoubtedly, contained in the story of *Don Carlo.* "What does *Don Carlo* have to do with the story of your life?" I asked. "My son died without having given me the chance of knowing him," he said flatly.

Vincent had not mentioned in the year I had worked with him having had children. In fact, I remember quite distinctly that during a psychological history intake of Vincent in our first few sessions he had eschewed any mention of marriage.

I looked outside the window, as if I expected to find the mystery of how his son died in the muddy field below my window. It had been raining heavily for the past three days. The mud had formed deep funnels of water, giving the impression of canals of wet clay. As I searched the mud in idle thought, I imagined that three days of downpour on the decaying leaves and vegetation of early winter would have caused the canals to flow with odious debris. It also occurred to me that every secret had its own real or imagined odor. I suspected that this had to do with the association of secrets with dank and forbidden places of the psyche. Also, each home has its familiar smell. I asked Vincent what odor he associated with his mother's home. "The sense of foreboding and despair. It followed me throughout the war and every day afterward. It overwhelms me. I have never known if I will be able to avoid it before it finally drowns me," he said with a deep sigh of resignation. The sound of his words conveyed the same feeling that I had experienced moments before in regard to the climate of the room.

I now finally recognized the surge of my emotion as resentment. I was able to control my expression of feeling only by repeating to myself some basic principles of psychological interviewing. "Tell me about your son and what happened to him," I said, hearing my voice as it may have sounded in my first year of clinical training.

Vincent's words no longer conveyed any surprise. Yet the lack of emotion with which he spoke was harrowing. Vincent told me:

"I think I killed him. I never found out how he actually died. I was afraid to really know. He was just an infant. My wife was away from the house on an errand. I was trying to meet a deadline on a news story. The writing was not going very well. He kept crying. I raised my voice, shouting at him to shut up. He was too young to understand. I immediately realized that yelling at him would only make things worse. I went over to his crib and just tried to reassure him. Soon he became quiet. But he stared at me like he felt abandoned by me. After I went back to my desk I soon forgot about him. The story I was working on started to fall into place. When my wife came home she looked in on him. Then, I heard the most anguished scream I've ever experienced. Nothing I've ever heard in war sounded so indignant. *(What a strange word to use here, I thought).* I went over to her and looked at the child. I instantly knew that he was not breathing. I also realized that I must have killed him. But I didn't know how or why. But, then, it would not have mattered whether or not I had intended it. My son's death was like a horrible nightmare. It was the inevitable unfolding of my fate. I had until that moment been able to keep my depression from overwhelming me. But when my son died it was unavoidably obvious that my ability to feel adequate and good about myself would always elude me. My fate long before my birth had destined that I would never have a confidant and friend. My father never spoke to me of his sister's death or the other unfortunate griefs in his life. I have come to suspect that he caused his sister's death by somehow trying to break up her affair. Oscar Wilde wrote, 'Each man kills the thing he loves.' *(What Vincent should have added, but did not fully realize, was that he only kills what he loves when he believes he does not deserve it).* I became ashamed of a man I had always so highly admired. What I had regarded as his dashing ways I realized was really cowardice. I guess I am loyal to my father's character that way. I was never the son he wanted. I, too, have been denied a son with whom I can share the painful entrails of my life. There will never be anyone to understand me, or anyone who even would care to try!"

My agitation with Vincent was alarming to me. Intellectually, I recognized that this disturbed man was revealing his painful suffering. My task was not to determine what really happened to his son or, least of all, to adjudge guilt. Nevertheless, I kept focusing on his bland and controlled manner and, especially, his lack of compassion for his child. Why was I being so critical of Vincent? I have treated vicious criminals before. Several of them had brutally raped and murdered. I did not admire or respect them, but I did not regard them with the intense resentment I felt toward Vincent at that moment.

A second thought kept intruding upon me. It seemed to feed on my need to justify my resentment. I felt unwilling to let go of the realization that Vincent had largely ignored and excluded me during the session. It was unlike me to be so egocentric in a therapeutic session. Yet I self-righteously reviewed in flashbacks the many occasions that I had made myself available to give Vincent a session within a few hours of request, at considerable inconvenience, when he incurred some particular stressful event. I recalled the times Vincent had the police call me after he was arrested for making a public disturbance. Usually it involved trying to get to see a public official, who Vincent knew from his successful days and who he believed owed him a favor. Vincent would always calm down within a few minutes, after we began to discuss his agitation. I kept asking myself how he could treat me this way, effacing all my hard work in trying to understand him!

During the last few minutes of the session I sat in self-contained silence, afraid to speak, lest my unreasonable resentment erupt. If I permitted it to happen, it would embarrass me, harm Vincent's precarious self-esteem, and irretrievably contaminate our working relationship.

Because the intense resentment I was experiencing toward Vincent was not my usual feeling toward him, I assumed that my own unresolved conflicts were somehow involved. My progressive understanding of my clinical work has taught me that I frequently encounter unfinished aspects of myself in a therapeutic impasse, as I was having with Vincent. Of course, there is a natural tendency for all of us to identify emotionally with the people with whom we are closely involved. This identification, however, is generally suppressed when we become threatened by a subliminal sense that we share certain unacceptable traits or, on the other hand, are struggling unsuccessfully with the same issues as the other person.

In most situations in life we avoid people who evoke uncomfortable reactions in us. Quite obviously, the analyst can ill afford to ignore annoying feelings about his patients.

His reactions to his patients, both those of which he is readily aware and those which he has suppressed, are the tools of his trade. He must continually search his own reactions for his unresolved fears and aversions. Indeed, by using a deeply subjective understanding of himself, the analyst has the most potent human instrument available for understanding human nature, and for knowing how to respond compassionately to the hurt and suffering of his patients. So if I am unwilling or unable to find and examine my own suppressed similarities with a patient, I cannot work effectively with that person. Without knowing precisely what is bothering me about being in the same room as my analysand, I will be too fearful, blinded, and limited to be present, active, and available to help.

I trust that if you have followed me so far you will understand my concern that I needed some time to figure out what conflicts I was bringing in from my own past before I would be appropriately able to work analytically with Vincent.

Vincent called my answering service very early the next morning and left the message that he needed to cancel that day's appointment. He had never cancelled a session before. Although I was concerned about the reasons for not attending, I was more relieved in not having to see him. I spent his analytic hour sitting alone in my consulting room, looking again out into the mud. The rain finally stopped. The tranquility of the morning after the rain served me with an awareness that the mud below had special meaning for me. I found out why a few minutes later.

Each analyst has a favorite, trusted medium for exploring the hidden meanings of analysands' communications. Many practitioners share with Freud the conviction that the interpreted dream provides the golden road to analytic understanding. For me, on the other hand, it has always been the cadence and resonance of the spoken word that convey meanings that transcend their literal connotations. Just as Vincent was trained and comforted by operatic harmony, poetry is a form of expression to which I have always been drawn. I trust it, without reservation, for the evocation of hidden truths about the human psyche. Expanding on the images and moods offered in a verse has provided me with invaluable clues to the riddles posed by the disturbed lives of many of my analysands.

Sitting in my consulting room, visually probing the mud from afar, the words of a poem came to my mind with a profusion of disturbing emotion. The precise words were as follows:

The wind is still now after the tempest of the night;
Yet I can not set aside my fear;
For I have been driven into the burial place of my soul;
The rain falls now, slow and cold;
The mud is thick and red;
How gray is the sky and the sea beyond still grayer
   fields;
How come I see the fields as gray
When I know they should be green?
I fear the rewake of the wind!
It serenely ushers the call to my tomb.

Upon recitation, I understood why I had seen the room as dark and the walls as gray in the previous day's session. I also realized that properly I should have revised the last line of the poem to read, "I fear the rewake of the wind; it serenely ushers a call to my father's grave and to my own tomb."

I had written the poem the day of my father's funeral, a year before. Apparently, some communication Vincent had conveyed about the death of his son and the loss of hope of their companionship had joined in my own psyche with the resentment I have always harbored toward my own father for not giving me his understanding and, thereby, not accepting who I was. My father left me with the feeling, similar to Vincent's father, that I was inadequate and couldn't take proper care of myself.

The resentment I felt toward Vincent, I assumed with shameful realization, was being shaped by the animosity I held toward my father for his viewing of me as a person who will not leave his mark on the world. Vincent's excluding me in the session had reopened a psychic wound for me.

I came to realize in these moments alone in my consulting room, in a way that I never have before, that the
practice of psychoanalysis isn't for everyone. It takes a
special kind of person to be an analyst. Although a person
may be highly intelligent, insightful, interested in other
people and concerned about their well-being, these factors
alone are not sufficient to be a competent practitioner. My
viscera informed me that being a competent practitioner
involves the willingness to touch upon one's own personal
conflicts and uncertainties, because clinical work absorbs
the analyst's entire being, often in very intensive ways. At
this perturbing moment in my session with myself, I had to
question whether I was willing and able to do this. I told
myself, with uneasy conviction, that I would try. I probed in
the remainder of the session with myself the relationship of
my father's death and my intense reaction to Vincent.

Many analysts believe that if they were simply to list all
the books and scholarly papers they have ever read, one
could sufficiently grasp why they practice as they do. It is as
if they were claiming that their life story offers little insight
into their work. But I don't believe that this is true. In the
following pages I will discuss aspects of my life that analysts
rarely, if ever, reveal. Not to speak of these events would
make it difficult to understand why Vincent has such a
disturbing effect upon me.

I experienced my father as strong and resourceful. As
long back as I can remember, my father worked six or
six-and-a-half days a week at the most difficult and unsa-
tisfying types of labor. Among the many jobs he held was as
a railroad worker, longshoreman, and cab driver. He often
worked fifteen-hour shifts.

Until my father's last breath, I waited for him to be the
caring father I needed. Standing on the edge of my father's
grave at his funeral, I realized that it was too late. My fervent
wish about my father would never come to pass. A feeling of
hopelessness overtook me. I experienced my father's death
as my own epitaph. To me it signified the end of all hope of
ever feeling like a confident and loved son.

During my despondency, my clinical and observational
skills did not desert me. As I might search the face of a

patient in the assessment period to appraise what the new situation might hold, I looked around the gravesite. There were a few men with shovels in their hands and a rabbi reciting the Kaddish, the Jewish prayer of mourning. This rabbi had been hired hastily to recite the service. He had not met or had not even heard of my father before this day. Except for me, my mother, and some of her relatives, there was no one at the gravesite who had been close to my father. I realized that my father did not have any close friends.

My eyes were then drawn to my father's casket. I questioned my own perceptual judgment. I had always regarded my father as a powerful man. What astonished me was the diminutive size of the box. Was he a small man? Gradually I realized that my father had never been the powerful, resourceful, and capable person I wished him to be. On the other hand, I also recognized for the first time that my father had probably been terrified by the promptings in his own psyche. He didn't know himself very well, having been born in an age in which psychological awareness had not pervaded human life to the extent it has in contemporary society. My father must have gone through his life with a modicum of exploration of his own feelings and attitudes. He, like Vincent's father, undoubtedly regarded himself as a prisoner of his life situation. His emotional pain was expected to be borne alone—silently and unflinchingly. Apparently, like Vincent's father, mine also had been adept at concealment and creating false impressions, such as that he didn't need my friendship.

It was I who always had been the strong person. Despite my own self-doubts, I had pursued my mission to examine the human psyche, if not with the effectiveness I ideally wished for, then at least with realistic, admirable conviction and persistence. I resolved at that moment that I must and would become a real and compassionate friend to others— the confidant that I had sought to find for myself. I vowed never again to allow fear to isolate me from others. I did not wish someday to die like my father, with no one around who had ever truly known and cared for me. I felt resolute and believed at the time I had placed all matters of importance in their proper place.

In my clinical work after my father's death I had believed that I had been able to disengage myself from resentment toward my father.

In the session with myself I become aware that I had not finished my work with my psychological father. Vincent's ostensibly emotionless description of his son's death had brought back disturbing aspects of my relationship with my father that, apparently, I had not sufficiently worked through and resolved.

I mentally scan the psychoanalytic literature for help with my predicament. A review of psychoanalytic theory suggests that as long as my father had been alive I had cherished the hope that someday we would finally have that cozy chat and, as if by magic, an everlasting warm camara- derie would result. But now he was gone. Analytic theory counseled that I must forgive my father for not being the all-wise, all-caring, available person I had desired. I must see him realistically as an ordinary person, prone to the same human frailties as other men.

In reviewing theory with my own situation, I realized that analytic explanations did not adequately account for my distress. This is to say, I had thought that I had realistically come to terms with the impossibility of cama- raderie with my real father. In fact, I had developed a number of warm male friendships in the past year to provide what had been missing in my relationship with my father. Yet, clearly, something was still amiss in my understanding of my situation, and this factor was seriously interfering with my analytic work with Vincent.

Vincent's strange use of the word *indignant* flashed into my mind, together with the intense resentment I had felt being left out in my efforts to help Vincent during our last session. The word *indignant* used by Vincent provided a key clue to my side of the shared mystery with Vincent. A wise supervisor had indicated early in my clinical training that good sessions attract good words. The session yes- terday morning probably had been more constructive than at first I had believed it to be. From the following set of clinical deductions the phoenix of self-understanding emerged from the ashes of my self-recrimination. My understanding of human relations, shaped by analytic theory, was one-sided. Analytic explanation, I came to realize, focuses almost exclusively on the child's being neglected by the psychologically unavailable parent (Goldberg 1991b). But what, I asked myself, recalling Vincent's sadness in not being allowed by his father to share his father's pain and comfort him, about the child not being caringly available to the father? Of course, as a young child I didn't have the wherewithal to be a real friend to my father. Yet, as an adult and especially as an analyst, I should have recognized him as a man both too proud and too unskilled in reaching out for his own friendship needs to allow me to know that he wanted my companionship. As my self-scrutiny continued, I became aware that my identification with Vincent consisted of shame and anger at myself for suspending my analytic acumen by childishly continuing to regard my father as the all-powerful person he never was. Was my father indignant and resentful that I hadn't permitted myself to recognize him as the lonely and hurt person he was? Shamefully, I became aware that I had denied an important part of myself—the opportunity to be a friend to my own father. In recognizing the presence of my own shame I became aware that a large part of my motivation in becoming an analyst was to help people with their misery in ways as a child with my own parents, I had neither the skills nor the knowledge to do. I ended my session with myself with that thought.

THE ROLE SHAME PLAYED IN VINCENT'S LIFE

I met with Vincent regularly, three times per week. Not having heard from him for a week, I knew it was important that I contact him. He reported having felt extremely humiliated in telling me of the circumstances of his son's death. He said that he was at the present time unable to face me and to return to analysis. I reminded him that he would be lying on the couch and we would not be looking at each other. That didn't matter, he said, because my physical presence was like a mirror to him. As a way of explanation, he reported that he had stopped brushing his hair and trimming his beard. He could not tolerate seeing himself in the mirror. The sight was unbearable.

Although he didn't want to be in my presence, he also didn't seem to want to get off the phone. Vincent went on to tell me that he realized that he had been living a colossal lie for twenty-five years. He had continued to believe that if somehow he could raise his courage and confess his guilty deed he might finally rid himself of his suffering.

After the death of their child his wife had implored him for weeks on end to speak about their loss. He sensed that complying with her request might have been wise. If he could have confessed to her they might have found some solace together, perhaps even the intimacy that had eluded their marriage. Yet some perplexing need to hold onto painful secrets prevented openness with her. His depression began to feed on itself, eroding his last remnant of self-regard, until there was no self-esteem and pride left in him. His despondency and need for protective solitude drove her away and, finally, the last of his friends as well. He recognized what was happening, but felt powerless to act on his realization that those who will not share their painful secrets with others suffer their terrors alone.

His career held together a while longer than his personal life. He had always been able to control his voice and to convey an image of assuredness as a reporter.

In the past two and a half decades he had consulted several therapists. None, he believed, had the slightest notion of what he was suffering. He had heard me speak in a public forum about the psychological trauma that ingresses from guilt. He chose to regard his attendance at my talk as a fortuitous omen. He had come to me for analysis because he believed that if he could finally confess his secret to an uncritical and caring authority figure he could rid himself of his painful guilt. But our last session ripped away the cloak of pretense and revealed his humiliating duplicity. His confession hadn't been sufficient. Indeed, he now felt worse after confession than he had for the twenty-five years he had held onto his guilty secret.

I was quite puzzled by his intense distress. It was evident that the explanation of guilt being the cause of Vincent's

suffering wasn't accurate. If it were, then Vincent's confession to me should have relieved much of his despondency.
Instead, his confession served to augment his bad feelings.
Moreover, Vincent's description of himself—his dread lost
sense of self, the feeling that his personality had crumbled
away without any personal protection from how other
people saw him, which led to relegating himself to a restricted life, experiencing social isolation, regarding himself
as discredited and believing himself to be unwelcome to
others—was not indicative of one suffering a guilt reaction,
but that of shame and humiliation.

It is reasonable to infer that throughout his life Vincent
had been ashamed of his bouts of depression and despair.
He had difficulty believing that other people would want to
develop a close friendship with him because he had assumed that they, like his father, regarded him as a coward.
The feeling that other people disrespected him had always
contaminated his life. However, the feelings of inadequately
caring for his son, if not actually killing the infant, so
pervasively undermined his self-regard that after the
tragedy he could no longer function adequately in the areas
in which he once held consummate skill. Over the years he
had become more and more of a recluse.

But why, you may well ask, couldn't Vincent confess his
shameful sense of himself, just as he finally did his
supposed guilt? Yes, there is agreed-upon language to
confess and to express one's guilt, which enables the
sufferer to speak about his deed and to begin to find ways of
redeeming himself. Such a procedure enables the guilty
person to find some solace for his hidden terrors and
uncertainties. The same, however, cannot be said of the
experience of shame. Human experience futilely cries out
for ways of articulating our shame and humiliation. For
people like Vincent, shame is experienced as impossible to
communicate and to share with another human being.

RESPONDING TO VINCENT'S SHAME

I searched for a long moment on the phone for a way to
best reach Vincent and to deal compassionately with his

shame. I realized that because his profound shame and humiliation had closeted him from other people, that what Vincent needed from me at that time was the opportunity for friendship that had been denied to him by his father and his son. If I wouldn't share genuine friendship with Vincent, then who would?

Poets and psychoanalysts should be the two types of people who, because of their sensitivity to the exquisite nuances of subjective experience and their skill in expressing these experiences in words, best offer the experience of shame a voice. Consequently, I needed to speak to Vincent from my own experience in such a way that he would no longer need to feel totally alone in his shame and loneliness. It was from the realization of my failure to be a friend to my own father that I could give voice to Vincent's shame.

Because Vincent was inattentive to his shame, he had unwittingly fashioned for himself a "proper" punishment for his guilt. I realized that I must free him from this unfair punishment before we could deal effectively with his shame. Until that moment I had not been actually aware of what his self-imposed punishment was. This was because I had always regarded entering psychoanalysis as a person's recognition of his wish to liberate himself of his neurotic suffering. As such, I had believed that in spite of whatever ambivalent loyalties people may have to the parents of their neurosis, becoming an analysand was a clear statement of one's feelings of legitimate entitlement to a more satisfying life. But this wasn't true of Vincent. It was the first time in my clinical work that I realized the possibility that many patients may compulsively attend psychotherapy without hope. They regard therapy as their just punishment because of their failure to be an adequate and competent person. Such patients derive little or no benefit from therapy.

In our prolonged telephone conversation I told Vincent that I was not sure how I could help him because I had become aware in listening and responding to his pain that I shared some of his issues. At the same time, I added, I recognized the need and permission in myself to feel compassion for myself during those moments in which I felt inadequate and didn't know what to do. I believed that Vincent had the right to do the same for himself.

I told him that I cared about his struggle and what would come of it. However, if the only way he could protest his unfair punishment of himself and his legacy of despair was by not returning to analysis, temporarily or permanently, he had my permission if he needed it.

However, I also said that if he ever wanted someone to struggle with him who didn't have all the answers and could not guarantee him success, I was there. Vincent was silent for a moment. He then ended our conversation by saying that he would think about what I said and call me back.

Why was I so baldly self-disclosing to Vincent? To face the mirror of the psyche squarely and probingly, courage is required. Courage is the willingness to take those actions necessary to change that which can be changed and the serenity to accept without resentment that which cannot. Before entering analysis, almost all the patients I have ever worked with suffered from the lack of courage of their convictions and a reluctance to stand up for what they believed and deserved, which comes from a lack of self-esteem. The analyst indirectly, sometimes even directly, must offer his analysands the courage and conviction he has found in struggling with his own mirror.

Vincent called back some days later. He told me that he had appreciated that I had spoken to him from a struggle with my own convictions. He had never experienced any significant person in his life, he said, who had rendered himself vulnerable on his behalf. He conveyed his belief that he had found a friend with a shared mission and, as a result, he was experiencing the awakening of his own hope. For the first time in his life he felt free to explore his inner being. He ended the phone conversation by stating confidently and unhesitatingly that he was ready to return to analysis.

In addition to a growing friendship between us, Vincent needed to offer his friendship to someone sorely in need of his, Vincent's, considerable strengths. An inherent problem with psychoanalysis is that the extraordinary emphasis given to the patient's concerns frequently results in the magnification of self-importance. For Vincent to come to terms with his morbid destiny, he must become involved with other people's suffering, not only his own. He must learn by direct experience that the world doesn't begin and end with him. Moreover, by realizing that he could do much to help others he would learn the ways that he could help himself and also earn the right in his own mind to ask others to assist him.

Shame mirrors the awareness of the conditions necessary for self-worth. We become embarrassed and humiliated from catching ourselves in the act of trying to deny the ways of living we regard as proper.

Vincent had always been a man of strong humanitarian sentiments. His social and emotional withdrawal in recent years had prevented him from compassionately touching the lives of others. In the sessions I had with Vincent following his telling me that he was ready to return to analysis, I suggested that he find some way of helping other people. After some investigation he volunteered time with the Big Brother program in his city. He offered his companionship and guidance to a 14-year-old black lad named Junior, who lacked a male mentor in his life. Vincent's work with Junior proved gratifying. His face seemed more relaxed, and his choice of clothes reflected a more liberated sense of himself. It also allowed Vincent to proceed with more confidence further into the real world.

Then, during one session Vincent said to me, "I have the best news of all today. You remember my telling you that a public relations firm asked me to pull together my news stories and clippings? Well, last night they called to ask me if I would consider letting them arrange a lecture tour for me. I surprised myself. I said, without any hesitation, that I would be delighted if they did. I think I've abandoned my myth of destined suffering."

Our sessions ended soon afterward. Vincent's lecture tours were taking him all over the world.

11

THE HUMILIATING CLINICAL CASE CONFERENCE

Deep shame has struck me dumb.
                    —William Shakespeare

Psychoanalysts want to be perceived not only as competent practitioners, but also as compassionate and caring people. Few of us involved in psychotherapeutic endeavors view ourselves as lacking sincere concern for those who petition us in our professional role with their burdens of hurt and suffering. Yet consumers of psychotherapeutic services have become increasingly vocal in their contention that many psychotherapy practitioners do not act in a caring and compassionate manner toward their patients.

The issue I am concerned with in this chapter addresses the specific ways the unhappiness and suffering of another person whom I encountered in my personal life had an impact upon my role as an analyst. The story I will share with you in the following pages reveals my own examination of the underlying conditions and the vicissitudes in my own capacity and willingness to express compassion. Consequently, an important reason for relating my story is to further develop my thesis that analysts bring to the treatment situation the positive benefit of the values gained from their own life experiences. Whatever wisdom I have brought to the analytic hour was only partially shaped by my professional education and clinical training. More significantly, my own maturity both as a person and as an analyst was acquired by witnessing and participating in my analysands' struggles and, especially, those events in my personal life in which I was not in the role of analyst.

My ambition, in addition to practicing analysis, has always been to teach. Several years ago I was appointed to the clinical teaching faculty of the department of psychiatry at a medical school. During my first year of appointment several senior psychiatric residents asked me if I would be the faculty discussant at a clinical case conference. I was flattered by the request. The discussant in this psychiatric department has overall teaching responsibility for the case being evaluated at a clinical conference. If my assessment of the patient being presented and my manner of regarding the circumstances of the case make clinical sense to residents and staff involved in the patient's care, it will be used as a guide for treatment. The discussant is expected to teach by either clinical explanation or clinical demonstration. This is to say, the case discussant directs how to treat the patient by discussing didactically the dynamics and issues involved in the patient's condition, or he demonstrates how to work efficaciously with the patient through his own style of interviewing the patient.

Of course, the particular circumstances of the case determine which approach the discussant will use. If the resident interviewing the patient is skilled, or if the patient is relatively cooperative, the discussant may choose not to interview the patient during the conference. He may instead just ask a question or two, broaching material that has not been already asked or ask the patient to elaborate on information already discussed and still unclear.

On the other hand, if the patient is highly resistant to being queried in front of an audience, the discussant is required to demonstrate how skillful interviewing can elicit relevant information needed to understand the case properly. In this eventuality, the discussant assumes the roles of both interviewer and supervisor.

Dr. Levy, the resident who would be interviewing Mrs. Franz, the patient to be presented, was a supervisee of mine and we had developed a fond friendship in the six months we had worked together on his psychotherapy cases. I was not surprised, therefore, when he called me at home the Sunday before the conference. We both were aware that the policy for clinical conferences dictated that no prior information was to be given to the discussant before the actual conference. In this way residents could most readily appreciate how the discussant formulated his clinical impressions on the spot.

Dr. Levy said that he would not disclose any data about Mrs. Franz. But out of friendship he wished to warn me about the case. He did so with a typical resident-type of pun. "She is a tough nut to crack." He then added in a mock whisper over the phone, "You better not use anything heavy to crack her! Dr. Danton (an influential faculty member) is a friend of the Franz family." I was being told that the case I would be discussing would not be an ordinary one.

The conference was held in a room filled with psychiatric residents, medical students, psychiatric staff, and a few members of the teaching faculty. The room itself was not very large. A long conference table with three rows of chairs on all sides of the table occupied most of the space. Almost all of the audience had arrived by the time the case history was to be read. Inevitably, however, two or three faculty members arrived late, having taken time off from their private practices to attend the conference. Prior to the reading of the patient's case history, an attractive nurse of perhaps 35 laughed uncomfortably as she straightened her short skirt and leaned over to whisper to a middle-aged psychiatrist in a three-piece suit, sitting stiffly in his chair and fidgeting with his maroon tie. A tall, lanky, young medical student coaxed on by the encouragement of smiles and grimaces he received from the rows of occupants, pushed the window on the far end of the hall up and down, finally reaching a level satisfactory to alleviate the stuffiness of the room. He slid into a seat next to a slim social worker, devoid of cosmetics, seated in the last row of the circle. She was writing up a report, undoubtedly an intake evaluation past due. The inpatient unit psychologist, a heavy, bosomy woman with a painted smile, furtively studied the others in the room. She is a person who almost always takes an oppositional position to the discussant, in regard to the patient's treatment, particularly if he is a psychiatrist.

Dr. Snowden, the chief resident of the psychiatric inpatient unit, a loquacious but mild-mannered fellow, initially presents the patient's psychiatric history. Mrs. Franz is a middle-aged, upper-middle-class woman, highly intelligent and well educated, who owns a well-regarded art gallery in the city. She had been brought up by rather rigid and punitive parents, who used humiliation and ridicule to discipline her. An overriding motif of her upbringing was that she should associate exclusively with people of high moral and intellectual character. She was taught that people who have not developed sufficient intellectual and aesthetic sensibilities are prone to be derisive about what they cannot appreciate or understand. Mrs. Franz had conducted her life and her art gallery accordingly. She had been unwilling to sell or to even show her paintings to anyone whom she regarded as uncultured and unable to understand fine art. Mrs. Franz was married and the mother of two grown daughters. Her husband, described as a very attractive and urbane man, was an academically unsuccessful college professor.

Mrs. Franz was hospitalized ten days before the conference by Dr. Danton at her family's request. She had become increasingly guarded, secretive, and hostile. Neither her family nor Dr. Danton had been able to reach her. She flatly refused to communicate with anyone about what was troubling her.

When the reading of her psychiatric history was completed, Mrs. Franz was led into the conference room by a medical student and given a chair at the far end of the conference table. I was startled by Mrs. Franz's drab attire.

Dr. Snowden had told us that she was a very stylish dresser, who wore expensive diamond earrings and rings. She was now dressed in a dark gray hospital outfit, with no jewelry. In the midst of the assembled mental health professionals peering inquisitively at her, Mrs. Franz, looking quite pale, seemed lost and alone. I experienced an immediate sense of sadness for her.

My eyes canvassed the audience, resting for a moment on each of them. The tension in their countenances conceded a plea to Dr. Levy to get the interviewing process going and then to skillfully unearth interesting details about the patient's condition. Few of the audience, unless they were directly involved in Mrs. Franz' treatment, would remain in the room unless the case was stimulating or if not, unless there was considerable heated controversy among the prominent professionals in attendance about how to understand and handle the case.

Dr. Levy now took over the interviewing of the patient. Although he had spoken with Mrs. Franz several times before, she remained mute to Dr. Levy's questions about the reasons for her hospitalization. Throughout his attempts at interviewing the patient, I heard hushed whispers of annoyance and disapproval around me. Recalcitrant patients do not make stimulating conferences!

Dr. Levy had been flushing with exasperation throughout the ordeal. After a few indecisive moments he turned to me and asked if I would take over the interview.

I had studied Mrs. Franz closely. Her appearance was remarkably similar to the qualities of her guarded self. She was quite thin for a woman her age. I surmised that her slender build had resulted neither from a lack of appetite, nor from salubrious considerations of dieting. I suspect that her slight appearance was tied into some moral requirement of her upbringing in the home of highly critical parents. Her presence seemed to convey a belief that it was foolish and unseemly for anyone to see too much of who she really was.

Because I sensed that she was proud of her ability to stay thin, asking her about her diet seemed to me to be a less threatening line of questioning than to inquire about other aspects of her life. Nevertheless, she said nothing to my question about how she went about dieting and exercising.

I was not overly concerned at the moment. I next asked her about how she had found the conditions to be in the hospital. (I generally have found that this sort of question is effective in getting many angry and withholding patients to speak freely, because it provides an opportunity to complain about hospital conditions, rather than to initially discuss painful and embarrassing aspects of themselves. Few patients, even in a well-run hospital as this, enjoy their stay in a psychiatric unit.)

To my dismay, Mrs. Franz refused to respond to my questions about the conditions in the hospital. For that matter, she would not converse on any subject I broached. Although I felt that my questions and my manner were clinically sensitive and caring, it was to no avail. She made it clear by her contemptuous expressions and gestures that she did not want to be in the hospital, nor did she want me to be interviewing her. The few words she *did* render said, in effect, that she did not belong in the hospital, did not want to be discussed in a clinical conference, and if she ever needed any help, that I was not qualified to assist her. How she came to this determination, I was unable to ascertain.

I was becoming increasingly self-conscious about how poorly I was doing in trying to reach Mrs. Franz. Needless to say, my idealized imago of myself as a competent analyst was being threatened under the critical gaze of my colleagues. I was experiencing a serious concern that this clinical conference would have an adverse effect on my teaching career in the medical school. Resentfully, I told myself that what was happening to me was grossly unfair. I regarded my ostensibly poor performance, unfairly, as a result of Mrs. Franz's psychopathology—not due to any lack in my clinical skills. I would realize the absurdity of this belief only later in the interview.

The embarrassment of my position caused me some sort of stage fright. For a few moments I was uncertain about what I should do or say to Mrs. Franz and the audience. In my hesitation I was aided by a strange inner resource.

The anxiety of how poorly I was performing in my capacity as a clinician loosened in my mind an association of memories of other humiliating moments during my life. These events flashed through my thoughts in a rapid kaleidoscoping of emotions until my attention focused on a particular memory. I realized only afterward that the atmosphere of the conference room had directed my recollection. My colleagues' disdain for a difficult patient was part of this coterie of factors that revived the event. So, too, was my sense or perhaps my hope, that despite Mrs. Franz's guardedness there was a hint from her of a desire to be understood. These factors served as a bridge from the conference room to a difficult moment I had shared with a disturbed woman in my private life.

I considered my recollection of this difficult moment with mixed emotions. My memory of the incident was an amalgamation of pride at my clever dispatch of a disturbing social situation and, at the same time, chagrin at the deceit I perpetrated in utilizing a disturbed woman's psychopathology to avoid her unpleasant presence. I must tell you about this incident before we return to the conference and Mrs. Franz. What eventuated in my subsequent dealing with Mrs. Franz was directly influenced by my behavior during the earlier event.

Some time before Mrs. Franz's conference I consulted to a hospital in the upper reaches of the Bronx, in New York City. The trip to the hospital was long and unpleasant. I rode an old, dirty, and crowded subway train from my home in midtown Manhattan to where I consulted. One of the few distractions from the disagreeable train experience was getting involved in reading *The New York Times.*

Early one morning as I began reading the newspaper I observed a heavy, middle-aged woman entering the subway car, garbed all in black, with a strange sort of bird's nest hat worn to one side of her head and holding a black-covered Bible. The sight of her set off a queasy feeling in my gut. I had worked with many such seriously and chronically disturbed people in my career as a psychotherapist and a consultant to federal and state psychiatric hospitals. Now I wished simply to read my newspaper. The day would be long and demanding. I would be supervising psychiatrists in training and other mental health professionals. I also would be consulting to a couple of psychiatric programs during the day. Later in the afternoon I would be taking the same long trip back to my office in Manhattan to work with my own analysands until late into the evening.

There were a few empty seats in the subway car. The woman with the Bible did not move toward any of these seats. Instead, she slowly strolled back and forth the length of the car, with a slight rocking cadence to her stride, calling out in a loud, flat voice, "God talks to me. God talks to me."

People in the train, mostly Blacks and Hispanics on their way to work or school, tried to ignore her. I, too, attempted to avoid her by concentrating on my newspaper. It was to no avail. Her loud, monotonous voice rendered me unable to remain heedless to her actions. After ten or fifteen minutes of her religious recital, I was willing to try anything, short of getting off the train in some unknown (to me) part of the Bronx and, by doing so, missing or being late for my teaching assignments. The cars were locked, so that I could not readily change cars.

Why, I resentfully thought, can't someone take care of this annoying situation. I was fully aware, however, that it was unlikely that there was anyone in the subway car, except me, who was trained to handle a disturbed person. Consequently, I decided to try something radical. I called the woman with the Bible over to where I was sitting and asked her, "Did you say that God talks to you?" She replied in a loud voice, although she was standing close to me, "God talks to me."

"Well," I replied, "God speaks to me, too. And, if you believe in God you will listen to what He said to me. He told me to tell you that you should get off at the next station stop."

She looked straight at me for the first time. Her appearance seemed somewhat altered. Perhaps it was due to the fact that her eyes no longer held the glassy, fixed gaze she had while she walked up and down the subway car. When the train stopped at the next station she promptly left the train. I didn't know whether she believed me or whether her leaving the train was due to a coincidence between my assertion and her destination. I assumed at the time that she believed that God had spoken to me.

I felt a sense of considerable relief when she departed. I assumed that I would have some tranquility for the remainder of the train trip. I was mistaken. I didn't feel at peace. A disquieting feeling arose in me, that I, by using my technical knowledge about psychopathology to insulate myself from my annoyance with her, had acted uncompassionately toward this hapless person. I uncomfortably sensed that I was denying her my humanity.

Nevertheless, I questioned whether my self-castigation was overwrought. I realized that most of us are more uncomfortable with the suffering of children than with the adult homeless, as the Bible woman appeared to be. Children are born into their disadvantage and can do little about it. If they are not responsible, then their condition strikes us as grossly unfair. We can, on the other hand, rationalize our lesser concern for people like the lady with the Bible, because we can plainly discern the annoying and dysfunctional things they do to influence how others treat them.

Was I being too self-reproachful about effecting an intelligent solution to an unpleasant situation? Of course not. Intelligence and wisdom are not integral. I had shown cleverness, not wisdom, in the situation I have described above. Possessing factual knowledge does not make one a caring person. Wisdom has an emotional component that factual knowledge often does not. Wisdom consists of compassion, decency, and common sense. Unless we are able to combine our technological knowledge with wisdom, we will experience our efforts at touching and being touched emotionally as elusive to our efforts.

If I had manifested more wisdom than cleverness on the subway trip to the Bronx, I might have realized that the disturbed woman on the train, like the rest of us supposedly "sane" people, endures her daily struggles, frustrations, and disappointments in the silent hope that her suffering will someday bring her to an intimate closeness with another person. She hopes this intimacy (my previous clinical experience with people suffering disturbed ideas of reference suggested) will enable her to experience herself as a competent and self-sufficient person.

I now believe that the woman's heeding of my contrived command came not from a religious delusion but because she desperately wished to believe that my stating that God speaks to me, too, was a statement of communion with her. I surmise that she fervently needed to believe that I understood her and, as a consequence, cared about her. She was willing to get off at the wrong station, to what considerable inconvenience I'll never know, as the price she was willing to pay for communion with my caring. My chagrin is that my statement to this woman came from convenience, not compassion.

For the following few days after the subway incident I felt badly that I had not recognized the Bible woman's desire for communion with me. I came to realize, in a very personal way, that frequently in modern life the technological skills and factual knowledge we have acquired are not effectively helping us with our daily struggle. Too often, as I did in the subway incident, we utilize our technological knowledge not to find humane solutions to our societal problems but rather to fashion momentary respites from social annoyances and internal dissatisfactions. Generally, we do not concern ourselves, even if we are aware, with the impact our behavior has upon others. Not certain how to use my realization, after awhile I willingly pushed the incident into the back of my mind.

In turning my attention back to Mrs. Franz at the conference, I realized at that moment I had the opportunity to utilize my experience on the subway to reach another human being in a meaningful way. I recognized however, to offer communion with another person's suffering, I could no longer present myself as a professionally aloof being, but as a fellow sojourner. Therefore, I needed to reveal my own candid feelings about my difficult impasse with Mrs. Franz. Yet, to openly disclose my feelings to the patient I would, at the same time, be revealing my personal vulnerabilities to the scrutinizing eyes of my colleagues assembled around me, who were intently judging my every word and action. I felt at the moment considerably more comfortable divulging uneasy aspects of myself to Mrs. Franz than to my critical colleagues. It was best, therefore, that I turn my thoughts and concerns away from the audience and pretend that Mrs. Franz and I were alone in my consulting office.

My discomfort with Mrs. Franz had come from my need to act as if I were in control of the clinical situation, and in so doing, deny the obvious awareness by everyone present that she was directing the interview and that I was ineffectual in gaining a working alliance with her. I further recognized that my need to conceal my feelings of professional ineptitude were increasing my anxiety in a dysfunctional way. I decided, whether or not I succeed in doing a better job of interviewing the patient, it made no sense for me to remain anxious—certainly not if I could do something about it!

I indicated to Mrs. Franz that I had been asked to interview her because supposedly I had some expertise in cases like hers. I added that I had no idea from where this foolish notion had come. I smiled and pointed to the audience, while saying to the patient that she must now be aware, as was everyone else in the room, how poorly I was doing.

For a moment Mrs. Franz appeared not to know what to make of my statement. Then, for the first time in the interview, she began to smile. Her smile evolved for a while into a quiet laugh. The softening of her face conveyed a warm and approachable demeanor. I told Mrs. Franz in earnest that I appreciated her tolerating my ineptness. Her smile became broader and her body appeared more at ease.

In the process of liberating myself in order to express myself more freely, I became aware that I had been more concerned during the interview with my persona to the professionals present at the conference than in how difficult

and shameful this exposure of herself in front of so many
strangers must have been for Mrs. Franz. If I felt uneasy
revealing my vulnerabilities to colleagues, some of whom I
already knew, her embarrassment must have been even
more manifold. I felt ashamed at being concerned with my
own professional reputation at her expense.

Curiously, as I spoke to Mrs. Franz of my embarrassment, she became more and more responsive to me. She
indicated, "Dr. Goldberg, I am now willing to talk with you."

But before she spoke of the emotions and disturbing
events that had caused her to become recalcitrant, Mrs.
Franz told me the following, as if she were commenting
upon a work of art hanging in her gallery:

> I should tell you that you are not doing such a poor job
> interviewing me as you have represented yourself to me
> and to the doctors here. My lack of cooperation, if you
> want to call it that, is simply because I don't want to be
> the only person in this room who is going to admit to
> having feelings. To speak of my troublesome feelings in
> a room of professionals, who are all acting inaccessibly,
> makes me feel ashamed of my problems and terribly
> alone.

After a moment of hesitation and with a deep sigh or two,
she spoke of what drove her into seclusion. Her words were
an admixture of sadness and venom:

> I know that my husband is having an affair with a
> younger woman. I assume he no longer finds me inter-
> esting and attractive. Just like the doctors in this hospi-
> tal, he expresses his concern about me as if his caring for
> me is some damn formal obligation rather than from
> some personal warmth and interest. He has been rot-
> tenly cold and indifferent to me. I have this dreadful
> feeling as if my personality is crumbling away, without a
> sense of something else to replace it. I feel gripped by the
> feeling that I am unwelcome to anyone. I feel doomed to
> living a limited life. I guess it is because my husband has
> been the only person I have ever completely trusted. His

THE HUMILIATING CLINICAL CASE CONFERENCE

betrayal has devastated me. There is no one else who cares for me or understands me. I feel isolated and don't know how to reach out to anyone.

I was aware, of course, that Mrs. Franz had been behaving less fearfully in the last few minutes. I asked her how she was feeling at that moment. She told me that my adjusting my style of interacting with her made a profound impression on her. By expressing my feelings of embarrassment, she had become freed up to express her own vulnerable concerns with a fellow commiserate. I only realized through her telling me this that by freely expressing myself, I was also conveying to her my conviction that it is both proper and safe to express dissatisfactions with oneself at the clinical conference.

Only a few minutes after I started speaking of my own anxiety, she and I were involved in the kind of intimate dialogue that an analyst may not achieve until after several months of analysis. Unfortunately, the conversation had to be terminated. The diagnostic conference had drawn to a close. I never saw or heard from Mrs. Franz again. Nevertheless, my time with her has left an indelible impression on how I practice my profession.

12

THE THERAPEUTIC USE
OF INTERSUBJECTIVE SHAME

And in that shame still lives my sorrow's rage.
—William Shakespeare

Inevitably, the psychotherapy office is a place of shaming. The patient who comes to us for treatment is ashamed because his presence in our consulting room is experienced as an indication of his incompetence as a person. Moreover, our very presence magnifies the patient's shame. Our presence during the recitation of his secrets compels the patient to reflect upon unworthy and mortifying aspects of himself. In turn, the ashamed patient shames the practitioner. The practitioner who cannot meaningfully reach and help to heal his suffering patient is vulnerable to feeling shame. The inexorable shaming of the therapeutic encounter awakens unresolved personal concerns and conflicts of the practitioner (Goldberg 1990).

The intersubjectivity of shame has a potentially constructive substratum. It is my thesis that the presence of therapeutic shame provides the sine qua non for a meaningful examination by the therapeutic participants of the existential dilemmas of human existence. I believe that there is a crucial interrelationship between how the analyst uses his own shame and the patient's willingness to express and to work through his despair (Goldberg 1986). To illustrate this I will candidly present my own existential condition several years ago when I worked with a very troubled patient.

Before I present the clinical material it is necessary to offer a brief perspective on the existential dilemmas that analytic work poses for its practitioners.

The Existential Basis of Psychoanalysis

The recurring theme of human existence is the self's striving for personal identity, significance, and unification. It seems to be the nature of the human animal to require some intelligible sense of purpose for his existence. A loss of purpose or an inability to achieve a sense of meaning for one's existence results in feelings of denigration of self-worth. If this existential malaise persists, it develops into a state of anguish and despair. It would follow that psycho-pathological symptoms of any sort are, in their most profound sense, synonymous with an inability to find life meaningful. In short, people who find their way into any brand of psychotherapy are seeking, regardless of their specific complaints, an answer to their quest for personal meaning (Goldberg 1986).

Generally, people come to psychoanalysis and other forms of psychotherapy as a last resort—the final respite before giving into terminal desperation, in the form of murder, suicide, or some other less severe solution to the problem of making sense of their lives (Goldberg 1977).

In my view, each of the therapies other than psychoanalysis, amends the direct, bald, search for purpose with a structural endeavor to help the patient develop some type of social or psychological skill, in order to cope more successfully, or even just adapt to the expectations and demands of other people. Ideally, psychoanalysts (or, at least, the more existential practitioners) are unique among healing professionals in eschewing efforts at developing social and psychological coping skills for their analysands. They regard such activities as diverging from the only authentic task of psychoanalysis, which is the examination of the meaning of a person's life through a dialectic dialogue with the personal unconscious of the analysand.

THE ROLE OF THE EXAMINED LIFE FOR THE PRACTITIONER

The analyst, by choice of his career, is affirming his faith in the proposition that the examined pursuit of the intrapsychic world is the ultimate and only true means of finding meaning in one's life. In this regard, analytic practitioners are a select cadre of people. It is my thesis that for most analytic practitioners, deeply committed to meaningful therapeutic work, psychoanalysis is not a conscious and rational choice of career. It may sound unscientific, but in many ways I believe that it is accurate to regard the choice to practice analysis as a spiritual calling. I approach this issue from the point of view of practitioners and theorists such as Carl Jung, who contend that psychotherapists do not choose their profession by chance. Those drawn to analysis are impelled by the instinctual disposition of their psyche, a psyche whose vulnerability has never been fully healed and is continually in search of a more comprehensive understanding of human intentionality (Goldberg 1991a).

As a spiritual calling, analysis imposes certain concerns, problems, and hazards in the course of the practitioner's pursuit of a commitment to a way of life that transcends his professional hours. Some analysts develop a sense of fraudulence about the examined life. They feel that their commitment to analytic understanding of themselves has not harvested the savory fruits of the well-lived existence that their faith in psychoanalysis had promised. This is a subject that few analysts are willing to speak about publicly (Wheelis 1962). Their nihilistic feelings are reserved for conversations with close, trusted colleagues or for their return to the analytic couch.

One of the most difficult questions confronting the disillusioned analyst who regards his theory and practice as fraudulent is whether to try to resolve his troubles by returning to the couch, or by some other means. There is a thorny problem involved in this question: can a practitioner successfully find answers to questions about the limitation of his practice by using that practice to evaluate his dissatisfactions? For in doing so, is not the practitioner tacitly confirming that all his questions and doubts are not real, but rather countertransferential? Wheelis (1962) cautions us about the folly of assuming that despair is synonymous with psychopathology. For if this were true then all moral problems are dismissed and all troubling issues are relegated to psychological problems.

The meaningfulness of the life of the analyst who is in despair does not wane categorically. It departs from the confidence and sense of well-being of the practitioner, bit by bit (Wheelis 1962). Therefore, the seasoned practitioner, through the skills and tricks of the trade, may still carry on his professional duties almost competently, even when his convictions about the unsoundness of his theory and the illusory benefits of pursuing the examined life trouble him. For the seasoned practitioner these disturbing affects first may reveal themselves in a crippling manner in his private life. Inevitably, of course, they will manifest themselves in his clinical practice.

The Patient in Existential Anguish

Roy was, at the time I treated him, a 35-year-old, white male from a working-class family in the mid-Atlantic region of the country. He was the youngest of five siblings. His father had deserted the family when Roy was five. Roy had the classic Lombroso characteristics of the criminal physiognomy: he had a thick neck, a barrel chest, powerful torso, stood just over six feet, and had short-cropped blond hair, a square chin, and piercing blue eyes. Roy had spent half of his life in psychiatric and forensic institutions. Most of the incidents that sent him away involved the sadistic intimidation of women in situations that stopped just short of physical rape. The first such incident brought him into Fritz Redl's project for "acting out" children at the National Institute of Mental Health when Roy was 7 years of age.

Roy had dropped out of high school midway through. Despite his limited schooling, he was a highly facile speaker with an exceptional vocabulary. He was also especially observant of other people's behavior and able to offer rather plausible and astute assessments of their motivations.

Roy had come to see me, he said, because he sincerely wanted to get his life straightened out. However, the way he found out about my professional qualifications and then approached me for treatment was rather unusual, if not bizarre.

I had been involved in training the paraprofessional staff of the "Hot Line" crisis services in the county in which I lived and practiced. I remained as a consultant in instances in which the telephone worker was uncertain about how to handle a call from a person who appeared to be in a dire crisis.

Roy had been an obscene telephone caller for a number of years. He dialed the Hot Line service to say that he was concerned about his perverse telephone behavior. The young worker who took Roy's call became quickly intimidated by his obscenity, no less than by the frequent allusions to violence in his speech. She asked Roy to hold the line for a short while so that she could speak with a professional consultant about how to get Roy the help he was requesting. Roy shot back at her, "You can't help me, kid! Give me the doctor's telephone number!" The worker at first refused. Roy replied, smoothly and forcefully, "Little girl, I know who you are, therefore, I'll have no trouble finding out where you are. And as soon as I do, I'll come over and I'm going to rape you repeatedly."

The worker promptly gave Roy my home telephone number.

Roy called and asked if I would see him. He said that although he was a skilled auto mechanic, his finances were limited. But he said that he would find a way to pay me whatever my usual fee was. After a few preliminary sessions, I, with some reservation, agreed to work with him.

My two major misgivings concerned the nature of his motivation. First, as sincere as he presented his desire to examine closely what he was all about, his history was replete with numerous, short-lived forays into psychological treatment programs. Second, my office was located in my home. I could not dismiss the possibility that Roy's desire to come to my office for sessions was in part impelled by the opportunity to "case" my neighborhood for ripe access to objects for theft, or even rape.

You may well wonder, then, why I was willing to treat such an intimidating person as Roy and to work with him in my own home. I am not entirely certain even today. I am sure, however, it had something to do with the quality of my existential condition at the time. My inner nullity called out for an intensive challenge.

At the time I treated Roy my existence was almost entirely involved with my work as a psychotherapist, writer, and supervisor. I spent more time with patients and supervisees than I did with others. I recognized in myself, with no easy conscience, an apathy of personal concern in most areas other than psychological and intellectual functioning. This was at odds with the person I had been as a youth, who had been occupied with physical activity. I even had entered college with the hope of becoming a professional athlete.

I recoiled in horror, seeing in myself the identical malady that I struggled so arduously to enable my patients to transcend—the foreboding sense that living well would always remain elusive.

My existential malaise demanded a means of resolution. Practicing psychotherapy remained one of the few areas of my life that held some vestige of a sense of accomplishment.

It was an old and familiar route for me to make life changes with tenacity. Roy was a very difficult person. To deal with him would require a resurgence of vital energies on my part. This seemed a task I was willing to try. My willingness was attributable to a partial identification with Roy. Like Roy I had been a football player. I remember fantasizing during our earliest sessions of being locked in physical and psychological combat with him. These reveries revived memories of my adolescence, when I had matched my athletic skills and daring with intimidating opponents.

To my dismay, however, Roy would not cooperate with my need for accomplishment in our therapeutic encounters. His resistant behavior threatened my overvalued persona of competence as a practitioner. Roy would not allow himself to be analytically maneuvered. Whenever I tried to relate his present conflicts—such as the frequent times he was fired from jobs at garages because of violent altercations with supervisors—to events and feelings in his early life, Roy laughed at me. His sadistic-sounding snicker conveyed unmitigated contempt for me and my therapeutic technique— in a way that my more "civilized" patients would never dare to express. His laughter was frequently accompanied by such statements as, "Who are you trying to kid, Doc! You are no better than me. If I stay around maybe I will help you. But what can you do for me?"

During those moments I felt embarrassed and exposed. I wondered what he suspected about me. I had been acutely vigilant in trying to detect if my dissatisfactions with my own private life were beginning to reveal themselves to patients. I told myself that I had to keep my doubts and uncertainties to myself. If I didn't, my patients would seize upon even my best efforts at helping them as if they were of the same limited competence as figures in their past, who didn't know how to relate to them. I was apprehensive that in such an exigency my patients would break off treatment and leave me empty in the least conflictual domain of my life.

THE CRITICAL INCIDENT

There was a crucial incident in my therapeutic work with Roy, six months into its course, that brought our difficult encounters to an existential crisis. In the county in which I practiced there had been over the past year a series of rapes. The rapist, pretending to be a police officer, had lured women out of their cars at night.

I was concerned that Roy might be this "Beltway rapist." It seemed foolish not to ascertain how dangerous he actually was. But I did not want to ask him directly about his present (possibly, criminal) behavior. If he were the Beltway rapist and I asked him a direct question about his present behavior, I was sure that he would, despite my pledge of confidentiality, fear that I would report him to the police. Consequently to cover up his current illicit behavior he would then have to cumulatively mask, distort, and even lie about past behaviors and feelings. It was my main therapeutic responsibility, I believed at the time, not to concern myself with actual guilt, but *neurotic guilt.* Therefore, I needed to concern myself with the conditions of Roy's past life in which he remained pathologically stuck. I must do nothing, therefore, that might contaminate the free report of the past.

In our critical session, contrary to my usual practice, *I* began the session. I referred back to the episode with the crisis service's worker. I asked Roy, in regard to his having threatened her with rape, whether he had ever raped a woman. By my query I was questioning his truthfulness. He had told me previously that he had always stopped short of actual rape. However, I felt that he would be less reluctant to admit more remote behaviors than current criminal actions. And since serial violence rarely begins as such, there would most likely have been previous sexual crimes if Roy was the Beltway rapist.

To my great surprise, instead of his usual glib interaction with me, Roy sat with eyes downcast for a long moment. It was then that I first consciously realized that my willingness to take Roy on as a patient had meant a great deal to him. Before this moment I had believed that he regarded therapy with me as a "psychopathic gain"; this is to say, through intimidation, he had secured and was temporarily savoring the exclusive attention of someone who he assumed was an eminent professional. Consequently, I was taken aback by what followed my questioning of his honesty.

Roy looked up and said in a troubled tone, "I think you are afraid that I am that Beltway rapist. If I was that mug I would tell you so. Why do you keep trying to make me have a guilty conscience? I don't! That is not what is bothering me."

Roy went on to say that he had done many things in his life that most people would regard as immoral. He had been punished for most of them. He had no problem or resentment about that, he said, "That is the way the game of life is played!"

There was something that was bothering him, he confessed, that was more difficult to express than having committed a crime.

"Look," he indicated, "I am a real big, powerful guy. People are scared of me. And I am not afraid of anyone or any situation I have ever been in. Yet, inside I am scared shitless, lonely, and sad, all of the time. That is strange because I can have just about any woman I want and get her to do what I want. Like, for example, getting the woman I hang around with to pay your bill when I ran out of money. Yet, what bothers me most is that I am going to die and I am going to leave without really having been here. I am more ashamed to admit that I don't know how to live than anything you could point out that I have done that was immoral. I don't know what's missing in me. That is why I'm here. And, I've trusted you. Why the hell can't you trust me!"

I felt unprepared at that moment to responsively address Roy's anguish. My own personal therapy and clinical training had emphasized that unconscious, neurotic guilt (usually of an incestuous nature) was the major cause of human unhappiness. If my patients felt badly about themselves I had come to believe that they felt untoward because they harbored guilty feelings about some dastardly deed they had committed or even had only considered.

Yet, I recognized at that moment with Roy that there was

a real difference between the people I had treated who have identifiable issues of a guilty nature and those, like Roy, who my colleagues and I find the most perplexing in understanding and clinically treating.

In my uneasy cogitation I remembered Harold Searles's moving article, "Schizophrenia and the Inevitability of Death" (Searles 1961). Searles's message, as I remembered it, was that psychosis was a defensive strategy of fictitiousness. The person suffering from a psychotic condition pretends that he is neither alive or dead. To be alive is to eventually die. For a person whose life has not been fully lived, and who believes that it will never be lived well, the prospect of death is terrifying. I wondered whether the dread that Searles wrote of was true of all of us. I sensed that it was. I realized that what we assign the "mentally ill" as possessing and acting upon is inherent to being human. These feelings and moods are unavoidable characteristics of the person who is in touch with the frailties, paradoxes, and absurdities of the human situation. If this was true, then, despite our very considerable differences in background, Roy and I shared something psychologically in common. I realized that my identification with Roy would have to be examined closely if I was to reach him. This was an unsavory consideration. The thought of being more fully identified with Roy had a shameful quality to it. What made my discomfort most acute was the feeling that I would probably not be able to find refuge from the stirring-up of my own self-doubts and concerns that lurked in common with Roy as long as I worked with him.

Fortunately, my clinical experience had accentuated the importance of recognizing induced reactions in my responses to patients. I inferred that if I was feeling shameful with Roy, so might he with me. Some clinical cases earlier in my career had suggested to me that unrecognized shame plays a pivotal role in preventing some people from understanding and dealing with the dissatisfactions of their daily affairs. I had not given shame its proper due in Roy's life, nor in my own. Until this critical session I had bypassed Roy's shame and my own, experiencing it or, at least, labeling it, as something else.

Erikson (1950), as I have pointed out earlier, has emphasized that shame results from a crisis in trust between mother and child. Roy had not allowed me enough information about the conflictual aspects of his relationship with his mother in order to appreciate properly whether or not shame was deeply implicated in his despair. So I questioned him about what he remembered about his mother.

Roy spoke more openly about his mother at that moment than he had discussed any person in previous sessions. His words were fraught with resentment. He attributed his violent temper to having been "done in" by women like his mother and his sister. As a child he had looked forward to being with his mother. He felt safe in her guidance and support. Her dying, the way she did, when he was 7, changed all that. Unwanted, he had to go to live with an older sister overburdened by her own children and deserted by her husband.

THE DESPAIR OF SHAME

At age 7 Roy had been severely shaken from his tacit trust in his mother's ability to assure him a safe, predictable, and just world. He had naively believed, as children are apt, that by returning his mother's love with his unquestioning devotion to her he would be shielded from the uncertainties of living. He painfully found out that he wasn't safe and protected. Trust in one's self and in one's physical world develop together (Lynd 1958). Devastating to Roy's integrity of self-worth was the realization that he had misplaced confidence in the qualities of love, trust, happiness, and a desired response from a beloved person. The more fervently we believe in the benevolent qualities of love and find that these expectations are not substantiated, the more exacting will be the pangs of shame and despair (Lynd 1958). It left Roy feeling bitter and betrayed.

In listening to Roy's story I recognized that the shame

that is normally part of our lives usually does not come from someone's intentional meanness or even their ill-wishes. Ironically, it had been his mother's love that fueled Roy's sense of betrayal. She had tried to protect him by keeping her fatal illness a secret. Because of this she did not allow Roy to be of help to her, even in the small and important ways children are capable. Roy's hurtful shame derived from his inability to protect the person he most cared about. His not being allowed to care for her was tantamount in his own sense of himself to not being capable or worthy of assisting someone he loved. He felt betrayed by what he regarded as his mother's lack of confidence in his caring. His loss of a loving bond with her unfastened his desire to love and care for others.

Roy's intense anger and aggression toward other people since his mother's demise have been unsuccessful attempts to cast off the morbid feelings of impotence that derived from his not being allowed to try to change the course of his mother's illness. In short, Roy's shame resulted from his feeling separated from loving objects. It occurred when he was forced to leave his family and felt inadequate and insufficient to carry on autonomous functioning.

The Existential Despair of the Practitioner

Roy's expression of betrayal as the signifier of the shame and anguish in his life revealed the common bond I had with him. I realized that behind my existential despair was an anger that the examined life had betrayed me. I knew that if I dared to look back over the years of my professional career I would find that they had not been well spent. The dilemma I shared with other disillusioned practitioners was that having spent so many years in pursuing my craft it seemed now to be too late to turn back (Wheelis 1962).

In reexamining my commitment to analytic practice I recognized that the tenets of my faith in analytic insight required me not only to practice professionally the wisdom of the examined life, but to pursue my own life accordingly. My despair came from the realization that insight and analytic expertise about human affairs are not the finely attuned, rational tools that my faith in the examined life had led me to believe they are. I recognized that, as knowledgeable as I thought I was about human relations, my commitment to the examined life had not led me to living a more vibrant life than those people who appeared to be less self-examined than I.

Moreover, I seemed to have the same doubts about the meaning of my work, the impact it had on others, and its lasting importance as did my own patients about their own achievements.

My existential malaise had constituted a shift through the years from my being an active participant in life to becoming an observer who wrote numerous professional articles and books about my insights into the human condition. I had hoped that these works of scholarly pursuit would give my life some lasting meaning, that my clinical work, largely unobserved and subject to the mercurial vicissitudes of the lives of my patients, could not provide.

My devotion to producing scholarly works was an attempt to deny my uneasy realization, that like everyone else, I was essentially a vulnerable and finite being. There were moments, however, which baldly forced me to face the impermanence of the importance of my existence. One such incident was most telling. I had been asked to interview for a position as the director of a group psychotherapy training program at a large teaching hospital. The interviews for the position had gone well until the last of the day. The director of the outpatient clinic purviewed my resumé, with its listing of half-a-hundred publications. The bespectacled man looked up at me quizzically. "What is this all about?" he asked. I didn't understand his question at first. He elaborated his inquiry by cynically asking me, "Why do you have the need to write so much?"

I deeply resented the attack on the healthy legitimacy of my professional contributions implied in his reductionistic question. Such moments evoked for me considerable anxiety. This is an anguish that I believe is shared by most people. In its throes we become acutely aware of how fragile are the conditions upon which our hopes and aspirations depend. At these moments we realize how easily and quickly our desires may be taken from us. We may even painfully recognize that our wants will be empty, even if they are satisfied. Moreover, the terror of which I speak is concerned not only with our mortal being—it includes questions about our achievements, our reputation, and our remembrance by others. In short, the terror our vulnerability bares has to do with the fear of erasure or distortion of all that we worked for, struggled for, and created—in a word, the meaning of our lives (Goldberg 1989).

One of the motivational forces in my productivity as a writer has had to do with what I did not obtain from my father. Until I introspected about my anxiety in being questioned about the legitimacy of my writing I was not willing to acknowledge consciously what was driving me on. Among my shameful memories one was particularly vivid.

While in analytic training I wrote a professionally well-received book about my clinical work. I traveled back to my parents' home with my newly published book in hand at a rare moment when they were both at home. My mother excitedly opened the book, looked over every page, and commented about being impressed that I could write about such a difficult subject. I didn't value her comments about my book at that moment. She then called my father away from the television set.

He begrudgingly arrived in their small kitchen, and my mother eagerly showed him my new book, first carefully wiping off the cover with her apron. My father put on his glasses and quickly looked it over, saying with a shrug, "You should write a novel instead. People like to read about ideas in a story rather than in an academic book . . . *but* (he interrupted his literary concern with a more practical one) are you making some money?"

I nodded that I was (I really wasn't, of course, since I was just starting my career.) His response was, "Good!, Good!" and he returned to the television set in the living room. I again felt ashamed that I was still occupied with wasteful pursuits, as I had viewed my athletic and literary pursuits as a youth, while both my parents worked overtime at strenuous jobs so that I could go to boarding school and get an excellent education. I told myself once more that I must do something to show my father that his years of toil and personal sacrifice had not been wasted. I allowed myself to believe that if I tried again to write a better book he might somehow understand what I was trying to say in my literary efforts and he might, as a result, understand who I was as a person and why I chose the career I had. I never was able to write that book while he was alive.

After he died my mother told me that he had once said to her that I was the only right thing he had ever done in his life. He had never said anything like this to me.

THE TEMPORAL STATUS OF SHAME

Accepting the tragic sense of our existential condition is an onerous task for the practitioner, no less than for his patient. It is difficult to face, session after session, day after day, certain aspects of himself that the practitioner may wish to distance himself from and to deny. Yet, as practitioners we must use ourselves as mirrors to help our patients integrate. The mirror is reversible. It holds a threat to the bearer as well as to the gazer (Goldberg 1986). Consequently, as practitioners, the sense of our vulnerabilities is encountered in the eyes of our patients. The bold sight of our frailties evokes the discomfort of shame (Goldberg 1989a). Although we may avert our eyes from the bold view in our patients' eyes, during therapeutic shame our tragic sense remains painfully existent.

The most intolerable aspect of the practitioner's phenomenology during therapeutic shame is derived from the nature of his contract with his patient. This bond requires that he continue to try to help his patient heal suffering despite how badly he is feeling, at that precise moment, about himself. In essence, the agonizing existential dilemma for the shameful practitioner is that he must try to help the very person he resents for bearing witness to his vulnerabilities.

During the difficult moments with Roy in our critical session I experienced a loss of connection with what was familiar and safe. I felt stuck and unable to control or to escape the painful present moment. There seemed to be no refuge from my vulnerable feelings—no place to hide. Time seemed large and endless. I sensed no moment in the future when I expected to be beyond the present moment. A confirmation of my phenomenological experience of the nontranscendence of shame is found in a study contrasting shame and guilt by Lindsay-Hartz (1984).

But, strangely, my shameful phenomenology was illuminating. It helped me recognize that the key to my impasse with Roy resided in the *untranscendable* sense of shame. I realized that *existential time* was the ontological arena in which shame must be struggled with. The feeling that one is incompetent to find purpose in one's life is only meaningful to an existent—someone who is finite, whose time is limited and one day will cease to be. As clinicians we undoubtedly observe that the most disturbing psychological experiences are those that threaten the individual's relation to time. In the throes of emotional distress, "the most painful aspect of the sufferer's predicament is experienced as his inability to imagine a future moment in time when he will be out of [his] anxiety or [his] depression" (May et al. 1958, p. 68). I became struck by the awareness that our most profound human experiences, our joys and depressions, our ecstasies and our fears, are heavily influenced by differing phenomenologies of time.

No theorist that I am aware of has mentioned, let alone discussed, the very important fact that there are crucial phenomenological distinctions among the three existential anxieties in terms of their temporal dimensions. Guilt is experienced as a committed act, already past. The culpable subject experiences his guilty deed as one that he has *chosen.* Moreover, he may haggle or negotiate with the introjected representatives of authority as to when he will address his culpability. So, for example, in neurotic guilt the sufferer has chosen to remain in the past. Anticipatory (teleological) anxiety is the experience of uncertainty of some future moment. Obsessive concern with the future distracts the subject from the existential prerequisites of the present moment.

In contrast, in the throes of my shameful impasse with Roy I was suddenly and startlingly aware of how vulnerable I was at that moment. I experienced no choice in who I was. I was the shame. And I could not transcend myself. Time had stopped and I felt engulfed by the spectrum of the pervasive shaming moment remaining everlasting.

Seen from the phenomenology of time, the attempted avoidance of the present moment results in shame, because shame, in its constructive aim, alerts us to what is life-enhancing. Constructive shame is tied to the realization that each of us quite habitually tends to deny to himself the reality of time in his own existence. Nonetheless, our time is limited, and the past can not be held onto without cost to our present and our future (Goldberg 1977). An overemphasis on guilt, therefore, compels the analysand to discuss more superficial and often irrelevant material rather than the profound concerns both practitioner and analysand harbor about their own vulnerabilities in trying to foster the conditions of their self-worth at the present moment.

Wallace (1963) has pointed out that psychoanalysis has neglected shame because shame has to do with looking at and being looked at, whereas psychoanalysis has to do with listening and being listened to—which are more suitable for exploring issues of guilt than of shame. Anthony (1981) confirms this by reminding us that almost all Freud wrote about shame came early in his career, when he faced his patients. He wrote very little about shame after adopting the analytic couch.

The practitioner's need for a protective mask requires a congruent therapeutic technique to support the concealment of his narcissistic vulnerability. The vulnerable practitioner may switch from a reflecting mirror (his visual presence) to that of a voice mirror (the analytic couch) in magical hope that as long as his patients do not see the vulnerability in his eyes and only hear his more easily controlled voice, his troubling vulnerability has no reality. For him, like many of us, the reality of the diminution of our vitality and competence is not a reality until evidence of its symptoms is recognized by others (Goldberg 1989c).

The Constructive Role of Shame in Therapeutic Alliance

I realized that the only aspect of shame about which I had choice in my therapeutic impasse with Roy was whether or not I would renunciate any attempt to keep my vulnerabilities concealed. Upon consideration, I recognized that to the extent that I did not devote my energies to self-concealment, I would be free to explore the crucial determinants in finding a meaningful alliance with Roy. The most important of these would be found by examining how each of us was allowing the other to be known to ourself. With this in mind I asked Roy how he experienced my treatment of him. He told me, "In past sessions you have used the word 'discount' to explain how people put me on the defensive when I was a kid. Yet, that is just what you do to me."

Roy was hurt and angry that I had not confirmed his feelings as immediate and real. My shame had stood in the way of responding to his present needs. I had preferred that the therapeutic encounters stay with the remote shadows of the past and that I relate to Roy as an objective, detached detective in an archeological quest rather than a fellow sojourner with similar shameful despair for not having experienced life fully and well. In doing so, I was ignoring the mutual shaming that at that moment was transpiring between us. My focus on transferential distortion was denying my own real presence in the present moment. By focusing on the past I was eradicating any real importance to what Roy needed from me at that present moment.

What did Roy need from me? He needed me to bear witness to the unfair ravish of shame in his life. We must recognize that our feelings of shame in the presence of our patients are not only defensive. They also are testimonies to our conviction of *what ought not to be* in our patients' lives (Goldberg 1989d).

However, since we are guardians of what *can* be, as well as what should *not* be, we must be alert to the constructive aspects of shame. Struggling with the anxiety of shame requires the practitioner to be immediately present in a way that the other existential anxieties don't. Practitioners who acknowledge their own and their patient's shame open up vital avenues of existential options. It takes a responsive other to dialogue with in order to touch the deeper sources of our existence. To reiterate, shame experiences are vivid and painful because they foster an accentuated and disturbing self-consciousness. These are moments in which we become aware, albeit fleetingly, of aspects of ourselves—our ambitions, longings, and sentiments—that are valuable to our sense of who we are. Shame provides a mirror for reflection of parts of the self that are typically hidden. Shame confronts us with the reality of our tenuous existence as human beings. Without this tragic sense we might mistakenly assume that we are fully taken care of in the world (Goldberg 1988a). Under this "vital lie" as Becker (1973) has referred to it, we act as if we need not better ourselves or to improve our world. Becker (1973) indicates that the profoundly disturbed person feels the dread of death more acutely than people who are able to maintain the vital lie that life on this planet is safe and predictable.

The shame I experienced with Roy enabled me to realize that I had a personal, as well as a therapeutic, obligation to take a more active, participatory role in my encounters with other people. Guilt tells the sufferer that he is at fault for a misdeed—shame that the subject has inhibited a necessary and legitimate action. In this way, shame mirrors the awareness of our neglected ego-ideals (Goldberg 1989a).

To redirect my therapeutic efforts I needed to find a way in which my presence would matter to Roy. I realized that people who enter the practice of psychotherapy generally share with their patients, like Roy, an exquisite sensitivity to the suffering of others. They strongly differ from Roy, however, in that they have found from their personal experiences that human conflict can be successfully handled by psychological means (Goldberg 1986).

Roy's life had been replete with the betrayal and duplicity of the countless psychological treatment regimes to which he had been subjected. One such incident that left him with a bitter resentment against psychiatry was being subjected to electroconvulsive therapy while incarcerated in a forensic hospital. He had been involved in psychiatric treatment since the age of 7. He well knew that ECT was clinically contraindicated in his case. His treatment, therefore, constituted abusive punishment. To shield himself from his psychological vulnerability he developed a characterological shamelessness to his own feelings by severing empathic identification with others.

I needed to offer Roy some existential options based upon the constructive influence of psychological examination. This was a paradox in that I, myself, had found the examined life deficient.

However, my growing understanding of shame conveyed the realization that the feelings of helplessness, vulnerability, and transparency the practitioner shares at the proper time, rather than keeps silent about, are the crucial sine qua non of meaningful healing for those suffering from the devastation of despair. To permit transparency I needed to be less critical of myself. I would try, therefore, to feel compassion toward myself during those moments in which I felt that I could neither help my patients nor myself. If I could not feel compassion for myself, then neither could I regard my feelings of compassion for my patients as genuine statements of my capacity to care. On the other hand, if I would regard my own struggles with helplessness and vulnerability during the therapeutic hour not as weakness, but as the pangs of caring and concern, they would best offer my patients a meaningful therapeutic experience. In short, it is only when practitioner and patient share their humanity with each other can the road to finding meaning in human existence actually begin. Dealing with the shame and the guilts of the past cannot proceed in any meaningful way until therapist and patient trust each other in the present. This is a reversal of the usual psychoanalytic procedure. However, a reappraisal of shame mandates this consideration.

My therapeutic task was now clear. First, I needed to guide Roy by showing him that emotional maturation can succeed by reliance on psychological examination and a willingness to use this psychic data to struggle with untoward aspects of one's self. Second, I must acknowledge to Roy that I was no less invested in how we were making ourselves known to each other than he was. And third, that I had to offer a psychological scrutiny of myself as a means of repairing our therapeutic alliance.

I told Roy about my interview at the teaching hospital and my reaction to the outpatient clinical director's question. I went on to tell him that in self-examination I had come to realize that my anger at the director's words came from the painful recognition that I was living a lie. I had resented being forced to face the realization that my efforts to give my life permanent importance had been futile. All attempts at everlasting meaning would be for me, as for everyone else, illusory sand castles in the dunes of time. On the other hand, it was my relations with other people that would give my life meaning—although this meaning would be shifting, mercurial, and subject to the whims and vicissitudes of life. I added that I was willing to try to use this understanding of myself to help him make sense of his own life.

Eyes, we have been told, are the windows of the psyche. We avert our eyes to conceal the desolated domain of our psyche. Similarly, we avert our eyes so as not to have to concern ourself with the tribulations in the psyche of the other (Goldberg 1989a).

We raise our eyes to allow our psyche to intermingle with the psyche of the other—to permit the other to dwell in the domain of our psyche. It was when I allowed my eyes to meet and hold Roy's intense gaze that I sensed that the shaming between us held hope for Roy's healing. I sensed that he wished to assure me that I need not feel ashamed of what I had revealed to him. I asked him about this. He nodded his head and agreed. But he also wished me to assure him that he was an acceptable person to me, although he had not contributed anything of value to anyone.

I indicated that each of us was a separate person and must someday go his own way. So the more openly we would be able to share our feelings and concerns about how we were making ourself known to the other, the more we would be able to appreciate what we were currently sharing together and the preciousness of that moment. And, although we would never fully understand each other, nor agree fully with each other, this, I believed, was the best we could do. And, most importantly, the effort had been worth making if we recognized and responded to the humanity of the other.

A couple of weeks after our crucial session I left town for a professional conference across the country. I was away for a few weeks. Upon my return, among the messages on my phone answering machine was one from Roy. He had decided to turn himself in for a criminal act that he had committed a couple of weeks before he started psychotherapy with me. The incident involved exposing himself to two adolescent girls who were sitting in a parked car. He had been ashamed to tell me about it before. He had throughout his life tried to impress others with his sexual powers with mature women. But he had come to recognize from our last several sessions that the only thing he had to be ashamed of was not being willing to live his life openly and to the best of his capacity. He said that he could take whatever punishment they gave him. He would then get on with his life without fear. With what sounded like a quiet resolve, he added that he was confident that he would succeed. The message ended.

13

Overcoming Pathological Shame

What, must I hold a candle to my shames? They
are in themselves, good sooth, too too light.
                                    —William Shakespeare

As a psychotherapist, I asked myself continually throughout
the past 25 years, what are the underlying conditions that
threaten the personal identity of my patients. I have
searched for the dimensions of psychological life that are so
basic that they traverse all interpersonal and relational
situations. I have sought out the standards and motifs that
lie at the heart of human endeavor, regardless of whether
these acts are directed toward the world of ideas, natural
phenomena, or are rooted with the framework of interpersonal relations.

What seems most basic to human endeavor is that each
of us craves a sense of meaning and unification to his
existence (Lecky 1969). In order to survive, each of us
attempts to make some semblance of meaning from our
experiences by creating standards to live by, thereby regu-
lating and ordering an otherwise inexplicable world. Thus,
Oedipus dashed out his own eyes. In a particularistic sense,
he could not be held culpable for his tragic deeds. He had not
known his father prior to his fateful encounter on the road to

221

Corinth. Moreover, he had slain his father in an act of self-defense. But in a universal sense, Oedipus realized that patricide was an unpardonable crime. He had done the deed. A price had to be exacted. He realized that it was just.

All societies, subcultures, and groups establish normative systems that regulate exchanges among their members. These exchanges may be regarded as psychosocial formulas for social utility. Without such systems of exchange, interpersonal relations would be bombarded with haphazard, chaotic, and unexpected demands and consequences. When the standards of the system are not shared, or when they cease to function as they were intended to, individuals experience difficulty communicating with one another. They are unable to make sense of their existence and, consequently, failing to experience their existence as having been lived harmoniously and well, are subjected to feelings of shame and despair (Goldberg, 1977).

THE IMPORTANCE OF EQUITY IN HUMAN ENDEAVOR

My psychological study has revealed the concept of *fairness* as a ubiquitous motif underlying the human endeavor to create standards that give our existence meaning. Fairness is a basic issue that runs through the course of history. Indeed, it is rather difficult to conceive of any theme that is more fundamental to the transactions of persons involved with one another than fairness, be these exchanges brief encounters or durable, lasting relationships. People tend to perceive the universe in terms of their early relationships with significant others. To reiterate, individuals who were made to feel powerless and incapable of establishing fair exchanges with significant others tend to perpetuate these feelings into contemporary relations. As long as an individual believes that he is incapable of freely contracting in a fair manner, he must either remain dependent, as a patient or as a child, or be involved in aggressive active manipulation, changing the rules to his own advantage. The individual's "awareness of the existence of *in*justice in the world comes from infantile feelings of deprivation, a recognition of all the frustrations inherent in being human . . . the child in each of us still expects *automatic justice,* a spontaneous gratification of its feelings of unfairness" (Meerloo 1959, p. 9).

It is my impression that all of the patients that I have ever seen in community clinics and psychiatric hospitals, as well as in private practice, essentially are seeking either justice from the social institutions that regulate their lives or equity (fairness) in their relationships with significant others. Intellectually, while they may be asking for help in changing themselves psychodynamically, at an emotional and functional level they prefer that others change in regard to them, because they experience others as treating them arbitrarily and unfairly. For example, with a married couple, one marital partner will experience the taking of increased responsibility for resolving the marital conflict as unreasonable unless he experiences his partner as taking increased responsibility also.

In addition, I have observed that conflict between alienated and troubled significant others, such as parent and child, husband and wife, employer and employee, is exacerbated and perpetuated by the infusion of each agent's personal system of equity into the interpersonal system. It is my impression that each of the agents in chronic conflict operates from an arbitrary moralistic structure that implicitly suggests that the other agent is supposed to act in particular ways. For example, in cases of spouses or parent and child, each agent expects actions that indicate respect, consideration, caring, morality, and so forth. When the other agent fails to act in the prescribed manner, he is blamed for causing conflict. The blaming agent tries to induce shame and anxiety in the other. In turn, the blamed other generally reacts with anger and resentment. With some persons, the reaction toward the blamer is a passive-aggressive one and the issue in conflict cannot definitively surface so that it can be dealt with and resolved. With still others (and this is most often manifested in marital conflict), reaction to blame and manipulation takes the form of a tit-for-tat retaliation in which the major payoffs are hurting the other or learning skillful strategies for slipping out of the attack. None of these strategies, of course, effectively deals with the issues at hand or harmonizes the relationship.

Gorman (1974) has suggested that the sense of justice is not a hallmark of only certain societies but has the valence of a universal psychosocial "obsession."

Most of our actions are based upon *justification*. That is to say, our behavior has reference to some standard or guideline that legitimizes our actions. So often in our conversations, to say nothing of our thoughts, we employ concepts of "deservingness," "reasonableness," "justice," or "fairness." The individual who refuses to refer to and abide by shared standards of conduct and common justifications, that is, "I do whatever I want—I don't need anyone to tell me what to do"—is regarded as dangerous to a regulated society. Shaming sanctions are applied to such persons to induce them to provide socially acceptable justifications for their behavior.

Even among societal deviants, it is well substantiated that a need for justification exists. These individuals feel that they experience mitigating conditions that require them to bend or break societal codes. The drug addict justifies his palliative on the grounds that he was born weak; the alcoholic his imbibing because he is misunderstood; the criminal his violation because he has the courage to do what other men only dare in fantasy. By justifying the violation of social codes, the "exploiter" restores psychological equity. Rosenquist (1932) indicates from his study of Texas convicts that the vast majority of the prisoners directed their excuses for their crimes at society at large, and they felt that their excuses either completely exonerated them or strongly mitigated their guilt for their crimes. This is hardly an isolated instance. Joost Meerloo, a psychiatrist interred in a Nazi concentration camp, reports (1959) that "one of my most astonishing experiences as a prisoner of the Nazis during World War II was observing the appeal made by both prisoners and jailors to the abstract principle of 'justice.' The masters of the torture chamber spoke more of their

'sacred rights'—justifying their crimes with various mythical theories, than the victims themselves" (p. 7). Apparently, then, even those who violate serious social mores are
concerned with the need for justification.

Our emotional being, then, is integrally related to our
evaluation of the equity and inequity on the part of others in
their actions toward us. We perpetually ask whether we are
being treated justly. Instinctually, we react in terms of gross
threats to our physical survival. However, these instinctual
reactions have become modified by social compromises.
The philosopher Rawls (1971) has pointed out that "if men's
inclination to self-interest makes their vigilance against one
another necessary, their public sense of justice makes their
secure associations possible" (pp. 4–5). This means, for
example, that potentially, every angry gesture by another
person, every sign or display of force or coercion, poses a
threat to our physical safety. The socialized individual,
however, has been led to believe that his physical survival is
in jeopardy from others only at such times as he intentionally or seriously violates society's codes. "What is 'justice'?
Only a legal code of mutual behavior" (Meerloo 1959, p. 9).
Consequently, as long as he abides by social codes vis-à-vis
others, he expects that others will not subject him to harm.
On the other hand, when he meets with hostile or uncaring
treatment, which he believes is undeserved in terms of his
understanding of social convention, he feels betrayed and
unprotected by the social order and is shamed.

If an individual cannot derive desired commodities in
accordance with what he has come to regard as his referent
system of equity, then frustration, resentment, and finally
"acting in" or "acting out" behavior occurs. At such times
as these, he experiences the urge to return to instinctual,
that is, primitive, manners of survival in which he no longer
concerns himself with treating others decently and fairly.
Emotionally and socially disturbed behaviors are, from this
perspective, attempts by the individual to restore protection
to himself in situations in which he feels shamed by the
social order treating him unjustly.

GROUP PSYCHOTHERAPY WITH SHAME-SENSITIVE PATIENTS

Group psychotherapy is designed precisely to resist rules and directives of social and interpersonal life that have frustrated the individual's attempts at a consistent and gratifying sense of personal identity. Therapeutic groups provide the opportunity for group members to recognize consciously the interpolation of whatever intrapsychic discomfort they are experiencing in an interpersonal situation and the roles, attitudes, sentiments, and defenses they evince in response to these feelings (Goldberg 1973).

Theoretically, group psychotherapy should be of benefit to people suffering from shame because of the opportunity it offers to examine psychologically the conditions that cause people in stress and conflict to shame and humiliate one another. Of course, the added proviso is that the experience of learning will be healing rather than hurtful as long as the interactions and responses occur in a safe and trusting environment.

Aye, there's the rub! In fact, with the notable exception of Pines (1987), few theorists actually recommend group psychotherapy as a viable treatment option. Group therapy theorists and practitioners alike erroneously have assumed that shame-sensitive patients' vulnerabilities will be exacerbated by their masochistic premature exposure or by sadistic probing by other group members. No less an authority than the standard text in the field (Yalom 1985) cautions against the danger of having patients who are shame-sensitive in a therapy group. Yalom indicates that the subtleties of shame are such that the practitioner may not recognize their manifestations in angry and dominating group members. By not being alert to the vulnerability to hurt and shame in ostensibly well-defended group participants, serious harm can come to them from the irritation and fury of other group members' attempts to make meaningful contact with them.

As we have learned in earlier chapters, theorists and practitioners alike confuse shame with its humiliating and embarrassing variants. It is the *private* shame kept enclosed in secrecy in the isolated psyche that is the source of human misery. The skilled group practitioner, who recognizes the role unfair and abusive treatment and regard play in the development of a painful personal identity, will relate to potentially shaming experiences constructively rather than neglectfully in a group treatment modality. Led by a shame-enlightened practitioner, the group will provide the shame-sensitive patient with the opportunity to practice altruism, correct intersubjective distortions, and refine skills in emotional attunement (Alonso and Rutan 1988). Development as a member of a well-functioning group will enable the shame-sensitive patient to tolerate group experience. As he does, "so does a tolerance for the imperfect self and vice-versa. Shame and other painful affects come to be viewed as part of the human experience, rather than corrosive stigma that lock the individual into greater isolation and despair" (Alonso and Rutan 1988, p. 13).

In my clinical experience, group psychotherapy serves an important role in healing the wounds of shame and despair. However, the practitioner needs to be especially appreciative for when and how group experience will be of help for the shame-sensitive person and when it won't. Abe's story will illustrate these clinical considerations.

Abe is a man of short, slender stature. He wears thick glasses, has wavy hair, a full beard, and very large hands for a man of his height. Abe begins speaking with a swift motion of his right hand across his eyes, conveying his shyness. His typical attire is checkered outdoors shirts and suit vests, deceptively presenting him as an absent-minded professor. Actually, Abe is mindful of how others perceive him. Like Vincent, he simply is uncertain about how to influence their positive regard.

When Abe joined a psychoanalytic therapy group I conducted early in my private practice, he was a scientist in his late forties. Abe had a brilliant intuitive mind of mature cognitive development and the wants of a child, as his emotional needs were not met at the proper time in his early maturation. At the time he consulted with me,

Abe had a child's curiosity, but one of a restrictive nature. He had a need to know—purely and simply—without any commitment on his part ever to use his knowledge on his own or anyone else's behalf.

Abe was romantically drawn to a young woman in his group. Laura was a schoolteacher, sophisticated and coolly alluring. Abe, in contrast, was unsure of himself, especially with women. He had been married from early adulthood to a woman in whom he had lost sexual interest many years previously. Abe had gone from mother to wife-mother without a loss of stride. He never had with either of them, nor with any other woman, even his young daughters, for that matter, an intimate, caring relationship.

Laura was the embodiment of everything Abe passionately dreamed of in a woman. But he was unable to express his feelings directly to, or even about, her in group sessions. His fear of actual intimacy with a woman confined him to fantasies in which he enacted hundreds of "What if?" questions—such as, "What if she found him attractive?" and, "What if he left his wife and had an affair with her?" Abe's preoccupation with romantic possibility was unconsciously designed to embellish his fantasy world with Laura, without having to examine his fearful vulnerabilities and self-doubts. As long as Abe held Laura only as a romantic fantasy he could avoid facing his mistrust of the motives of the women—his mother, his wife, and his daughters—upon whom he depended for supporting his tenuous sense of self-worth.

Abe did not regard his fantasies about Laura as empty. That is, until Laura, speaking about the scarcity of suitable men she had met recently, indicated in a group session that she was ready to go as far as a man wanted in a relationship, as long as he had enough courage to openly take the initiative. She told us, moreover, that she could never get involved with a person who was unwilling to tell her directly about how he felt about her.

Abe was caught off-guard. He was forced to grapple with the shallowness of his fantasized images of "the perfect woman." Laura was real! She had desires of her own. She had bluntly stated that she was available and provided the precise conditions she required for having a relationship with a man. If Abe wanted to get involved with her, he realized, then he had to come to terms with the demands of a relationship with a woman, unlike those with whom he had been previously associated.

Fearing the disapproval of the women and the competitiveness of the other men by speaking of his sexual feelings for Laura in the group, Abe surreptitiously called her at home. In their brief conversation Abe shyly alluded to his romantic feelings about her and asked her out to dinner. She politely but firmly refused. She also insisted that he bring up his feelings for her in the next group session.

Laura's declining of his invitation came as no surprise to Abe, although, of course, he had hoped that she would accept. Her rejection merely reflected his lifelong sense of himself—that because he was so needy, he was unattractive and bothersome to women. He was, however, quite disturbed that she expected him to discuss his sexual feelings for her in front of other people. He perceived Laura as having encouraged him to initiate a relationship by her speaking about what she wanted in a lover. Furthermore, the others in the group had indicated repeatedly that Abe would make no real progress with his conflictual issues until he directly revealed his feelings without intellectual rationalization. Groups instill in their members pride or shame, in regard to how these members conform to important group norms (Zander et al. 1972). Self-esteem is based on the way the self experiences success or failure in achieving the ego-ideal of its desired self. To a considerable extent, the self tests its competence by what is reflected back to it by one's peers (Chasseguet-Smirgel 1985). Freud (1921) indicated that in becoming committed to a group, the individual replaces his ego-ideal with the group-ideal represented by the group leader. Abe had obediently complied with what he believed was expected of him. But, instead of reward, he was being punished. He felt that the way he was being treated by the group, sanctioned by the therapist, was quite unfair.

Confluenced by an inability to escape from old patterns of behaving and experiencing the dread of attempting new ones, Abe felt betrayed by the process of group psychoanalysis. The group had become a dire place for Abe, in which taking psychological risks seemed foolhardy. He later told me of a fantasy in which I protected him from rejection and competition by arranging with Laura to get together with him. Since I hadn't fulfilled his magical wishes, he was angry at me, also.

Abe's feelings of shame and betrayal festered in him in the days before the next group session and became transformed into hurt and resentment. Since he was a fearful man, he panicked at the prospect of either speaking directly of his sexual feelings or expressing his resentment at Laura in the group. Instead, Abe stayed away from therapy. In his absence, Laura reported Abe's telephone call to us.

After the second session that Abe missed, I telephoned him. He confessed what had happened. He reported feeling too humiliated to be able to face the people in the group. Since his phone conversation with Laura, he told me, he spent his time alone, avoiding family and co-workers.

He described his reluctance to return to the group because of "the condemning, judgmental eyes" of the group members, who, he believed, were intent in exposing his inadequacy as a person and, especially, as a man.

Abe sounded to me like a frightened adolescent. It is in adolescence that we are most inclined to feel unable to protect our vulnerable inner being from hostile eyes. In reviewing his history, my impression seemed valid. The natural rebellion of adolescence had been denied Abe. He rebelled only in his fantasies—masturbating to scenes of being sexually intimate with the females who came to visit his mother and sisters.

Abe was trying to rebel more openly than he could as an adolescent. He regarded me and the other group members as comprising a massive and strict conscience that denied him the right to act upon his forbidden wishes. He felt that he was not legitimately entitled to be as free as he perceived other people to be, because he was an unattractive and awkward person.

I did not try to offer him explanations for the difficulties he was having. I recognized that this extremely shame-ridden man, who claimed that he could remember every bad thought that he had ever had about himself, did not need any interpretations from me of the underlying reasons for his misery. Abe, who had nearly as many years of therapy, as I had years of living at the time I was his therapist, had enough intellect and psychological expertise to provide that for himself. Indeed, I realized that he would obsessively ruminate about the reasons for his current plight without any encouragement to do so from me.

My personal and professional conviction held that I should in no way obviate a patient's freedom to decide for himself how much suffering he must tolerate. Accordingly, my foremost clinical responsibility was to act in the best possible way in order to foster Abe's freedom of choice.

In our phone conversation, I said to Abe that if the only way he felt that he could sufficiently rebel against his miserable feeling was by not attending the group, then he should come back only if and when he felt he had made an adequate protest.

Instead of asking Abe to examine his avoidant behavior, as therapists typically do when patients act in resistive ways, I wished him courage in protesting the misery that for so many years he had passively accepted as his destiny. I also confirmed Abe's right to rebel, if he needed to, against all the years of therapy and analysis he had undergone since childhood, and which he now regarded as worthless. I added that I hoped that he could rebel against his miserable feelings and still attend sessions, but that was up to him.

I told him, as I had Vincent, that I cared about his struggle and what would come of it. However, if the only way he could protest his unfair punishment of himself and his legacy of despair, I repeated, was by not returning to the group, temporarily or permanently, he had my permission, if he felt he required it.

If ever he wished to return to analysis, he would be ready when he was willing to accept himself as being strong, as well as intelligent. He had survived a bizarre childhood, but now he must use his strength to go forward rather than to guard against the encroachment of past ghosts. I told him that he would be ready to come back to therapy when he no longer continued to ask only to understand himself. He must learn also to *do* something with his understanding.

What Abe was being told is a reversal of what we usually would expect to be the reason for someone attending psychotherapeutic treatment. Abe was told to come back to analysis when (because) he was strong. Typically, we believe people should be in therapy when they are disabled (weak) and to leave when they are strong and able. In a way, I was asking Abe to forget all he had learned in his many years of therapy and analysis and simply to come back to the difficulty he might face in the group as an act of courage.

In helping their patients overcome pathological shame, practitioners need to devote sufficient attention to fostering passionate attributes such as courage in their analysands, as well as encouraging an understanding of the analysand's behavior (Goldberg and Simon 1982). The analyst who suggests and supports the notion that analysis is *only* a preparation for life—that the analyst's consulting room is the place where the analysand learns about the psychological skills he *someday* may use to become the kind of person he would like to be—does his analysand a serious disservice. Abe's story vividly demonstrates that group psychotherapy is not only preparation for life; it is also a series of experiences in the real world.

Unless Abe could express his fears and desires openly in the presence of a supportive community—the other partici- pants—he would continue to experience himself as a divided self. Abe had never been able to accept himself as being strong as well as intelligent. The paradox was that unless Abe could endure his fearfulness he could never experience his strength. Courage is not a character attribute, an essen- tialistic entity, or mysterious quality bestowed at birth. Courage is an empty and illusory concept, except as a term used to describe a series of specific behaviors and activi- ties—behaviors that can be observed and described. Indeed, it is the illusory belief that courage is a character trait that some people have and others don't, which, in fact, disables people who don't regard themselves as courageous from carrying out acts and behaviors that they are capable of performing if they didn't impute the requirement of courage (Goldberg and Simon 1982). Because Abe had been uncou- rageous in the past he did not necessarily have to be now. He had to take each situation and event one at a time. To free himself up to be courageous he needed to realize that he had in the past acted at various times in ways he and others regarded as cowardly. Each moment, however, he had the freedom to act as his desired self indicated, regardless of what he had done before.

Abe called back a few sessions later. He told me that he had found strength and contentment being alone outside of the group. He realized, however, that these feelings would be short-lived unless he learned how to attain this state of being with people he cared about. He said that although he was never before able to put his feelings into words, he cared deeply about the people in the group. He wanted to tell the others in the group to their faces how he felt about them. He had some issues with me, especially. He told me that he had felt humiliated with what had happened with Laura. I should have known how she affected him and should have protected him from making a fool of himself. If he were the therapist he would have acted differently than I had. He told me that there was much I could learn from him.

When Abe said this to me, I remembered a story about

Trigant Burrow (1958), an early psychoanalytic practitioner who had radically changed his therapeutic understanding about human behavior after changing places with one of his analysands and encouraging that person to use some of their sessions to analyze Burrow.

I accepted Abe's challenge. When Abe returned to the group I told him that I would like to know how he would have handled his situation in the group if he were the therapist. I invited Abe to change chairs with me in the group and assume the role of the therapist.

After sitting in my chair, he told us that changing chairs had been one of the most remarkable events in his life. He had fantasized since starting therapy as a child of being the therapist and turning the tables on the self-confident, all-knowing people who occupied the therapist's chair for so many years of his life.

Yet Abe could only remain in my chair for about twenty minutes. He realized that it had its drawbacks. It wasn't all it seemed to be. He became rather anxious about having to take care of everyone else's needs rather than just his own. This was not a role he had been encouraged to take by his family.

I recognized at that moment that both Abe's and my sensitivities to shame had been cast from very different molds by our families. Like so many who eventually become members of the healing professions, my role in life had been cast for me long before my birth. I had been imprinted with the desires and worldview of preceding generations. My grandmother admired men of learning and compassion. As a small child, I loved to sit by her side as she served me wonderful meals at her diminutive chrome-topped kitchen table in her small apartment. Preparing the food, she told me exciting tales of the old country. I was especially fond of stories about her father. My namesake had been a lover of books and of the human spirit. People from all segments of society—Jew and Gentile alike—had come to him for encouragement and advice.

Without conscious realization, until Abe spoke of his fearful, superstitious grandparents, who advised against excessive charity and concern for others, I had directed myself to studying other people's motives and concerns, starting from those ardent moments I shared with my grandmother in her warm and snug kitchen.

I also was affected by my parents' attitudes toward caring and compassion. My parents were very different personalities, yet what they shared in common was generosity and concern for other people. One of the most memorable experiences of this kind occurred one evening when I was a child. My mother and I visited my grandmother in a city-operated hospital. All of the patients on my grandmother's ward had visitors but one. She was a frightened, blind, old woman. The nurses' aide had simply put her food on a tray and left her to her own resources for feeding herself. The old woman seemed unable to do so. She fumbled with the food, spilling it all over herself and the bedcovers. My mother said in Yiddish that it was a pity to be treated like that. She went over to the old woman, fed her, speaking comfortingly to her as she did. When I heard the nurse's aide who was supposed to be taking care of the old woman laughing in the hallway, I felt sorry for the old woman and angry at the aide. But, unlike my mother, I have never been as comfortable with people physically ill as those who were emotionally disturbed. The helplessness of serious physical illness seems unfair and has always made me uncomfortable. My discomfort was a bridge to Abe's plight.

Abe's discontent in the "helper's" chair came from his not having been given the necessary permission and trust in his competence to help others from family and other authority figures in his life. Without his providing help and care to others, his view of himself was as of an uncharitable and constricted person.

My associations to the acts and sentiments encouraging caring and concern for others afforded by my family enabled me to recognize that Abe needed permission and support for overthrowing the very considerable degree of shame he harbored from perceiving himself as an uncompassionate man.

A therapy group is a propitious place to address the

issues of compassion and concern. I asked the others in the group how they saw Abe. Interestingly, none regarded him as lacking caring or concern for them. They provided numerous instances of how Abe in his shy and gentle manner had touched their lives. I added to this that I would appreciate Abe's help whenever he cared to assist me in the group.

His subsequent behavior in the group suggested that he had accepted my offer and had taken in and believed what he had been told by the others in the group.

14

THE PSYCHOTHERAPIST
AS A MENTOR OF FRIENDSHIP

Whoever is in possession of a true friend sees the
exact counterpart of his own soul.

—Cicero

The working alliance is a central construct of clinical work.
However, practitioners widely differ as to which model of
interpersonal functioning should be the basis of the constructive features of the working alliance. Through the ages,
most traditions of healing have been predicated upon the
tutelage of friendship. While modern psychotherapy has
parted company with many aspects of traditional healing, as
I tried to demonstrate in Chapter 7, several important
similarities are shared by modern psychotherapy and
friendship. Psychotherapy is a private affair. Unlike family
relationships, it requires no official announcements, public
ceremonies, or any traditional rituals to mark its rites of
passage. It is a continual arrangement in which the participants negotiate the terms of their association. They must
earn the rights and privileges of their roles and status that
family members acquire by birth or marriage. There is no
obligation in psychotherapy, as with friendship, to others in

relationship with one's therapist or one's patient. This dimension, of course, is the binding force that holds families together—often at the baneful cost of freedom of action among family members.

Despite psychotherapy's close semblance to the strengths and good character of friendship, the psychotherapy profession still predominantly employs the model of family rather than friendship as the crucible of clinical work.

THE THERAPEUTIC CRUCIBLE OF FRIENDSHIP

A close examination of the concept of friendship will help us better understand the motivation of our patients. Rubin (1985) points out that "Just as with love, the *idea* of friendship stirs yearnings from our infantile past, bringing to life the hope that somewhere, sometime, perfect love, trust, security and safety will be [finally] ours . . ." (p. 7).

Yet, just as there are societal and subjective factors in the world-at-large that mitigate against friendship, so there are professional and personal factors in the practitioner holding him back from genuine friendship with patients (Goldberg 1989d). I believe that the five most basic reasons for the lack of genuine friendship in psychotherapy are:

1. Practitioners have indicated that when real relationships are encouraged, countertransferential impulses more easily get out of hand than when the practitioner is a nonactive participant. Moreover, it is difficult to define what is technically and ethically proper in a real relationship between a patient and therapist.
2. Many practitioners would also contend that they have something far more profound to offer than friendship. They further would indicate that special training as a psychotherapist is not required to be a friend. Almost anyone can offer companionship.
3. Many therapists would be embarrassed to be paid for friendship. This would be especially true if friendship

implied mutual, although not necessarily equal, benefits to each of the people involved.

4. Most psychotherapeutic theories teach us that patients learn best psychologically by frustrating their impulses rather than by gratifying them.

5. The problem with calling for friendship in psychotherapeutic practice is that many practitioners have considerable difficulty with making friends themselves. Many people who are drawn toward practicing psychotherapy struggle conflictually with issues concerned with relatedness. A wise practitioner, Alan Wheelis, thirty-five years ago wrote that the problem of intimacy is for many analysts the principal determinant to their careers. The problem, he indicated, is "the conflict between the tendencies that lead to closeness and the fear that is evoked by closeness." Becoming a psychoanalyst, Wheelis indicated, is a compromise between these vacillating needs. The analyst achieves intimacy "by hearing secrets none other can hear, not even a priest; for a priest can not take so much time. He [the analyst] will enter hidden recesses of another life none other can enter; for no one else is possessed of such sensitive technique. At the same time he will maintain the isolation he requires. Indeed, it seems that psychoanalysis not only permits, but demands isolation" (Wheelis 1956, p. 180). It is understandable, then, that patients have increasingly become vocal in their contention that many doctors do not act in caring and compassionate ways toward their patients. The sort of practitioner Wheelis speaks of far too frequently responds to his unhappy patients with a superficial relationship, referred to, cynically, by many mental health professionals, as the "purchase of friendship" (Schofield 1964). In these overly formal professional relationships, the patient is provided with medication and advice, or thrown back to his/her childhood for the source of the problem. On the other hand, there is

minimal or no opportunity to learn about genuine friendship.

GENUINE FRIENDSHIP IN PSYCHOTHERAPY

I am sure that there are many psychotherapists who would react to what I have said so far by indicating that competent practitioners are by definition friends to their patients. This is to say, they demonstrate their friendship by their expression of caring and concern about the conditions of the patient's well-being. These concerns are generally personally felt, exceeding that of simply doing professionally responsible clinical work. In Emerson's words, these practitioners are people with whom the patient may speak sincerely and openly without fear of condemnation (Emerson 1951, p. 145).

I would respond to the above point of view by indicating that the practitioner's friendship *toward* his/her client is a necessary, but not sufficient, condition of *genuine* friendship. Genuine friendship can not be onesided. Friendship without *reciprocity* is inconceivable (Lepp 1971). Without the experience of being of assistance to others and being recognized and appreciated for these efforts, interpersonal relations remain sterile and ungratifying (Goldberg 1973).

The provocative nature of friendship was a pervasive theme in the life of Daphne, a person I will discuss in this chapter.

Some years ago I attended a reception for the cast of an off-Broadway play. Daphne, the female lead, told me prior to its opening that her feelings of success in overcoming personal conflicts and experiencing success as an actress would be dampened if I did not attend.

As I stood and spoke with members of the cast, their families and friends, I asked myself why I was attending this reception—why had I not departed with the fall of the curtain on the play?

Daphne is a talented and troubled actress, who I saw for psychotherapy for about seven years when I practiced in

the mid-Atlantic region. She is 5′10″, with long straw-
berry blonde hair that drapes her shoulders and deeply
set, striking blue eyes. Up until about a year before the
play opened, it would have been rather inconceivable
that she would have permitted herself the auspicious
fortune of being the leading lady in an off-Broadway
show.

My presence at the reception, and my smile of acknowledgment when Daphne's friends thanked me for helping
make possible that successful evening, confirmed for
Daphne that her accomplishment was real and I was willing
to affirm it publicly.

Daphne had been relatively successful as an actress
earlier in her career. In subsequent years, however, her
stage accomplishments oscillated along the shaky
grounds of her quite chaotic and troubled life. For a
number of years she had virtually abandoned the stage
and had tried to support herself with secretarial work.
Nevertheless, dramatic art was central to Daphne's personal identity. It was the sustaining breath of her existence.

What brought Daphne to consult with me was the
aftermath of seeing a Broadway show that she regarded
as phony and a debasement to the integrity of acting that
she felt she had worked so arduously to uphold. The
featured actor had done the worst acting job she had
seen on stage in recent years. He talked with his hands as
if he could not speak and was relegated to communicating in sign language. He also grimaced with his
mouth agape as he used his hands. Daphne believed that
she was the only member of the audience who did not
join in a standing ovation.

She fled from the theater and flew home (she lived
several hundred miles away). On the flight she became
floridly inebriated. After a few drinks, when in despair,
she had the urge to break everything in view. Arriving
home, she went to her cupboard, picked up several of her

prized crystal glasses and hurled them against the wall. The smashed glasses, she said, were a metaphor for the shattering of her life. In humiliation—fury at what she had done to herself—she grabbed some broken glass and drew it across her wrist.

There are few psychological conditions in which the prognosis is more guarded and pessimistic than Daphne's. Her self-destructive feelings can be viewed in the context of shame, as Daphne's inability or refusal to come to terms with her human condition. Daphne was a person who was continually in serious crisis and subjected to periodic bouts of personality disintegration, marked by such clinical features as: a confused sense of identity; low and debasing self-esteem; considerable vacillation in terms of her immediate and long-term goals; poor control of anger leading to rage and fury; lack of contact with what she was feeling at the moment these feelings were evoked; and a chronic sense of emptiness.

Daphne was referred to me for psychotherapy by her lover, Barney, an internist who was a personal friend of mine, as well as a professional colleague.

Barney had wanted to break off his relationship with Daphne for some time. It wasn't just that his wife would no longer believe that it took two hours to find a parking space (these were the opportunities he gave himself to meet with Daphne). He also was concerned about her instability, alcoholism, and suicidal potential. He regarded her as a person who would always be close to an abyss of uncertainty and despair. No matter how well she might be doing at one moment, a desperate or angry profusion of feelings might, the next moment, provoke her to suicide. In case of suicide, Barney did not want to be identified as having been associated with her. He was frightened by her desperate response after seeing the play.

One evening shortly after the Broadway incident, they were sitting in a cafe and Daphne began to cry uncontrollably. He asked her what was wrong. She said that she felt that she would soon die. He told her that if she had a better therapist her life might seem worthwhile. Daphne had been seeing a woman psychiatrist for about five years for her depression. Barney recommended that Daphne discontinue with the psychiatrist and go to see me instead. He told her that I might be able to save her life and also that I was interested in the arts and the theater.

She felt heartened by my artistic interest, in the aftermath of how her psychiatrist had reacted to her suicide attempt. After ascertaining that the cut on her wrist was not life-threatening, the psychiatrist made an appointment with Daphne for the next day. During their session she indicated that she was bewildered by Daphne's emotional turmoil. She had been advising Daphne for years to give up her acting aspirations. Instead of feeling depressed as a failed actress, she should be deriving the satisfaction of supporting herself with a good-paying job. This advice infuriated Daphne. The psychiatrist tried to convince her of the soundness of her opinion by indicating that at the heart of Daphne's drive to be a successful actress were reparative feelings toward her mother.

Daphne had always had a contemptuous relationship with her mother. From early in life and well into adulthood, her mother would shout at Daphne, "There is something wrong with you! There is SOMETHING WRONG WITH YOU!" Often in these incidents, her mother would express her rage by grabbing a large kitchen knife and menacingly approach her daughter. Daphne would flee and hide in terror.

Gertrude, Daphne's mother, is a rather blunt and egocentric person. She is often dramatic in the ways she gets what she wants from others. Once she telephoned her brother-in-law and told him that there was an emergency at his home. When he rushed over to his house he was greeted by Gertrude in the buff, with no one else at home. Gertrude also enjoyed performing a "bump and grind" dance at parties, during which she lifted her dress to reveal no underclothes.

Daphne's psychiatrist indicated that Daphne had been unable to succeed in her acting career because of the conflict she had with her mother. Daphne was entirely dependent upon Gertrude for financial support as well as companionship. Her mother had always wanted to be an actress herself, but didn't have the opportunity or talent. While Daphne was trying to fulfill her mother's fantasies and vicarious ambitions, at the same time she was continually inwardly enraged at how Gertrude treated her. Instead of allowing herself to become accomplished in her career, her psychiatrist told her, Daphne was left with a sense of depression, that her life was a failure, and guilty about sexual feelings she harbored toward her stepfather.

Daphne's natural father had left her mother a few months before Daphne was born. He joined his college fraternity buddies in the Army at the outbreak of the Second World War. Because he did not return from the war, he never saw his daughter. Daphne was unable to learn much about him. Her mother virtually refused to discuss the relationship she had with her husband or even tell Daphne anything significant about his background. Daphne felt deprived of an important source for her personal identity. It resulted in a frantic search to find men who would confirm that she was a worthwhile person. She tried to secure this affirmation from each of a continuous series of men with whom her mother was involved. Gertrude's highly accentuated need for exclusive attention and admiration, however, prevented these men from getting emotionally close to Daphne.

One of the few men that Gertrude was unable to keep completely away from Daphne was Michael, the man Gertrude married when Daphne was 12 years of age. There was an unspoken sexual tension that existed between Daphne and her dashing stepfather. However, Michael was an old-fashioned gentleman who regarded lascivious thoughts and feelings as contemptuous as actions. The tension between them prevented Daphne from obtaining the love, guidance, and encouragement she desired from a father.

I surmise that to deny what he was feeling toward Daphne, Michael was unwilling to see her as a woman. On one occasion when Daphne was 18 and enjoying her budding maturity by wearing a low-cut dress, he snorted at her, "You will never be a woman."

Daphne's psychiatrist also stressed her limitations. She told her, "I am going to get you on your feet for the first time in your life." She indicated to Daphne that it was now time to be realistic about how she conducted her life. If she stayed with acting, by the time she worked out her guilty feelings, she would be long past a real opportunity for a successful career. It makes more sense to abandon her acting ambitions and to get a well-paying job, Daphne was told, so that she wouldn't have to be so dependent on her mother for financial support.

Daphne felt that she was being told that the world of the theater was for her an illusion. "Everything I stood for," she told me, "as a creative, honest, performer was reduced to a piece of shit."

Daphne's psychiatrist was trying to humiliate Daphne into feeling ashamed of her unrealistic ambitions, the passionate pursuit of her ego-ideals. It seemed to Daphne that her psychiatrist was trying to deprive her of the crucial meaning of her life by telling her that her desire for creative expression as an actress was not authentic, but simply a manifestation of her Electra conflict. By shaming Daphne into feeling guilty for having been a failure, her psychiatrist may have believed that Daphne would turn around and take a more realistic attitude toward her life. Understanding the mechanisms of shame, as we should by this point, would suggest to us that this therapeutic strategy would fail. Daphne's intensified preoccupation with suicide following her psychiatrist's confrontation confirms this contention.

The "put-down" she felt from her psychiatrist vivified the pervasive loathing she continually received from her mother. Despite her most conscientious efforts to do the right thing and to please others, Daphne was constantly told that she was a failure. When boys didn't ask her out again or girls stopped calling her, her mother would yell accusingly, demanding to know, "What did you do this time? Why can't you have any friends?" She was made to believe that because there was something wrong with her, she was different from and unacceptable to other people. Although her mother was always there, intruding, scrutinizing, and critically judging everything she did, Daphne felt like an abandoned child in search of her personal identity.

She viewed herself like a rough diamond with exceptional potential, who needed to be discovered, inspired, supported, and guided in order to shine brightly. She desperately wanted a mentor and good friend to take her by the hand and lead her to the promised land of self-realization.

The men she had sought as friends were temporary or replaceable. They never stayed around long enough to serve as mentors. As a child, her mother kept men away. As an adult, Daphne had found her own ways of discouraging men's interests. If she responded favorably to a man, she was rarely aware of how she was actually feeling at that moment. On the occasions she was conscious of strong sexual attraction, she became indifferent or even hostile. She believed that men were primarily interested in sexually scoring and not interested in becoming an intimate companion. She regarded sex as a battleground between combatants, who are adversarial and self-protective at all times.

Even the women Daphne has turned to for friendship, her glamorous aunt, her acting coaches, and fellow actresses, retreated from Daphne, as she was quick to feel misunderstood, betrayed and strike out at her friends.

People like Daphne harbor feelings of lack of legitimate entitlement, so when they experience disappointment, they create a belief system that says in effect that *their suffering is meant to be* (see Chapter 15 for a discussion of the "myth of suffering").

Daphne's Psychotherapy

When I first saw Daphne she regarded her life as useless. She was physically exhausted by her continual anger and despair. She also felt hopeless, as she was unable to envision a life that would be any better than what she was suffering. She later told me that during our first few sessions she was preoccupied with the various ways that she could take her own life. She wondered, if she bought a gun, if she would have enough courage to pull the trigger. However, she denied present suicidal ideation when asked during our early work together.

I cannot describe in comprehensive detail in a single chapter the long and difficult work required to heal Daphne's intense shame and despair. I will focus instead on the *special* features of Daphne's treatment.

The Treatment of Shame and Despair

As I have already mentioned, one of the factors that promoted a therapeutic misalliance with her previous therapist was the psychiatrist's criticism and discouragement of Daphne's raison d'être. I have no doubt that my encouragement, advice, and deep interest in Daphne's theatrical career had to do with my own creative experiences. I had written short stories and poems as a child. I also had done some amateur acting at the same time.

In working with Daphne, I was not only supportive of her artistic aspirations; I also explored the specific problems she incurred in regard to the business, political, and interpersonal aspects of her work that were required to pursue her ambitions successfully in the theater.

In addition to the practical aspects of acting, we spent large portions of sessions, when she was not feeling upset or desperate, discussing philosophy, psychology, sociology, physical health, and athletics, as well as acting theory and personalities in her field.

I found Daphne to be highly intelligent, curious, and extremely well-read. She had been an education major in college. She also showed considerable capacity for psychological understanding of what motivated other people—but, of course, very little about her own inner promptings. Therefore, whenever possible in our discussion of intellectual ideas or psychological principles, I suggested to Daphne that she apply what we were discussing to how it might relate to her own life.

Even during those times when she became desperate and upset, she was able to hold onto many of the ideas we had discussed during quieter times. This fund of knowledge—at first abstract, but gradually more personal—served as an anchorage for Daphne during the Sturm und Drang of her more difficult days and nights.

I did not push helping her if she was unwilling to accept my assistance. I simply inquired if she wanted my help at that moment. These statements calmed her. She said that no one had ever asked her that question.

An important agreed-upon goal was to help Daphne directly experience and understand the meaning of her feelings when they occurred. Until our work together, she was rarely aware of what she was feeling until after an interaction had occurred or a decision was made. Only then would she realize that she had allowed herself to be humiliated, but had been so numb and detached that she had not recognized what was happening to her. Periods of intense self-recrimination followed her awareness that she didn't know how to take proper care of herself and had allowed herself to be mistreated. Once she had allowed an angry stranger to paw her breasts while she was standing at a bus stop. She didn't realize what had happened until some people passing in the street spoke to her about what they had observed.

When she was mistreated, she felt that she had no right to expect better, because she had not done anything with her life to deserve the kinds of relationships that other people enjoyed. Seeing her drowning in her own awful self-loathing was painful to observe. I often had to abandon a psychological scrutiny of what had happened to her, because it served to exacerbate her feelings of shame. At those times I soothed and reassured her with whatever positive attributes about herself she was willing to admit possessing.

I took two different, but related, approaches to help her take better care of herself. First, to confirm her right to feel legitimate entitlement, I acknowledged that I would feel and would express indignation if I were being treated as awfully as she often was. I added that I wouldn't feel that I would have to take my life because someone had mistreated me. This approach is concerned with the therapist helping the patient temper a tenacious personal identity. Fortunately, psychotherapists are not only listeners of their patient's tales of despair, they also live in the same world as do their clients. It is the practitioner's enlightened presence in their shared world that holds hope for a more optimistic life for the patient. It is the thesis of this chapter that genuine healing requires more than the wisdom of understanding. It also demands that the practitioner extend to patients the caring, goodwill, and friendship that are derived from the practitioner's firm place in the world outside the consulting room. This is indispensable for developing the shamed-debilitated patient's feelings of legitimate entitlement to the benevolent qualities of interpersonal relating (Goldberg 1989d).

In my second approach with Daphne I indicated to her that I suspected that those who humiliated her had less confidence and less omnipotence than what she ascribed to them. To help her realize that other people weren't neces-sarily more powerful than she, I told her that I believed that rather than being nefarious, they were ignorant and des-perate people who didn't know how to respond appropri-ately to others. Therefore it was her responsibility to define herself in positive ways and to let her humiliators know clearly how she expected to be and, indeed, insisted on being treated. She later told me that one of the most important skills she acquired in therapy was learning how to break off with people, in nonrageful ways, when she wasn't given what she needed. Accompanying this new faculty came a willingness and an ability to ask more of others without feeling ashamed.

The Building of Trust

The building of trust is essential in a friendship, and, of course, it is no less salient in a therapeutic relationship. This is especially true of clinical work with easily shamed and mistrusting patients. Without her first allowing herself to explore openly her vulnerable feelings in our sessions, Daphne would never have been willing to share these feelings with significant people outside.

Building a safe "holding environment" in our sessions posed a quandry for me. I am a person whose emotions are often not well masked. If I feel annoyed, displeased, or angry, it generally shows. For an easily humiliated person like Daphne, a disapproving look can cause considerable self-recrimination. Therefore I needed to find a constructive way to make safe my own display of emotion. This was vital in terms of the desperate phone calls she made to me.

During the first four or five years of treatment, Daphne would call me whenever she was upset. She had convinced herself early in life that she could not tolerate pain and suffering. She had no trust that her suffering and desperation would end, because she had no sense of her own competence to take care of herself. Consequently, she expected and, even demanded, that I respond immediately to her telephone calls.

On some days this might happen two or three times. Sometimes Daphne would call in a panic at two or three in the morning. If I didn't respond the way she wanted, or if she assumed that I was annoyed or angry at her calling me, she would slam down the receiver. Sometimes she would call right back—sometimes not, if she was embarrassed that she had bothered me. When she did not call back I had to phone her. It was an uncomfortable position for me to be in. I always had Julie (see Chapter 8) in mind, so I knew it was a dangerous time for Daphne.

To deal with this difficulty constructively, I made two agreements with her. One was that she was free to call regardless of the hour, whenever she felt upset and desperate and wasn't certain that she could handle her feelings. At those trying times, I told her, she was in no state of mind to evaluate whether or not it was an appropriate call. Making that type of decision was my job. But if I felt that it wasn't necessary to speak at length with her when she called, I would at that time make an arrangement to see her face-to-face, or speak at length with her by phone in a short while (for example, later that morning).

I don't charge patients for phone consultation, unless a prior arrangement has been made to have a session over the telephone. I don't want a patient in desperation or crisis to hesitate to call me because of payment concerns.

Because of Daphne's periodic bouts of confusion and desperation, therapy frequently had to be done over the phone in addition to office sessions. These telephone sessions had both a reassuring and a practical aim. I focused on precisely how she could take care of herself in the specific situation that had overwhelmed her.

Over the years, her ability to take care of herself improved. In the year or so before her off-Broadway performance, it was a rare occasion to receive a frantic call for help from Daphne. Instead, she would call to get some information about issues she was working on between sessions, or to make an appointment for an extra session. Occasionally, she called to inform me of a radio broadcast or television show that was at that moment on the air and she thought would be of special interest to me, or was relevant to our work together.

Yet even into the latter part of the middle phase of therapy it wasn't "roses, roses, all the way." Periodically, Daphne felt misunderstood by me. At those moments I became one of "them"—those who had lied, manipulated, betrayed, or never cared about her. At those bitter moments, she both doubted my words and claimed to be able to read my "real" feelings from my gestures and facial expressions.

Because of Daphne's basic mistrust of everyone, it was necessary to make the second arrangement with her. I indicated that she did not have to try to decipher how I was responding to her by means of my nonverbal communication. All she needed to do was ask me. Upon her request I would let her know precisely how I was feeling toward her at that moment. If she knew that I was willing to inform her if I was put off by something she had done, she would then have a reasonable basis for accepting that when I said I was not annoyed I meant it.

I am not suggesting that it is advisable for psychotherapists to share with their patients the content and full account of all their personal feelings. Nevertheless, there are some vital responsibilities practitioners must always keep in mind. They should never distort or deny reality. Patients have sufficient problems finding confidence in their own judgments, without additional confusion brought on by their therapist misleading them, no matter how benevolently intended.

Consequently, the practitioner must acknowledge all concerns that affect the therapeutic relationship. If a patient says, for example, "You look terrible. I am concerned about you," the practitioner should inform the client if the observation is valid, that there is a conflictual issue in his life and he is, one hopes, dealing with it. Moreover, the practitioner must express at least a tacit appreciation for the patient's concern and then explore how the client's perception might affect their working and being together. Shifting the patient's concerns about the therapist to similar feelings in the client's developmental years, while having potential usefulness, is too often defensively used by therapists. I believe that expressions of caring and compassion rarely should be discouraged in patients by reducing them to defensive mechanisms. Obviously, there are limitations on how these feelings may be acted upon appropriately in the therapeutic situation. The same holds true about the therapist's feelings and responses to the patient.

Psychotherapy with shame-sensitive people requires a careful examination of how to act appropriately upon caring and concern between therapist and patient. A very important way of healing Daphne's despair was through my identification with her feelings by means of sharing my own experiences. A psychotherapy practitioner is, ideally, a person who is affected by similar feelings as are his patients and is able and willing to communicate his understanding of these feelings openly through sharing how these emotions have effected him.

My willingness to share my feelings when asked served as a sharp contrast with the behavior of her longtime companion, her mother. As a corrective emotional experience, my self-revelation awakened numerous scenes of humiliation that she suffered from her mother's inability to separate psychically who Daphne was from how her mother saw herself. My sharing some of my experiences enabled her to be with someone who defined himself as different from her, but, at the same time was responsive to who she was trying to become. In sessions in which shame scenes and their interpretive script were elicited, we spent considerable time formulating words and messages for talking back to Daphne's negative inner voice in order to modify radically her interpretive script.

At first, as an actress who felt that the author's words were unimpeachable and should be exactly reproduced by actors, she was reluctant to alter her inner voice. However, as she became increasingly aware of how much of her negative inner voice was an actual expression of her mother's angry indictments of her, she was more wont to change her script. She also found several self-growth books and audiotapes reassuring and instructive for soothing herself and changing her inner voice between our sessions.

During the middle phase of my work with Daphne, Gertrude would call and complain that I wasn't helping

Daphne. She would launch into a detailed description of how Daphne had lost her temper and embarrassed her and others.

As a child Daphne had been controlled and well behaved. Her so-called "temper tantrums" during the middle years of treatment were the first time in their long-running relationship that Daphne had directly expressed anger at her mother for the past hurts she had incurred and was even still being subjected to by her mother.

I encouraged her mother to join us in conjoint sessions at those times when Daphne was willing to be seen with her. During these encounters both were quick to feel hurt and anger and to launch vicious attacks on the other's intentions and state of mental health. Despite the usual vituperation of those sessions, we were somehow able to negotiate agreement about how each could respect the other's personal boundaries and sensibilities.

Also, during the middle phase of treatment, I saw for a few months at different times, two of Daphne's boyfriends in conjoint sessions with Daphne. Each of these were sad, no-growth relationships. In our dyadic sessions afterward, we did quite a bit of laughing over the kinds of relationships Daphne was allowing herself.

Humor and *laughter*, at these moments, as well as at other times in our work together, suggested that Hegel was only partially correct about healing shame. Laughter, as well as love, is a means for transcending shame. These light moments served as a safe container in which Daphne's faults and my occasional failures of empathic attunement to her could be broached without condemnation or contempt.

The Turning-Point Incident

Daphne told me that the turning point in therapy came when she realized that I was her friend as well as her therapist. Although I had tried to provide all the nurturance and understanding that a responsible therapist should, this was not sufficient by itself.

About a year before her play opened, Daphne was given an opportunity to perform in a series of dramatic readings, skits, comedy routines, and musical sessions in an experimental theater. These performances covered a three-day period during the holiday season. Each performer was given one hour on the stage. Daphne's hour, quite inconveniently, was scheduled for 2:30 A.M. on New Year's Day. Many of her friends, family, and acting colleagues had promised to come to see her perform at that very important moment in her life. None showed up. The director and I were the only members of the audience she knew.

A significant issue was involved with this event. I wished to pay for my ticket because I wanted Daphne to know that I valued her work. I told her that I was not at the theater at 2:30 in the morning just to add support to her, but because I was genuinely interested in her work as an actress. I believed that by paying for my own ticket, rather than accepting it free for my extra-therapy work, I would give credibility to this intention. When we discussed the issue of payment for the ticket, Daphne told me that she wanted me to attend not only because I was her therapist. She wanted my opinion about her work, because of my interest in the theater. She said that I was doing something special as a friend by staying up late to see her work. I thanked her and said that I would accept the ticket as a friend.

Therapeutic Progress

Daphne had achieved by the time she opened in the show, a much clearer sense of who she was and felt much better about her personal identity. She still had periods of sadness and occasional bouts of depression, but no longer felt gripped by panic about what was happening to her or whether she was able to take care of herself properly. Moreover, her circle of acquaintances had widened; a few had become close friends. And while she had not yet secured a satisfying romantic relationship, she found herself more drawn to a man's wisdom and kindliness than to his physical attractiveness, as in the past.

Of course, no matter how well-intentioned we are toward our patients, we cannot insure that a genuine friendship will develop. This chapter is not meant to imply that I developed a friendship with every patient I have worked with. Not by a long shot! Yet on the other hand, I believe that we should allow ourselves to be open to the possibility with each and every one of the people with whom we work. We should not allow our theory or our character to preclude the possibility of friendship. We are never someone's friend in spite of ourselves (Lepp 1971).

The goodwill and exchange of friendship plays a crucial role in healing loneliness, suffering, and despair. It also contributes to our understanding and enhancement of who we are, as well as providing the vehicle for our caring and support of others. I believe that unless a genuine friendship is allowed to develop in the therapeutic situation, meaningful healing and personal growth for the client is in important ways mitigated. It has been pointed out that we only come to know another person meaningfully through friendship (Lepp 1971). It seems to me that the impressive discoveries of psychological insights in psychotherapy need to be matched by warm and moving responses of friendship.

15

A Guide to the Healing
of Shame

If a man shames me once, shame on him.
If a man shames me twice, shame on me.
—Asian Proverb

Psychological healing rarely occurs in one decisive, broad leap. It almost always requires many small steps along the way. Shame-imbued people have had their debilitating condition evolve over a lifetime. Moreover, the treatment of shame, at the present time, is not an exact science. At best, it is a creative and compassionate art. Often, we can make only small gains in the lives of our despairing patients. Yet it is better to light a single candle in the journey toward self-understanding, a wise and forebearing supervisor taught me during my apprenticeship as a practitioner, than forever to curse the darkness. It is with this humble ethos that I pursue the exploration of personal identity and the healing of shame.

The previous clinical chapters provided accounts of working with shame from a phenomenological perspective. Here specific guidelines are provided for clinical procedures with shame-sensitive patients. This approach is conceptualized in the following phases of therapeutic work:

257

- Intake and Evaluation
- Treatment Plan
- The Steps Required to Heal Shame
- Working-Through

Signs and Symptoms
of Shame during Intake

The mother's expressive face reflects the earliest indication of the quality of the emotional attunement between infant and parent. Similarly, the *patient's* face registers his degree of rapport with the psychotherapist—in regard to whether he feels optimistic and trusting, or is responding with shame-anxiety and doubt.

Symptoms of shame also are noted in the patient's *affective response* to the therapist, expressed in his verbal material. I take special note of the metaphors patients use in revealing themselves. I listen for constriction in the free expression of feelings and for passive statements about self that seem bound with secrets and well-concealed fantasy lives implied in their metaphors. Shame-bound people frequently speak about themselves in *allusions* rather than make direct personal statements. In William James's (1890) bifurcation of knowledge, they speak from an *acquaintance* with themselves, rather than a knowledge from within. They make references to themselves and significant aspects of their lives as "it," rather than conveying the centrality of these events as having been directed from a personal identity that is experienced as "me." Often there are so many *impersonal pronouns* used in their accounts of the events of their lives that it is difficult to ascertain whether they are referring to themselves, someone else, an inanimate object, or a hypothetical construct. There also is an overabundance of *power* words like "must," "have to" and "can't" contained in their speech. On the other hand, the expression of volitional experience, such as "want to," "choose not to," "will," or "won't," are absent.

SOURCES OF SHAME
EVOKED BY THERAPEUTIC EXPERIENCE

Nergaard and Silberschatz (1989) found in a study of brief therapy that patients with high ratings on shame and guilt did not make substantial progress in their treatment. They demonstrated a negative therapeutic reaction, doing less well on all therapy outcomes measured by the investigators, than did a patient population that had low scores for shame and guilt. There is clinical evidence that this finding is valid for all forms of psychotherapy (Lewis 1971).

Let us examine how shame produces a negative therapeutic reaction. Early memories of being shamed that are revived by therapeutic interactions by patients with a higher order of defenses (see Table 3–2) are available for conscious recall and exploration. On the other hand, shame-debilitated patients have more deeply repressed memories of early hurtful shame, and rather than explicitly recounting these experiences that have been jarred loose by therapeutic encounter, they express their symptoms through the mechanisms of acting out or acting in (Gorsuch 1990).

There are five aspects of the therapeutic situation that contribute heavily to shame-debilitated patients indirectly and dysfunctionally expressing their experiences of having been shamed rather than recalling it in such a way as to maximize therapeutic examination. First, being looked at or seen evokes painful memories in shame-bound patients about their flaws having been ridiculed and their personal identity condemned by others for their inability to achieve a desired self (Gorsuch 1990). Second, primitive defenses are ushered forth by the regressive experience in therapy that recounts a shame-bound patient's symbiotic dependence upon caretakers (Gorsuch 1990). Grinker (1955) pointed out, "One of the dangers in uncovering therapy of any type is the patient's confrontation with the quality of his unsatisfied needs, his failure in growth, and his inertia characterized by a compulsive search for unchanging goals" (p. 251).

Alexander (1938) indicated, along the same lines, that the failure to develop higher-level defenses is due to the patient giving in to regressive wishes and, as a result, feeling ashamed. Third, competitive comparisons with the therapist fosters feelings of helpless rage and humiliation-fury by highlighting the shame-debilitated patient's failure to be the desired self and, as a result, feeling inferior to the therapist (Gorsuch 1990). Fourth, a patient's efforts to discuss painful material may result in blocking and inarticulateness. These feelings give rise to an intense *secondary* shame and a sense of incompetence and failure (Levin 1971).

There is yet another important source of shame in therapeutic encounter that if not detected and resolved severely impairs therapeutic efficacy, if not resulting in the patient's complete unwillingness to come to sessions. A patient's behavior in psychotherapy is never solitary—insulated from that of the therapist. Therapeutic interaction always is *intersubjective*. Morrison (1989) suggests that when the therapist encounters what he regards as negative therapeutic reaction, he should ask himself if the patient is responding transferentially, or whether he actually is reacting to the therapist's failure of emotional attunement to the patient. Therapeutic approaches that emphasize conflict-resolution too early in the treatment of shame-debilitated patients raise the patient's shame-anxiety. Lewis (1971) has impressively illustrated the numerous ways in which unanalyzed and countertransferential shame occurs in therapy sessions, exacerbating the patient's symptoms.

Throughout my therapeutic work, I try to understand how the patient is relating to me within the context of how I may have been unwittingly shaping what he says and how he responds to me. This task requires examining what I am assuming about the patient and how I am responding to these assumptions, as well as what he seems to want from me and how he experiences me responding to his needs. In every therapeutic encounter the underlying issue is how each person is allowing the other to make himself known. Awareness of how this disclosure is taking place helps the therapist recognize how he may be managing the behavior of his patient in ways that antagonize the patient's own intentionality.

Many instances of what has been termed "resistance" on the patient's part are due to the therapist having unwittingly opened a painful wound, evoking the patient's defenses against being shamed (Lewis 1989).

The therapist's untoward behavior gives rise to retaliatory, hostile, and derogatory thoughts by the patient about therapy and about the therapist, such as: "He can't help me. Therapy doesn't work. He is insensitive and uncaring. Therapy makes me feel worse."

I regard behaviors such as missed sessions, lateness, aloofness, coldness, defiance, long silences, emotional blocking, and wanting to terminate treatment prematurely not necessarily as manifestations of resistance. Often they are signifiers of shameful feelings evoked by the therapist that the patient is unable to deal with or express.

As we learned from earlier chapters about how shame develops and is maintained by shame-imbued people, the therapist's failed empathy with the patient's feeling-state is turned into derogatory feelings by the patient about himself. It fits congruently with his interpretative *script* about his relationship with painful caretakers in the past. Particular scripts were developed early in life to avoid or escape painful shaming situations. These scripts contain specific rules for responding and controlling potentially hurtful social situations (Tompkins 1987). The therapist who has shamed the patient reinforces the predictions found in his interpretative script consisting of such beliefs as, "They all felt that I was too sick and needy to be helped. They were right!"

A PLACE OF SAFETY AND TRUST

There is an especially important requirement in working with shame-bound people to create a safe environment in which to explore the sources of shame. Shaming can be unintentionally induced even before a prospective client makes himself known to the therapist as a patient. For example, some practitioners do quite a "number" on callers by answering the phone during a therapeutic session and indicating in an irritated tone that the caller has intruded into the sanctuary of the therapist's office. To insure a meaningful sanctuary for therapeutic work, the therapist needs to recognize fully not only how his countertransferential feelings affect his clinical work, but also the influence of his values and characterological attitudes. This is particularly important in working with clients from a different culture than his own.

The providers of mental-health services are predominantly middle-class and college educated. Their orientation toward resolution of problems is usually by means of rational discussion and compromise, working within and accomodating to the established social order. The middle-class mental-health professional's attitudes best prepare him to provide ameliorative modalities that are insight-oriented and directed toward clients who have a conscious philosophical stance toward life. These clients are capable also of abstract and symbolic reasoning and have sufficient conflict-free areas of psychological functioning to withstand day-to-day frustrations, tensions, and problems, enabling them to struggle with the meaning of their existence and to develop a viable sense of identity.

The clients we treat may come from cultures with very different value orientations and attitudes toward being helped than our own. Some attention should be given, therefore, to the specific communication between the middle-class professional and a client from a different culture from himself. The verbal symbols that the psychotherapist uses may do more to put some clients on guard than to establish a meaningful communication. The psychotherapist's symbols may unwittingly imply critical evaluation and diagnosis to the client. It is extremely difficult, if not impossible, for a client not to feel shamed with a therapist when his behavior is critically regarded as inappropriate. An obvious example of this is the psychotherapist's viewing the client's lack of punctuality in attending sessions as resistance and lack of motivation, when time commitments may have dissimilar meanings to the psychotherapist and the client from a different culture. Because the therapist "knows" what is appropriate and the client doesn't, the client's feelings of inferiority are aroused (Goldberg and Kane 1974).

THE REAL RELATIONSHIP IN TREATMENT

Mother–child interaction studies have contributed to our understanding of shame in our patients' lives. This understanding mandates that the *real person* of the psychotherapist should be the source of therapeutic progress in working with shame-sensitive patients. Theory does not heal shame and despair. It is the therapist's attitude and personality, more than his knowledge about the etiology of shame, that heals suffering. We need to be emotionally responsive and available and not cloak who we are behind the anonymous persona of neutrality if we are to reach those who have been painfully shamed by emotionally unavailable caretakers in their developmental years.

Adult shame has at its roots the feelings of abandonment by caretakers in the patient's past. To undo shame, attachment to compassionate figures needs to be regained or, perhaps even for the first time, secured. Overcoming shame is best achieved in a trusted and intimate relationship in which the therapist is a fellow sojourner, able to be emotionally touched by the patient, rather than being an objective expert interested in an archeological quest of mummified demons.

One of the most serious problems in the training of psychotherapists is that we are oriented to look for and to believe only in what is *wrong* with the patient. Many psychotherapy training orientations focus too exclusively on what is hidden, denied, or pathological in our patients. I strongly believe that we need to balance the search for what is wrong with what is right, healthy, and hopeful in the lives of those with whom we work if our consulting room is to be viewed by our patients as a sanctuary. This is because our very emphasis on pathology will indelibly mark us, despite our manifest concerns about our patients' suffering, as little different from those who have painfully crippled them in the past.

One of the parameters of clinical practice that reinforces an emphasis on the pathological is the clinical *language* used to describe and explain our patients to our colleagues and to ourselves. Clinical language seems more accurately descriptive of physical objects than of the motivations of psychotherapy patients. Our therapeutic communications must be free of cant. If we conceptualize the people with whom we work in dehumanized terms, we are likely to treat them accordingly.

The importance of using the *language of health* rather than that of pathology is because the patient's overriding need in struggling with shame and despair is to find positive qualities about himself and his life that will establish his personal identity in a self-enhancing way. The most difficult task, and when achieved, the turning-point in healing, is getting a shame-imbued person to believe and trust in *his own goodness.* The absence of a sense of personal goodness is the major source of depression and despair. If our patients cannot secure the recognition of their own worth from their interactions and impact on us, their therapists, then from where else will it come?

From my initial contact with patients I accentuate what is hopeful and positive in their attitudes, behaviors, and intentions. In doing so, my responses to how they reveal themselves to me are conceptualized and expressed in *positive connotation.* I try to avoid attributing their behavior to negative and pathological causes. In my interactions as well as my statements, I underscore my interest in helping them find the healthy direction from which I believe they may be responding to their sense of the world. Their personal stories are helpful in this endeavor.

THE PERSONAL STORY

To treat the despair of shame we need to understand how our patients see themselves. To understand a patient's intentionality, I encourage the prospective patient to speak from his experience of what it is like for him to be in-the-world as he, himself, experiences his world. I don't interrupt as the patient tells his story, as long as I experience his account as heartfelt and uncontrived. I do intervene, however, to ask questions, make comments connecting aspects of his story, and to share a desire to better understand how he feels about himself when he presents himself as another might describe what is happening to him rather than from a personal statement from the deep recesses of his own psyche.

Revealing one's personal story openly is often a difficult task for patients. From having for over two decades asked patients during their initial consultation to "tell me how you see yourself," I have discovered that otherwise highly articulate and thoughtful patients find themselves at a loss to convey a meaningful sense of self. Freud's most important discovery was that the greatest cause of emotional disturbance is the fear of what one might learn if one knew oneself intimately. It is not surprising, then, that those who consult with me about shame-afflicted conditions have a need to hide from themselves and, consequently, from me, their sense of themselves as incompetent to live fully and well.

It was because of the difficulty of many patients to present a coherent sense of themselves to me that I devised a projective approach to facilitate their presentations.

It is inimical to human experience to regard the events of one's life evaluatively. We are meaning-oriented beings. One's personal identity is constituted in ways expressed by the *stories one tells oneself* about what has happened in one's life. Each of us has, if not a favorite story about oneself, then, at least a prototypic story that has direct implications for how we regard the world, its resources, opportunities, and impediments to the achievement of our desires.

These stories derive from a wide coterie of sources. Since we cannot empirically acquire absolute truth about our world, each of us attempts by using the events, legends and myths of family, and society to create a reliable guide for living. These stories generally undergo considerable elaboration and modification through time. Nevertheless, myths in story format reveal rather succinctly how our patients navigate their lives through the straits and vicissitudes of daily life. These stories provide the psychotherapist with a working hypothesis for understanding what is directing a patient's sense of personal identity in terms of the forces that drive his life—that is to say, what he wants from life, and what the obstacles are that prevent, and the resources that would enable, that person to realize and enjoy the intentions of his desired self.

In an intake or consultation interview, I ask the prospective patient to relate a story about himself that best represents what his life has been like for him. Second, I ask the prospective patient to describe the situation in the story in regard to what each person involved was thinking, feeling, and doing as fully as he is willing to describe. Like every coherent tale, the personal story should have a beginning, a middle, and an end. I inquire about important structural components missing. Finally, I ask the patient what he believes to be the moral, or significant message, contained in the story.

In examining the personal story with a patient we discuss:

1. What the story tells us about what is desirable and meaningful in life for him;
2. What he believes should be avoided;
3. The best means for obtaining the desirable and avoiding the untoward;
4. What will happen if the desired end is not achieved; and
5. What significant ways the story has been changed and what these changes exemplify about how he may begin to feel better about himself.

I will illustrate the capacity of the personal story to represent the shadows of emotionally laden shaming scenes that have invoked contemptuous inner dialogue, broadcasting to the psyche its lack of self-worth, in regard to Roger.

ROGER'S STORY

Roger is a tall, slender European, who wears thick glasses, without which he is nearly blind. He has a rapid,

English voice and a fidgety manner that initially induced restlessness in me. This 37-year-old man, although a gifted and highly trained actor and musician, experienced his life as empty and unsuccessful. He has held a paying job only sporadically in his life. When asked during our initial consultation session to tell a story that closely characterized what his life has been like, he told me that when he was 6 or 7 years of age, he took part in a reading comprehensive examination with the rest of his school class. Long after his classmates went to recess, he remained at his desk, unable to answer a question that he later realized was rather simple. He had difficulty with the question because he had misread the directions given about the situation.

I asked him what happened next. He said that his teacher came back to the room and found that he was still there. She asked him what was wrong. He said that he could not figure out the answer. However, once she read the instructions and the question aloud, the answer was readily apparent to him.

Asked what the moral of the story was, he indicated that the story vividly demonstrated how he typically fouls up his life by being conceptually confused by problems that he should be intelligent enough to understand. He indicated, then, that the only reason he came for therapy was he felt that it was irresponsible not to try to do something about his defective thinking. He also believed that it was too late for him. Everything he had read about psychology and sociology told him that one's cast in life is set early. How families treat their young, he believed, is irreversible. He went on to speak about the failures and mistakes he had made throughout his life because of the lack of proper guidance from his family. As he spoke, I had a sense of a person who felt that he was all alone in the world. Fittingly, in discussing the moral of his personal story, Roger had ignored the role his teacher played in helping him solve the problem and disengaging him from the solitude and humiliation that he had felt sitting there by himself. Roger, like so many shame-bound people, didn't recognize or believe that other people can be trusted to help or care about him. His teacher's assistance was cognitively dissonant with how he had been led to believe the world was for him. Incongruent experiences were disavowed by Roger. When asked why he had not requested help when he became aware that he did not seem able to solve the problem by himself, Roger shrugged his shoulders and said that he had met few people who cared about him.

The Myth of Suffering

Within every shame-debilitated person's interpretative script is a *personal myth* about the causes of his personal suffering. These myths have been examined systematically by Weisman (1984), who worked for many years with terminal patients. He contends that for patients in despair (and I would include all shame-bound people), it is the anticipation of *copelessness* that undermines their ability to feel alive and to thrive in a purposeful way. Their fearful apprehension is predicated upon the fallacy that one should operate at full capacity at all times. Consequently, when they become disabled by illness or other circumstances, they unquestioningly believe that their suffering is meant to be. The advent of illness or despair indicates that the force that controls the universe had decided their fate and no effort on their part can change this destiny. The feeling of copelessness for Roger resulted from personal statements he continually made to himself that if he didn't reach a state of ideal solution to his conflicts, then his lot in life would be one of failure, demoralization, and despair.

Roger had no vocabulary, despite his excellent education and stage training, to express articulately his myth of suffering from being betrayed and disappointed by other people. He simply expected to be verbally misunderstood. At these times, he communicated with me nonverbally. He crossed his arms across his chest, pulled his chin over the top of his chest, and grimaced bitterly.

Before we move to the next stage of clinical work with shame-afflicted patients, I should indicate that the personal-story approach is but one productive means of capturing

governing scenes and their interpretative script. Most patients respond to it readily, but not all. A projective method
I use for patients who have difficulty presenting coherent
and revealing stories is to ask for their family picture album.
This can be done literally by asking the patient to bring in
photos chronicling his development and the significant
people he met along the way, or even to describe these
scenes from memory. For patients who are more visual, are
cognitively concrete, or claim amnesia about their past, this
technique may be more effective than relating a personal
story. For example, Agnes, a chronically depressed 40-year-
old woman, consulted with me because she was concerned
that if she did not get help she would lose her job—her sole
support. She said that she had no interest in life, except for
being alone at home. She deeply resented having to leave
the house to interact with people to pay bills, to shop, and to
deal with the day-to-day hassles of living. She reported that
she could remember no interaction in her life that had ever
made her happy. Her childhood was a living hell of being
raised by two people unsuited to being parents who unmer-
cifully criticized her. Her family album suggested a rather
different early history. The photos she brought into sessions
revealed her, surprisingly, first as a smiling infant and then
as a happy-looking child, held by a mother and a father who
appeared to be proud of their young child. In looking over
the pictures with me, Agnes wondered about what had
happened to change all of their lives to the monolithically
unhappy one she remembered. A curiosity about her life
was stimulated from examining and discussing her photos.

PSYCHOLOGICAL INVENTORIES
THAT MEASURE SHAME-PRONENESS

The empirically minded clinician may be interested in a
number of shame-proneness measures as assessed by personality tests. The five scales that are reported to differentiate guilt from shame-anxiety are:

1. The Gottschalk-Gleser shame anxiety scale (Gottschalk et al. 1969).

2. The Binder shame-proneness scale (Harder 1984).
3. The Beall Situational Upset Scale (Smith 1972).
4. The Personal Feelings questionnaire (PFQ) (Harder and Lewis 1987).
5. The Internalized Shame Scale (Cook, unpublished).

An empirical investigation by Harder and Lewis (1987) found that the PFQ, a weighted-scale checklist, was the most promising objective measure among these inventories for detecting the presence of shame in a college student–population sample. A new inventory, The Self-Conscious Affect and Attribution Inventory (SCAAI), has been recently reported in the *Journal of Personality and Social Psychology* by Tangner (1990).

TREATMENT PLAN

In Winnicott's (1958) terms, the psychotherapeutic situation has the structure of a holding environment, or what Bion (1962) called a "container." It is this context that serves to permit both agents in the therapeutic situation to explore the full range of emotion. According to Winnicott, the emotional enactment within the holding environment is a process of *play*. In therapeutic play, the expression of the fantasies of each participant invites a response from the other. In the enactment of this liberated play the various aspects of the self are given permission to be revealed. The container and the free play represent the caretaking roles of human development. When they are combined in a meaningful manner, they serve as a normalizing, or corrective, emotional experience. However, the process within the therapeutic container would remain solely emotive and, at best, cathartic, without the imposition of *comment*. Explicit comment on the emotive experience between client and therapist reveals the meaning of the experience to the ongoing lives of its constituents. The therapist's "tool of empathy enables him to understand shame, depression and loneliness in his patients through the harmonic reverberation of the same affects in himself . . . the ubiquity of [these feel-

ings] enables the [psychotherapist] to recognize in his patients' symptoms landmarks of a country that he, himself,
has travelled" (Barry 1962, p. 589). The practitioner is
expected to relate the meaning of these troubling emotions
and moods to the client's place in the continuum of his life.
Whether the therapist has a historical, contemporary, or
teleological orientation, the practitioner is concerned with
the implications of the shared emotional experience of the
therapeutic relationship in terms of what the client intends
to be.

Therapeutic comment, which I regard as effective psychotherapy, generally moves from mirroring to transmutation to personal statement. In the *mirroring* phase the
practitioner empathically reflects to the client those aspects
of the self that have been frustrated and denied in relationship with caretakers. In doing so, the therapist reacquaints
the client with missing aspects of self, once deeply felt and
now disavowed and eschewed. Therapeutic skill is evidenced in the practitioner's ability to manipulate a series of
mirrors at different angles and perspectives—by expanding
upon and redirecting the client's metaphors and disguised
messages—to capture the client's premature integration of
self, the self-illusion that is derived from an inability to
obtain sufficiently nurturing responses from others. Therefore, the gradual acknowledgement and bodily reexperi-
encing of once deeply felt and yearned-for sensation and
emotional touch helps bridge and integrate the self and its
disavowed attributes. It helps the phenomenological self
feed itself, digest, and retain experiential nurturance (Goldberg 1991a). The remainder of this chapter describes the
steps necessary in the process of therapeutic integration
with shame-imbued patients.

During the second phase of treatment, the psychotherapist identifies for the prospective patient the themes, signs,
and manifestations of shame and its variants in the patient's
life. These are secured during the initial phase of treatment
from an evaluation of the presenting symptoms, assessment
of interpersonal data, assessment inventories (if used), and
verbal projective approaches (like the personal story). Ex-

ploratory discussion is given to how these themes of shame, now identified, are influencing the patient's life.

I then ask the prospective patient if he is sufficiently curious or concerned about his shame issues that he would be interested in exploring his concerns with me for a few exploratory sessions (usually three to five sessions). Only after this preliminary work together is a treatment plan and contract negotiated.

The treatment plan invites the patient to join the therapist in pursuing how his issues of shame impede him from living fully and well. This exploration includes shame experiences inside the consulting room as well as outside. I have found that patients become more curious about themselves and less frightened by their shame reactions once I discuss with them the basic psychology of shame, accompanied by the information that shame is an affliction that is shared by everyone in the world at some time. I also indicate that a capacity to experience shame consciously is an essential factor in their therapeutic progress (Ward 1972). Shame is like a thermostat (Retzinger 1989). If it fails to function properly, regulation of one's behavior and an ability to overcome dysfunctional patterns in one's life will be difficult to achieve.

Once we agree to work together I convey my *commitment of availability.* This means that I will be available between appointments for telephone and face-to-face consultations. This is an important therapeutic responsibility in working with patients in despair, since crises do not conform to a convenient schedule. The contractual issues that are important to an efficacious therapeutic partnership have been discussed in detail elsewhere (Goldberg 1991a).

The Steps Required to Heal Shame

To portray vividly the ways of recognizing and overcoming shame, let us return to the story of Richard and Jennifer discussed in Chapter 4. I will follow this account with a discussion of how these steps are translated into clinical practice.

Following the traumatic encounter with Richard, Jennifer retreated to her secluded studio apartment. She stayed home from work. She could not face her co-workers. She was certain that the terrible humiliation that she had incurred could be read on her face. She also shut off her telephone so that she wouldn't have to speak with anyone.

Susan, a concerned close friend and colleague, tried for several days to reach her. She knew that Jennifer didn't answer her phone when she was despondent and was unable to ask for help.

Susan went over to Jennifer's apartment. Jennifer reluctantly opened the door to her friend. After some gentle but probing questions, Jennifer plaintively told Susan:

"My life isn't working for me. I seem to be losing everything—including me." Jennifer then told her friend what had happened that past Tuesday at Richard's door. Susan looked straight at Jennifer. She gently placed her hand on her shoulder and said:

"Jennifer, you may feel at this moment that you are the only person in the world that gets treated badly. But, believe me, many of us have gone through the same awful experience as you. *I* certainly have. Let me tell you what happened to me. But remind me before I leave to recommend a book that I think can help you."

The volume Susan spoke of quickly captured Jennifer's curiosity. The stories seemed rather familiar to her. She wondered if it had come across her desk in manuscript form in her work as an editor at a publishing house.

As she more carefully read the stories, she began to become aware of a burning sensation in the pit of her abdomen. She had not seen the book as a manuscript. The descriptions, which seemed to leap off the page and lunge at her, frightfully captured many of her own life experiences.

In less than an hour's time at home Jennifer understood for the first time that the horrible feelings she harbored about herself had to do with her sensitivity to shame and humiliation. Feeling ashamed, Jennifer learned, is a powerful but unquestioned conviction that in important ways one is flawed and incompetent as a human being.

She thought back over the innumerable times she felt taken advantage of, but felt powerless to change the situation because she feared that protesting would cause other people to get angry and abandon her. Nothing frightened Jennifer as much as the prospect of being alone for the rest of her life. She had been willing to tolerate almost anything, including being treated badly, to avoid being abandoned.

As Jennifer delved into the stories, she was heartened to learn that many people like herself, who had experienced the unfathomable misery of shame, had overcome their oversensitivity to being shamed and had gone on to lead lives full of pride, competence, and feelings of self-worth. By giving her helpless feelings a name, Jennifer was for the first time in a position to do something about her troublesome emotions.

Shame, she read, is a normal part of life. As a complex emotion, it comes in a variety of shapes and has a multitude of different functions. Not all experiences of shame are deleterious. Quite to the contrary. In small doses, shame is a prod to self-improvement. In digestable amounts, shame spurs personal freedom by providing a means for penetrating self-discovery. Positive shame comes from the recognition that we do not know ourselves and the significant people in our life sufficiently well in order to live fully and with pride. Healthy responses to feeling shame derive from our willingness to examine openly, and to do something constructive about, those aspects of ourselves that cause us to feel badly and that we can reasonably change.

Jennifer chose to believe that discovering the book about shame was a propitious opportunity. If she were to overthrow her intense unhappiness, she must learn specifically how other people have successfully done so. From studying the cases in the book of those who have recovered from shame, Jennifer extracted the basic steps in overcoming debilitating shame and humiliation. They are:

First, you must learn to recognize the presence of shame in the ways you become unhappy and distressed; second, you need to learn the language of articulate emotion in order to give hurt and shame a clear voice; third, it is necessary to share your intimate feelings with a concerned and caring person; and fourth, you must halt the vicious cycle of being humiliated, feeling ashamed, hiding and not correcting the situation, or feeling weak and cowardly for tolerating the situation, which results in additional feelings of shame. To stop this destructive pattern you must learn skills in defining yourself positively and seeing to it that other people behave toward you in decent and nonhostile ways. Finally, you need to use the self-awareness and newly acquired skills from following the preceding steps to repair existing relationships and to explore challenging new ones.

Jennifer spent the weekend in her apartment carefully canvassing the specific ways that she related to people. In every interaction that she considered, with the notable exception of activities in which she excelled, she was embarrassed to recognize that if she was not inwardly calling herself harsh and terrible names for being unsure of herself, then she was allowing others to discredit her by treating her indecently.

She traced her current traumatic patterns of relating with people to how family members had interacted with her when she was growing up. Their profusion of negative criticism and harsh judgments had evolved into a *punitive inner voice* that rarely afforded Jennifer the acknowledgment that she had done something praiseworthy. Indeed, her reproachful inner voice hurled the very same accusations at her adult behavior that her parents expressed when she was a child.

She also discovered that her inability to feel legitimate entitlement depended on the denial of her hurt and other negative emotions. Her inner voice magnified the anger she harbored toward herself and, occasionally, others. At the same time, this voice ignored her feelings of sadness and loneliness for her failure to achieve the intimacy and closeness with others that she craved.

The book advised that reciting provocative emotional passages from poetry, literature, and drama has helped people give their inner voice an articulate vocabulary to represent the totality of their feeling states. Jennifer went over to her bookcase and drew out her favorite books.

She came across a passage in a novel by Somerset Maugham that conveyed sentiments about herself that she had been struggling to express with Richard but had never found the right words to reveal her actual feelings. In the novel *Of Human Bondage,* Philip, a young boy with a clubfoot, has been ridiculed by his classmates for his awkward limp. The school bully has twisted Philip's arm so painfully that Philip puts his foot out of the corner of the bedsheets, enabling the other boys to plainly see his deformed foot.

> Philip . . . had got his teeth in the pillow so that his sobbing should be inaudible. He was not crying for the pain they had caused him, nor for the humiliation he had suffered when they looked at his foot, but with rage at himself because, unable to stand the torture, he had put out his foot of his own accord. [p. 47]

Jennifer intuitively sensed that she had made a major breakthrough in understanding her hurtful feelings. She recognized that she was more afraid of self-criticism than she was of others' judgments about her.

Telling herself that she was a shy and easily embarrassed person had been just an excuse for not sharing with Richard and other people with whom she wished to get closer, unpleasant qualities in herself that she did not wish to face. She now recognized that she would only be able to root out and repudiate feelings about herself that were untrue, unreasonable, and unfair in the cleansing openness of speaking about her suppressed feelings with people who cared about her.

Jennifer's task now was clear to her. With considerable trepidation, yet no less firm resolve, she turned on her phone and dialed a familiar number.

"Richard, you didn't think that you'd hear from me again, did you?"

"I'm surprised. Why have you called?"

"I'm not going to tearfully plead about getting together again—I don't even know if I want to."

"Then I *am* puzzled why you're calling."

"Richard, you have been the person with whom I have been closest. I have made an important discovery about myself, and about you, too, for that matter. Are you interested in finding out what it is?"

"Sure! Fine! If you think you know something about me that I don't, why shouldn't I listen to you! By the way, there is something different in your tone, Jennifer—I think I like it."

Over the phone Jennifer gave Richard a cogent synopsis of what she had learned about shame and its consequences. Then her voice softened. She told him that she was no longer angry at him. She now understood that his distancing behavior toward her was probably indicative of his vulnerability to her pain and misery. She carefully discussed the concept of borrowed shame, giving a few examples from what she had read.

Jennifer's words struck a chilling chord in Richard's emotional memory. A vivid image of his father's eyes flashed before him. He felt the cold compress of what he associated as loneliness and sadness creep over him. These were feelings that Richard had never before consciously attributed to his father.

They arranged to meet at Richard's apartment the next evening. Jennifer brought over a simple dinner. They had no cocktails or wine. They agreed to set aside the entire evening without any unnecessary distractions.

The discussion continued on subsequent evenings. Richard began to feel impatient. Having discussed at length how hurt and humiliation had influenced their relationship, he felt that they now should be able to tell each other what they needed from one another.

"Jennifer, okay! Okay! I already understand the theory. Now, what about the practice? What can I do to help you feel better about yourself?"

"That, dear Richard, is precisely my problem. If I'm going

to grow up emotionally I'm going to have to learn to take care of myself. I cannot allow you or anyone else—as much as I may want to be taken care of—to continue to protect me from life's unpleasantness."

"Do you think there is any hope for us as a couple, Jennifer?"

"I don't know that. But I will tell you what I would like," Jennifer forthrightly stated. "In following the suggestions in the book on shame I have just read something by Rainer Maria Rilke, the German writer, that I would like you to think about. He says that love is the binding of two strangers, who step forth to disclose themselves, withholding nothing and risking all. If we are ever to get together again you are going to have to trust me. It is really all right with me if you are not always able to care for me in the way I would like. That is, as long as you talk to me about your feelings without anger or distancing yourself from me."

"You sound different from the Jennifer I used to know," Richard replied. "There have been some real changes in you in the last couple of weeks."

"Maybe," she said, "but I can't celebrate yet. It is going to take some time to heal the wounds that have taken a lifetime to acquire. It is just that I realize that hiding from my shame has deprived me of simply being human. What you and I have going for us is that we can care about each other because we are human—all-too human!"

When Jennifer left Richard's apartment that evening she had a vibrant sense of having crossed the line from being an avoidant person to one who was more willing to explore life's opportunities and to deal with whatever would be cast her way. Jennifer also sensed that having gained a considerable amount of insight into herself in negotiating a more shame-free relationship with Richard, she needed to get involved in activities that would increase her sense of competence and self-worth.

Two afternoons per week, Jennifer left the safe and familiar literary world she had lived in for so long, to be a volunteer in an after-school program for children with learning disabilities. It gave her considerable satisfaction to see how well the children responded to her.

She realized that being of assistance to others and being recognized and appreciated for these efforts went a long way toward reversing the destructive messages her inner voice had been broadcasting to her psyche about how incompetent, unworthy, and unwanted a person she was.

To remove the hazardous minefields of debilitating shame, each of us, like Jennifer, needs to influence our world, making it a better place for ourselves and others to express and receive caring and concern.

Undoubtedly, I have provided an overly optimistic account of how Richard and Jennifer might come to terms with the sources of their feelings of shame. I have done this in order to accentuate the constructive steps necessary in healing debilitating shame. Of course, if the events I describe were actually that smooth, then professional psychotherapy would be a less necessary healing endeavor than it is.

The Psychotherapy of Shame

Identifying the Narrative Voice of Shame

As I have already indicated, the person who suffers from shame usually is not aware of what he is suffering. Instead, he may feel depressed, aimless, easily offended, quick to get annoyed or feel hurt. To deal with something difficult one needs to know with what one is dealing. To overcome "toxic shame" the sufferer needs therapeutic experiences in which he first becomes able to recognize that he is indeed suffering from shame; second, what is causing the shame; and, third, specifically how he expresses his shame.

The purpose of this first step in treatment is to help the patient gain specific, trustworthy ways of recognizing the messages that broadcast his feelings of self-blame and worthlessness. A person recognizes his shame once he can designate a specific set of thoughts and feelings with that label (Potter-Efron 1989). In the early sessions of clinical work we trace these shaming messages to their original source as portrayed in governing scenes. We search for the interpretive script that comprises the negative inner voice. This script is found in the emotionally ladden shaming scenes that provoked contemptuous inner dialogue (Tompkins 1978). Unfortunately, frequently there is *amnesia* about these governing scenes. Many patients have a great deal of difficulty recalling childhood experiences. To abet conscious recall, I employ the following therapeutic activities early in treatment. I encourage my patients to:

- Have discussions with family members about their early life experiences;
- Examine their stream of consciousness for the governing force that directs them through a typical day. For example, is the patient compelled by matters and duties that have to be attended to that day, by a pleasant event the patient is looking forward to that day, or to a "voice" that broadcasts such authoritative messages as, "Keep busy!"?
- Probe the contents of dreams and day reveries for themes of shame;
- Write a daily journal about their thoughts, feelings, and behaviors;
- Learn to observe their thoughts, feelings, and actions objectively without making value judgments about these events, until the experience has been completed (Goldberg 1980b);
- Practice awareness exercises that I give them as "homework," such as a guided fantasy in which they are given a scene to fantasize about;
- Join a psychotherapy or professionally led support group.

Group experience, whether it is a therapeutic group, or a professionally led support group, is a vital accompaniment to dyadic psychotherapy. Robertiello and Gagnier (1990) cogently indicate:

A patient can make light of his individual therapist's acceptance of his most shameful secrets. The therapist may be an extraordinarily accepting person or he or she may even feel the therapist must play an accepting role. In a group when a person reveals his or her shameful secrets, his or her peers have no obligation to be accepting or to be kind. [p. 120]

In short, acceptance for the ashamed patient from a group of peers is more likely to be regarded as sincere and heartfelt than from one's therapist.

Giving Shame a New Voice

Once shame-imbued patients find the precise negative messages in their governing shame sessions that they are continually broadcasting to themselves, it is time to start changing these hurtful and shaming messages to give one's personal identity a new and reassuring voice. To give oneself a different voice a new language must be learned. It is the language of *emotionality* (Goldberg 1980b).

A very essential dimension of the therapeutic encounter has to do with the therapist's teaching the patient not only how to use emotionally expressive and meaningful words to communicate inner needs, but also to provide a discretionary guide for when it is appropriate and when ill-advised to express openly and directly one's innermost feelings to others. Methods I have found useful in this endeavor include:

- Having the patient role-model those people who are emotionally expressive;
- Reading aloud poetry, drama, and other literature that is especially provocative and emotionally articulate;
- Listening carefully to and learning to respect the soft voice of the desired self;
- Changing one's style of speech from excessive use of passive and powerless words to idioms that convey

passion, activity, and freedom of choice (see Chapter 12, Goldberg 1991); and
- Using a modified, forceful style of speech to inform the negative and pessimistic inner voice that its dark themes are no longer acceptable.

Learning the Skills for Constructively Defining Oneself

Shame and despair result from the bitter disappointment that are experienced when one realizes that one has lost or never had a clear direction about how to live one's life meaningfully and well. The third step of treatment affords the shame-bound patient specific ways of making definitive modifications in the quality of his sense of self-worth, competence, pride, and personal dignity.

One of the most effective approaches toward the goals of this stage of healing is teaching the patient a sound method of emotional dialogue from which to express his feelings to a concerned and caring person in his life. In this endeavor, I employ "Basic Emotional Communication" (BEC), an approach I developed over the years in working with couples and families and from teaching marital and family psychotherapy skills to psychotherapists in training.

BEC consists of a dialogue occuring between two or more individuals (usually two) involved in a significant relationship, in which the needs of each are both heard and responded to—emotionally, as well, as cognitively. BEC is based upon the principles of *Dialectics*—a concept popularized by Hegel but derived from the ideas and methods introduced by the ancient Greek philosophers. In BEC each alternate statement between patient and therapist should reflect the same basic theme the speaker has presupposed and, until that moment, not consciously realized. The essence of the BEC dialectic dialogue is a series of twenty-five principles for encouraging courageous and risk-taking responses from the therapeutic agents, so that more revealing and elaborate meaning can be produced from the progressive redefinition and understanding of oneself and the other.

The above approach enables the shame-imbued person to experience himself as an active agent in negotiating how he is regarded and treated by the other. A sense of inner strength, competence, and pride is fostered in this process. The interested reader will find a detailed discussion of BEC in Goldberg (1991a).

Other methods I have employed to help the patient constructively redefine himself include:

- Suggesting that he speak with a congruence between his desired self and his inner voice;
- Recommending that he regard personal attributes or circumstances about himself that are not easily changed with tolerance and self-acceptance;
- Exploring ways that he can modify existing family and friendship relationships; and
- Working on ways of creating new friendships.

DEALING WITH HELP-REJECTING PATIENTS

Our shame-debilitated patients are not only passive victims of others' humiliating behavior—some of them also are *active agents* of reproach. Shaming is not confined to intrapsychic processes in shame-imbued people, it projects outwardly, as well. A patient's reluctance to be a responsible partner in examining and correcting his negative personal identity may be manifested in such a way as to be intended as a challenge to the therapist's ego-ideal of being a competent healer (Leveton 1962). The crucial determinant as to whether psychotherapy will be simply another humiliating and failed episode that adds more shame and defeat to his life and leaves a bad taste of resentment in the person who has tried to help him, or becomes an experience that provides a life-changing and constructive impetus to the patient's existence, heavily depends upon how the therapist handles being reproached. Leveton (1962) indicates that in unsuccessful treatment of shame:

As the patient's demands and aggressive helplessness increase, the temptation to react with counterag-
gression also increases. The ultimate reproaching
aggression is suicide; the ultimate counter-aggres-
sion [is symbolic murder] in abandoning them. We
say, "He is not psychologically minded enough to
benefit from our treatment," . . . or "He is too sick,"
thus expecting nothing from him. We avoid the
shame of our therapeutic failure by placing the blame
on the patient. [p. 108]

Dealing therapeutically with shame-imbued patients requires helping them examine their *responsibilities* to other
people, as well as to themselves. I can understand why a
patient may treat me unfairly or "indecently" in our work
together. I do not, however, overlook the behavior or con-
done it. To do so would simply reinforce for the patient how
to absorb shame.

Shame-sensitive patients, for example, frequently terminate therapy by leaving a terse message on the therapist's
phone tape, or simply stop showing up for sessions.
Patients have the unalienable right, of course, to terminate
therapy whenever they choose to do so. At the same time, I
believe that it is my clinical responsibility to indicate to the
patient that he has an opportunity to terminate in a direct
and open way rather than like a fugitive stealing away at
night. If the therapist has treated the patient in a decent
and caring manner, he reasonably expects the courtesy of
being told the circumstances of the patient's decision, so
that he may understand his own part in these events and,
no less importantly, convey his well-wishes for the patient
in a personal, face-to-face way.

When Agnes left a message on my phone tape saying
simply that she was stopping therapy, I called her back. In a
paradigmatic statement intended to reach her pre-oedipal
rage about not receiving the love and caring she once
craved, and which I now believed to refuel her constant
depression and despair (Goldberg 1980a), I said to her,
"Don't worry about your decision to stop therapy! Who said

that your life was meant to be enjoyed? If you decide to think about what I am saying, I am sure you will agree with me. Well, goodbye and good luck!"

Agnes called back for another appointment. Her session started in the following way:

Patient: This is not helping.

Therapist: What did you expect to happen in your life by coming to therapy?

Patient: I don't know.

Therapist: You don't know and you're ready to leave? But then you've only come to eight sessions.

Patient: But that's enough to know it isn't helping.

Therapist: I believe to know that something isn't happening you need to have some idea of what will help. In my experience that takes more than eight sessions. It has taken you about forty years to acquire your feelings of despair. It will take a while to start effectively healing the way you feel about yourself.

Patient: I don't want to bother. I don't care what happens to me.

Therapist: You say that you don't care. But I believe that it is because you feel afraid and don't trust anyone's help with your fears. You have had a hard life. It has not been easy for you. But, rather than actively fight your despair and use my help, you are accustomed to feeling sorry for yourself.

Patient: I have seen other therapists. They didn't work out. No one can help me.

Therapist: Tell me about what happened with these other therapists.

Patient: (Discusses previous therapists.)

Therapist: (Indicates common pattern in how patient has defeated therapists by insisting that therapy should work for her without her being involved, assisting in the process, or even trying suggested modifications in how she lives her life.) You have been fighting my help, just as you did with your previous therapists. I guess you want to prove I can't help you, so you can blame the problem on other people and stop trying to get help for yourself.

Patient: You can't help me.

Therapist: What makes you think I can't help you? I have helped other people who suffer from intense shame and despair, why wouldn't I be able to assist you?

Patient: How can you help me?

Therapist: There are certain essential steps that are required to help you. I have found this to be true over and over again in my work with other people. You have to go through the shame you feel when you discuss your feelings and experiences with me to get past it. This is because, despite what you may feel in those moments in which you are embarrassed and humiliated, it is your private feelings of being ashamed that only you know about, rather than what other people see about you that cause you to feel the most badly about yourself. If you decide to work with me I will show you how to recognize and deal more effectively with the causes of your bad feelings about yourself. There are definitely things you can do so life won't be such a burden to you.

Patient: How long will this process take?

Therapist: This, of course, depends to a great extent on how actively you decide to work with me. Your trying to terminate therapy by leaving me a phone message, your not telling me how our sessions together affect you, and acting as if you are compelled against your will to be here are indications of your previous unwillingness to take an active part in our work together. I can tell you that the people I have helped who suffered from severe shame and despair I have seen twice a week for a number of years. However, when I began working with them I knew a lot less about shame than I do today. I have seen a patient for the past year who made considerable progress with his shameful self-feelings. He began to see meaningful changes in himself in about six months.

TREATMENT WITH SHAME-VULNERABLE MEN

Working with shame-afflicted patients is usually difficult. It may be even more trying with male patients than with females. Clinical evidence suggests that while women are more shame-sensitive, men appear to be more shame-vulnerable (Anthony 1981). In clinical practice we observe that women usually are more likely than men to become shy and embarrassed when sensitive subjects are discussed. Also, they are apt to blush or cry when they feel misunderstood. Male patients, on the other hand, more readily display counterdependent behaviors to conceal their vulnerability and shame about attachment and caring (Osherson and Krugman 1990). Lansky (1984) has found that men who become aware of being dependent upon another person frequently act out their feeling of shame through violence. Male patients who experience themselves becoming too close to their therapist (of either sex) may become competitive and combative, challenging the therapist's professional capacity to be of help. In contrast, a female patient usually is more concerned about the therapist's personal capacity to understand what she is feeling and with the willingness of the therapist to demonstrate explicit caring for her than with his intellectual and professional achievements.

In working with male patients several clinical considerations are useful in diminishing shame. First of all, interpretations are inherently shaming because they emphasize the status differences between therapist and patient (Alonso and Rutan 1988). Interpretations, at least those that are said with a firm certainty and that accentuate the therapist's superiority in being the knower, should be minimally used. Second, it would be wise not to regard the patient's "macho" stance as competitive and defensive, but rather due to his uncertain efforts to emotionally connect with another person. Therapeutic interventions, moreover, should clarify the patient's specific reasons for his competitive struggle in terms of past history and contemporary relationships (Osherson and Krugman 1990). Third, the therapist should provide a continual encouragement and reassurance for the patient's attempts to establish a relationship with the therapist. Fourth, the therapist should provide a role model by emphasizing the value of their relationship in therapy and showing the patient how to articulate his feelings of attachment and caring. Fifth, if the therapist is a male, he needs to impress upon the male patient that attachment and caring between men doesn't imply homosexual or sissified strivings.

WORKING THROUGH SHAME BETWEEN SESSIONS

Because shame is an emotional syndrome that is environmentally reinforced, it is ill-advised to wait out the patient's healing of shame from session to session in the consulting room alone. Usually, there is too much pain going on to sanction such a slow approach. The healing of shame requires active intervention by the therapist outside of the consulting room. Direct advice may be necessary, especially when the patient places himself in a position in which serious psychological and/or physical harm may ensue.

In working with shame-bound people it is necessary that the therapist's goals be modest and concrete. Interventions should address specific everyday instances of self- and other-induced shame. For what causes people to feel unhappy and dissatisfied with their lives, I will reiterate, is not what happened in childhood as much as what is tolerated in adult relationships. Therefore, what is most important to recognize about shame is not that these humiliating experiences originally happened early in the shaping of a negative personal identity, but that shame-imbued people continually allow these same unrecognized patterns to contaminate their daily adult lives.

I utilize what Levin (1967) has referred to as "shame mastery" to help shame-sensitive patients progressively expose themselves to what they previously have avoided in their ego-syntonic defensive stances toward the fearful world around them. In whatever ways we can help our patients gain more competence and self-pride in actively taking care of themselves, especially in ways they have eschewed before, progress toward healing debilitating shame has been further enjoined. Mastering problems in one's life that have previously caused a sense of incompetence can assert a positive influence on personal identity, even apart from a dynamic resolution of intrapsychic issues (Ablon 1990).

It is now time to lift the lid completely off hidden shame. Like the wise and benevolent spirit of the ancient Greek myth, Pandora, constructive shame waits to serve our self-discovery needs in the exploration of personal identity.

Shame serves as a sensitizer to both tragedy and inspiration in human consciousness. While revealing the tragic substrata of life, it simultaneously enables us to love and care for others and to strive for what we believe in. When our ego-ideal contained in our self-protective feelings of shame is liberated, we are enabled to express our heartfelt sentiments, in interpersonal interactions as well as in poetry, music, art, and all other forms of creative, intellectual, and constructive human endeavors.

REFERENCES

Ablon, S. L. (1990). Developmental aspects of self-esteem in the analysis of an eleven-year-old boy. *Psychoanalytic Study of the Child* 45:337–356. New York: International Universities Press.

Abraham, R. (1982/1983). Freud's mother conflict and the formulation of the Oedipal father. *Psychoanalytic Review* 69:441–453.

Achtemeier, P. J., ed. (1985). *Harper's Bible and Dictionary.* New York: Harper and Row.

Adler, Alfred. (1933). Advantages and disadvantages of the inferiority feelings. In *Superiority and Social Interest,* ed. H. Ansbacher and R. Ansbacher, pp. 50–59. Evanston, IL: Northwestern University, 1970.

Ainsworth, M., and Wittig, B. (1969). Attachment and exploratory behavior of one-year-olds in a strange situation. In *Determinants of Infant Behavior,* vol. 4, ed. B. M. Foss, pp. 67–104. New York: Wiley.

Alexander, F. (1938). Remarks about the relationship of inferiority feelings to guilt feelings. *International Journal of Psycho-Analysis* 19:41–49.

Alonso, A., and Rutan, J. S. (1988). The experience and the restoration of self-respect in group therapy. *International Journal of Group Psychotherapy* 38:3–14.

Amsterdam, B. (1972). Mirror self-image reactions before age two. *Developmental Psychobiology* 5:297–305.

Anthony, E. J. (1981). Shame, guilt and the feminine self in psychoanalysis. In *Object and Self,* ed. S. Tuttman, C. Kaye, and S. M. Zimmerman, pp. 191–234. New York: International Universities Press.

Antoni, M. H., Schneiderman, N., Fletcher, M. A., Gordon, D. A., Ironson, G., and LaPerriere, A. (1990). Psychoneuroimmunology and HIV-1. *Journal of Consulting and Clinical Psychology* 58:38–49.

Aquinas, T. *The Pocket Aquinas.* New York: Washington Square Press, 1960.

Aristotle. *Seven of the Most Important Books of Aristotle.* New York: Odyssey Press, 1951.

Ausubel, D. P. (1955). Relationships between shame and guilt in the socializing process. *Psychological Review* 62:378–390.

Babcock, M. F., and Sabini, J. (1990). On differentiating embarrassment from shame. *European Journal of Social Psychology* 20:151–169.

Barker, H. (1978). *Preface to Shakespeare*. Princeton, NJ: Princeton University Press.

Barry, M. J. (1962). Depression, shame, loneliness and the psychiatrist's position. *American Journal of Psychotherapy* 16:580–590.

Becker, E. (1973). *The Denial of Death*. New York: The Free Press.

Benedict, R. (1946). *The Chrysanthemum and the Sword*. Boston: Houghton Mifflin.

Benjamin, J. D. (1963). Further comments on some developmental aspects of anxiety. In *Counterpoint*, ed. H. S. Gaskill. New York: International Universities Press.

Bilmes, M. (1967). Shame and delinquency. *Contemporary Psychoanalysis* 3:113–133.

Binder, J. (1970). The relative proneness to shame or guilt as a dimension of character style. Doctoral dissertation, University of Michigan, Ann Arbor, MI.

Bion, W. H. (1962). *Learning from Experience*. London: Heinemann.

Bloch, D. (1966). Some dynamics of suffering: effect of the wish for infanticide in a case of schizophrenia. *Psychoanalytic Review* 53:530–554.

Blos, P. (1985). *Son and Father: Before and Beyond the Oedipus Complex*. New York: Free Press.

Bowlby, J. (1969). *Attachment and Loss*. Vol. I. New York: Basic Books, 1969.

Broucek, F. (1982). Shame and its relationship to early narcissistic developments. *International Journal of Psycho-Analysis* 63:369–378.

——— (in press). *On Being an Object—A Study in Shame*. New York: Guilford.

Brownmiller, S. (1989). *Waverly Place*. New York: Grove Press.

Burrow, T. (1958). *A Search for Man's Sanity*. New York: Oxford University Press.

Bursten, B. (1973). Some narcissistic personality types. *International Journal of Psycho-Analysis* 54:287–300.

Cattell, R. B. (1965). *The Scientific Analysis of Personality*. New York: Penguin Books.

Chasseguet-Smirgel, J. (1985). *The Ego-Ideal*. London: Free Association Press.

Cook, D. R. *Manual for the Internalized Shame Scale (ISS)*. University of Wisconsin-Stout, Menomonic, WI, unpublished.

Costello, E. J., Costello, A. J., Edelbrock, C., Burns, B. J., Dulcan, M. K., Brent, D., and Janiszewski, S. (1988). Psychiatric disorders in pediatric primary care. *Archives of General Psychiatry* 45:1107–1116.

Crouppon, G. A. (1970). Field-dependent-independence in depressive and normal males as an indicator of relative proneness to shame or guilt and ego-functioning. *Dissertation Abstracts International* 37:4669B–4670B. (University Microfilms No. 77-6292).

Darwin, C. (1872). *The Expression of the Emotions in Man and Animals*. New York: Philosophical Library, 1955.

Edelman, R. (1981). Embarrassment: the state of the research. *Current Psychological Review* 1:123–138.

Edelson, M. (1984). *Hypothesis and Evidence in Psychoanalysis.* Chicago: University of Chicago Press.

Edwards, D. G. (1976). Shame and pain and "shut up or I'll really give you something to cry about." *Clinical Social Work Journal* 4:3–13.

Ehrlich, A. (1977). *Hamlet's Absent Father.* Princeton, NJ: Princeton University Press.

Emerson, R. W. (1951). *Essays.* New York: Harper and Row.

English, F. (1975). Shame and social control. *Transactional Analysis Journal* 5:24–28.

Erikson, E. H. (1950). *Childhood and Society.* New York: Norton.

_____ (1980). *Identity and the Life Cycle.* New York: Norton.

Fenichel, O. (1945). *The Psychoanalytic Theory of Neurosis.* New York: Norton.

Firestone, R. W. (1988). *Voice Therapy.* New York: Human Sciences Press.

Fisher, S. (1985). Identity of two: the phenomenology of shame in borderline development and treatment. *Psychotherapy* 22:101–109.

Freud, S. (1887–1904). *The Complete Letters of Sigmund Freud to Wilhelm Fliess.* Trans. and ed. J. M. Masson. Cambridge, MA: Belknap Press of Harvard University Press, 1985.

_____ (1900). *Interpretation of Dreams.* Trans. James Strachey. New York: Avon Books, 1965.

_____ (1905). Three essays on the theory of sexuality. *Standard Edition* 7:135–244.

_____ (1921). Group psychology and the analysis of the ego. *Standard Edition* 18:67–134.

_____ (1923). The ego and the id. *Standard Edition* 19:3–63.

_____ (1928). Dostoevsky and parricide. *Standard Edition* 21:175–195.

_____ (1930). Civilization and its discontents. *Standard Edition* 21:59–64.

_____ (1935). *An Autobiographical Study.* Trans. James Strachey. New York: Norton, 1952.

_____ The Letters of Sigmund Freud (1907–1926). Ed. E. L. Freud. New York: Basic Books, 1960.

Freud, S., and Abraham, K. (1907–1926). *The Letters of Sigmund Freud and Karl Abraham.* New York: Basic Books, 1965.

Friedman, N., and Jones, R. M. (1965). On the mutuality of the Oedipus complex: notes on the Hamlet case. *American Imago* 20:107–131.

Gilligan, J. (1976). Beyond morality: psychoanalytic reflection on shame, guilt and love. In *Moral Development and Behavior,* ed. T. Lickona, pp. 144–158. New York: Holt, Rinehart and Winston.

Goddard, H. C. (1951). *The Meaning of Shakespeare.* Vol. 1. Chicago: University of Chicago Press. 1960.

_____ (1960). *The Meaning of Shakespeare.* Vol. 1. Rev. ed. Chicago, University of Chicago Press.

Goethe, J. W. *Faust.* In *The Works of J. W. Van Goethe,* trans. Sir Theodore Martin. Boston: Wyman-Fogg, 1902.

Goldberg, C. (1973). *The Human Circle—An Existential Approach to the New Group Therapies.* Chicago: Nelson-Hall.

_____ (1977). *Therapeutic Partnership.* New York: Springer.

_____ (1980a). Utilization and limitation of paradoxical intervention in group psychotherapy. *International Journal of Group Psychotherapy* 30:287–297.

_____ (1980b). A theory of emotions: emotionality as the expression of the self's intentionality. *Journal of Contemporary Psychotherapy* 11:104–128.

_____ (1986). Concerning human suffering. *Psychiatric Journal of the University of Ottawa* 11:97–104.

_____ (1988a). Replacing moral masochism with a shame paradigm in psychoanalysis. *Dynamic Psychotherapy* 6:114–123.

_____ (1988b). The role of shame in therapeutic misalliance. *Group Analysis* 21:339–344.

_____ (1989a). The mirror of your eyes. *The Psychotherapy Patient* 5:197–205.

_____ (1989b). The shame of Hamlet and Oedipus. *Psychoanalytic Review* 76:581–603.

_____ (1989c). The role of passion in the transformation of anti-heroes. *Journal of Evolutionary Psychology* 10:2–16.

_____ (1989d). The psychotherapist as a mentor of friendship. *Voices* 24:45–52.

_____ (1990). The role of existential shame in the healing endeavor. *Psychotherapy: Theory, Research and Practice* 27:591–599.

_____ (1991a). *On Being a Psychotherapist.* Northvale, NJ: Jason Aronson.

_____ (1991b). Why Hamlet could not love. *Psychoanalysis and Psychotherapy* 1:16–29.

Goldberg, C., and Kane, J. D. (1974). A missing component in mental health services to the urban poor: services-in-kind to others. In *Mental Health Issues and the Urban Poor,* ed. D. A. Evans and W. L. Claiborn, pp. 91–110. New York: Pergamon.

Goldberg, C., and Simon, J. (1982). Towards a psychology of courage: implications for the healing process. *Journal of Contemporary Psychotherapy* 13:226–232.

Gorman, W. (1974). *Psychotherapy and the Sense of Justice.* St. Louis, MO: Warren H. Green.

Gorsuch, S. E. (1990). Shame and acting out in psychotherapy. *Psychotherapy: Theory, Research and Practice* 27:585–590.

Gottschalk, L., Winget, C., and Gleser, G. (1969). *Manual of Instructions for Using the Gottschalk-Gleser Analysis of Content Analysis Scales.* Berkeley, CA: University of California Press.

Grinker, R. R. (1955). Growth inertia and shame: their therapeutic implications and dangers. *International Journal of Psycho-Analysis* 36:242–253.

Harder, D. W. (1984). Character styles of the defensively high self-esteem man. *Journal of Clinical Psychology* 40:26–35.

_____ (1990). Comment on Wright, O'Leary and Balkin's "Shame, Guilt, Narcissism and Depression: Correlates and sex differences." *Psychoanalytic Psychology* 7:285–289.

Harder, D. W., and Lewis, S. J. (1987). The assessment of shame and guilt. In *Advances in Personality Assessment,* vol. 6, ed. J. N.

Burcher and C. D. Spielberger, pp. 89–114. Hillsdale, NJ: Lawrence Erlbaum Associates.

Hattener, L. (1971). *Pleasure Addicts.* New York: A. S. Barnes.

Hawthorne, N. *The Scarlet Letter.* New York: Washington Square Press, 1972.

Hazard, P. (1969). Freud's teaching on shame. *Laval Theologique et Philosophique* 25:234–267.

Hegel, G. *The Logic of Hegel.* Trans. from *The Encyclopedia of the Philosophical Sciences* by William Wallace. Oxford, England, 1892.

Hinckley, J., and Hinckley, J. (1985). *Breaking Points.* Grand Rapids, MI: Chosen Books.

Hoblitzelle, W. (1982). Developing a measure of shame and guilt and the role of shame in depression. Unpublished predissertation, Yale University, New Haven, CT.

_____ (1987). Differentiating and measuring shame and guilt: the relation between shame and depression. In *The Role of Shame in Symptom Formation,* ed. H. B. Lewis, pp. 207–235. Hillsdale, NJ: Lawrence Erlbaum Associates.

Horney, K. (1950). *Neurosis and Human Growth.* New York: Norton.

Horowitz, M. (1981). Self-righteous rage and attribution of blame. *Archives of General Psychiatry* 38:1233–1238.

Izard, C. E. (1977). *Human Emotions.* New York: Plenum.

Jacobson, E. (1963). Guilt, shame and identity. *Psychoanalytic Quarterly* 32:475–477.

Jacoby, S. Hers. *New York Times,* April 21, 1983.

James, W. (1890). *The Principles of Psychology.* Cambridge, MA: Harvard University Press, 1983.

Jones, E. (1976). *Hamlet and Oedipus.* New York: Norton.

Kant, I. (1956). *Critique of Practical Reason.* New York: Liberal Arts Press.

Kardiner, A., Karuch, A., and Ovesey, L. (1966). A methodological study of Freudian theory. *International Journal of Psychiatry* 2:489–542.

Kaufman, G. (1989). *The Psychology of Shame.* New York: Springer.

Kaufman, G., and Raphael, L. (1984a). Relating to the self: changing inner dialogue. *Psychological Reports* 54:239–250.

_____ (1984b). Shame as taboo in American culture. In *Forbidden Fruits—Taboos and Tabooism in Culture,* ed. R. Browne, pp. 57–64b. Bowling Green, OH: Popular Press.

Kinston, W. (1983). A theoretical context for shame. *International Journal of Psycho-Analysis* 64:213–226.

Kohlberg, L. (1963). The development of children's orientations towards a moral order. I. Sequence in the development of moral thoughts. *Vita Humana* 6:11–33.

Kohut, H. (1977). *The Restoration of the Self.* New York: International Universities Press.

Kris, A. O. (1990). Helping patients by analyzing self-criticism. *Journal of the American Psychoanalytic Association* 38:605–636.

Lacan, J. (1980). Desire and the interpretation of desire in *Hamlet.* In *Literature and Psychoanalysis,* ed. S. Felman, pp. 11–52. New Haven, CT: Yale University Press.

Lansky, M. R. (1984). Violence, shame and the family. *International Journal of Family Psychiatry* 5:21–40.

Lecky, P. (1969). *Self-Consistency: A Theory of Personality.* Garden City, NY: Doubleday.

LeDoux, J. E. (1989). Cognitive-emotional interactions in the brain. *Cognition and Emotion* 3:267–289.

Lepp, I. (1971). *The Ways of Friendship.* New York: MacMillan.

Leveton, A. F. (1962). Reproach: the art of shamemanship. *British Journal of Medical Psychology* 35:101–111.

Levin, S. (1967). Some metapsychological considerations on the differentiation between shame and guilt. *International Journal of Psycho-Analysis* 48:267–276.

_____ (1971). The psychoanalysis of shame. *International Journal of Psycho-Analysis* 52:355–361.

Levinson, D., Darrow, C. N., Klein, E. B., Levinson, M. H., and McKee, B. (1978). *The Seasons of a Man's Life.* New York: Ballantine.

Lewis, H. B. (1971). *Shame and Guilt in Neurosis.* New York: International Universities Press.

_____ (1979). Shame in depression and hysteria. In *Emotion in Personality and Psychopathology,* ed. C. Izard, pp. 371–396. New York: Plenum.

_____ (1987a). Introduction: shame—the "sleeper in psychopathology." In *The Role of Shame in Symptom Formation,* ed. H. B. Lewis, pp. 1–28. Hillsdale, NJ: Lawrence Erlbaum Associates.

_____ (1987b). The role of shame in depression over the life span. In *The Role of Shame in Symptom Formation,* ed. H. B. Lewis, pp. 29–50. Hillsdale, NJ: Lawrence Erlbaum Associates.

_____ ed. (1987c). *The Role of Shame in Symptom Formation.* Hillsdale, NJ: Lawrence Erlbaum Associates.

_____ (1989). Resistance: a misnomer for shame and guilt. In *Techniques of Working with Resistance,* ed. D. Milman and G. Goldman, pp. 209–226. Northvale, NJ: Jason Aronson.

Lindsay-Hartz, J. (1984). Contrasting experiences of shame and guilt. *American Behavioral Scientist* 27:689–704.

Loevinger, J. (1976). *Ego Development: Conceptions and Theories.* San Francisco, CA: Jossey-Bass.

Lynd, H. (1958). *On Shame and the Search for Identity.* New York: Harcourt, Brace.

Mairet, P. (1969). Hamlet as a study in individual psychology. *Individual Psychology* 25:71–88.

Marsella, A. J., Murray, M. D., and Golden, C. (1974). Ethnic variations in the phenomenology of emotions. *Journal of Cross-Cultural Psychology* 5:312–328.

Maslow, A. H. (1963). The need to know and the fear of knowing. *Journal of General Psychology* 68:111–125.

Maugham, W. S. (1936). *Of Human Bondage.* Garden City, NY: Doubleday, Doran and Company.

May, R., Angel, E., and Ellensberger, H. F., eds. (1958). *Existence.* New York: Simon and Schuster.

McGill, A. (1982). Human suffering and the passion of Christ. In *The*

Meaning of Human Suffering, ed. F. Dougherty, pp. 159–193. New York: Human Sciences Press.

Mead, M. (1937). *Cooperation and Competition Among Primitive Peoples.* New York: McGraw-Hill.

Meerloo, J. A. (1959). Justice as a psychological problem. *Archives of Criminal Psychodynamics* 3:7–51.

Menninger, K. (1954). Regulatory devices of the ego under major stress. *International Journal of Psycho-Analysis* 35:412–420.

Middleton-Moz, J. (1990). *Shame and Guilt—Masters of Disguise.* Deerfield Beach, FL: Health Communication.

Miller, S. B. (1985). *The Shame Experience.* Hillsdale, NJ: Analytic Press.

———— (1989). Shame as an impetus to the creation of conscience. *International Journal of Psycho-Analysis* 70:231–243.

Morrison, A. P. (1989). *Shame: the Underside of Narcissism.* Hillsdale, NJ: The Analytic Press.

Mosher, D. C., and White, B. B. (1981). On differentiating shame and shyness. *Motivation and Emotion* 5:61–64.

Natanson, D. L. (1987a). The shame/pride axis. In *The Role of Shame in Symptom Formation,* ed. H. B. Lewis, pp. 183–205. Hillsdale, NJ: Lawrence Erlbaum Associates.

———— (1987b). A timetable for shame. In *The Many Faces of Shame,* ed. D. L. Natanson, pp. 1–63. New York: Guilford Press.

————, ed. (1987c). *The Many Faces of Shame.* New York: Guilford Press.

Natanson, M. (1983). An editorial fragment. *Journal of Medical Philosophy* 6:3.

Nergaard, M. O., and Silberschatz, G. (1989). The effects of shame, guilt and the negative reaction in brief dynamic psychotherapy. *Psychotherapy: Theory, Research and Practice* 26:330–333.

Nietzsche, F. (1887). *On the Genealogy of Morals.* New York: Vintage, 1967.

O'Hear, A. (1976/1977). Guilt and shame as moral concepts. *Proceedings of the Aristotelian Society* 77:73–86.

Osherson, S. (1986). *Finding Our Fathers.* New York: Free Press.

Osherson, S., and Krugman, S. (1990). Men, shame and psychotherapy. *Psychotherapy: Theory, Research and Practice* 27:327–329.

Ovid. *The Metamorphoses.* Trans. Horace Gregory. New York: New American Library, 1958.

Pandino, R., Labouvie, E. W., Johnson, V., and White, H. R. (1990). The relationship between alcohol and marijuana use and competence in adolescence. *Journal of Health and Social Policy* 1:89–108.

Pascal, B. *Pensées.* Ed. and trans. G. B. Rawlings. Mount Vernon, NY: The Peter Pauper Press, 1946.

Pianta, R., Egeland, B., and Erickson, M. F. (1989). The antecedents of maltreatment: results of the mother–child interaction research project. In *Child Maltreatment,* ed. D. Cicchetti and V. Carlson, pp. 203–249. Cambridge, England: Cambridge University Press.

Piers, G., and Singer, M. (1953). *Shame and Guilt.* New York: Norton.

Pines, M. (1987). Shame—what psychoanalysis does and does not say. *Group Analysis* 20:16–31.

Plato, *The Dialogues*. Trans. B. Jowett. Chicago, Great Books, Encyclopedia Britannica, 1952.

Potter-Efron, R. (1989). *Shame, Guilt and Alcoholism: Treatment Issues in Clinical Practice.* New York: Hawthorne Press.

Potter-Efron, R., and Potter-Efron, P. (1989). *Letting Go of Shame.* New York: Harper and Row.

Rank, O. (1964). *The Myth of the Birth of the Hero.* New York: Vintage.

Rawls, J. A. (1971). *A Theory of Justice.* Cambridge, MA: Harvard University Press.

Retzinger, S. (1987). Resentment and laughter—video studies of the shame-rage spiral. In *The Role of Shame in Symptom Formation*, ed. H. B. Lewis, pp. 151–181. Hillsdale, NJ: Lawrence Erlbaum Associates.

———— (1989). A theory of mental illness: integrating social and emotional aspects. *Psychiatry* 52:325–338.

Richards, L. O. (1985). *Expository Dictionary of Bible Words.* Grand Rapids, MI: Zondervan.

Riezler, K. (1942–43). Comment on the social psychology of shame. *American Journal of Sociology* 48:457–465.

Robertiello, R. C., and Gagnier, T. T. (1990). Shame, shame. *Journal of Contemporary Psychotherapy* 20:117–121.

Rosenquist, C. M. (1932). Differential responses of Texas convicts. *American Journal of Sociology* 38:10–21.

Rotenstreich, N. (1965). On shame. *Review of Metaphysics* 19:55–86.

Rubin, G. (1985). *Just Friends.* New York: Harper and Row.

Rycroft, C. (1968). *A Critical Dictionary of Psychoanalysis.* New York: Basic Books.

Sartre, J.-P. *Being and Nothingness.* New York: Washington Square Press, 1966.

Sattler, J. A. (1965). A theoretical, developmental, and clinical investigation of embarrassment. *Genetic Psychology Monographs* 71:19–59.

Scheff, T. J. (1987). The shame-rage spiral: a case study of an interminable quarrel. In *The Role of Shame in Symptom Formation*, ed. H. B. Lewis, pp. 109–149. Hillsdale, NJ: Lawrence Erlbaum Associates.

Scheler, M. (1954). *The Nature of Sympathy.* London: Routledge and Kegan Paul.

Schneider, C. (1977). *Shame, Exposure and Privacy.* Boston: Beacon Press.

Schofield, W. (1964). *Psychotherapy—The Purchase of Friendship.* Englewood Cliffs, NJ: Prentice-Hall.

Searles, H. F. (1961). Schizophrenia and the inevitability of death. *Psychiatric Quarterly* 35:631–665.

Seligman, M. (1972). Learned helplessness. *Annual Review of Medicine* 23:407–412.

Shakespeare, W. Hamlet. In *The Complete Works of William Shakespeare*, pp. 1071–1112. New York: Avenel Books, 1975.

Shane, E., and Shane, M. (1989). Child analysis and adult analysis. In *Dimensions of Self Experience*, vol. 5, ed. A. Goldberg, pp. 59–73. Hillsdale, NJ: The Analytic Press.

Shane, P. (1980). Shame and learning. *American Journal of Orthopsychiatry* 50:348–355.

Simon, J., and Goldberg, C. (1984). The role of the double in the creative process and psychoanalysis. *Journal of the American Academy of Psychoanalysis* 12:341–361.

Slochower, H. (1971). The psychoanalytic approach to literature: some pitfalls and promise. *Literature and Psychology* 21:107–111.

Smith, R. L. (1972). The relative proneness to shame or guilt as an indicator of defensive style. Doctoral Dissertation, Northwestern University, Chicago, IL.

Sophocles. *Oedipus the King*. Trans. B. M. W. Knox. New York: Washington Square Press, 1972.

Spero, M. H. (1984). Shame: an object-relations formulation. *Psychoanalytic Study of the Child* 39:259–282. New Haven, CT: Yale University Press.

Spinoza, B. *The Ethics*. New York: Hafner Press, 1949.

Spitz, R. (1965). *The First Year of Life*. New York: International Universities Press.

Spruiell, V. (1984). The analyst at work. *International Journal of Psycho-Analysis* 65:13–30.

Stamm, J. L. (1978). The meaning of humiliation and its relationship to fluctuations in self-esteem. *International Review of Psycho-Analysis* 5:425–433.

Stern, D. (1985). *The Interpersonal World of the Infant*. New York: Basic Books.

Straus, E. W. (1966). Shame as a historiological problem. In *Phenomenological Psychology: Selected Papers*, ed. E. W. Straus, pp. 217–223. New York: Basic Books.

Tangner, J. P. (1990). Assessing individual differences in proneness to shame and guilt. *Journal of Personality and Social Psychology* 59:102–111.

Thomas, A., Chess, S., and Birch, H. G. (1970). The origin of personality. *Scientific American* 223:102–109.

Thrane, G. (1979). Shame and the construction of the self. *Annual of Psychoanalysis* 7:321–341.

Tolstoy, L. *The Death of Ivan Illyich and Other Stories*. New York: Signet Classics, 1960.

Tompkins, S. S. (1962). *Affect, Imagery, Consciousness*. Vol. 1. New York: Springer.

_____ (1978). Script theory: differential magnification of affects. *Nebraska Symposium on Motivation*.

_____ (1987). Shame. In *The Many Faces of Shame*, ed. D. L. Natanson, pp. 133–161. New York: Guilford Press.

Twain, M. *Adventures of Huckleberry Finn*. New York: Norton, 1977.

Wallace, L. (1963). The mechanisms of shame. *Archives of General Psychiatry* 8:80–85.

Ward, H. P. (1972). Shame—a necessity for growth in therapy. *American Journal of Psychoanalysis* 26:232–243.

Weiner, M. B., and White, M. T. (1982). Depression as the search for the lost self. *Psychotherapy: Theory, Research and Practice* 19:491–499.

Weisman, A. D. (1984). *The Coping Capacity: On the Nature of Being Mortal*. New York: Human Sciences Press.

Wertheim, F. (1941). The matricide impulse: critique of Freud's interpretation of Hamlet. *Journal of Criminal Psychopathology* 2:455–464.

Wheelis, A. (1956). The vocational hazards of psycho-analysis. *International Journal of Psycho-Analysis* 37:171–184.

———— (1962). *The Seeker.* New York: The American Library.

White, R. W. (1963). Sense of interpersonal competence. In *The Study of Lives,* ed. R. W. White, pp. 73–93. New York: Prentice-Hall.

Wicker, F. W., Payne, G. C., and Morgan, R. D. (1983). Participant descriptions of guilt and shame. *Motivation and Emotion* 7:25–39.

Winnicott, D. W. (1958). *Collected Papers.* New York: Basic Books.

Wright, F. (1987). Men, shame and antisocial behavior: a psychodynamic perspective. *Group* 11:238–246.

Wurmser, L. (1981). *The Mask of Shame.* Baltimore: Johns Hopkins University Press.

———— (1987). Shame: the veiled companion of narcissism. In *The Many Faces of Shame,* ed. D. L. Natanson, pp. 64–92. New York: Guilford Press.

Yalom, I. (1985). *The Theory and Practice of Group Psychotherapy.* New York: Basic Books.

Yorke, C., Balogh, T., Cohen, P., Davids, J., Gavson, A., McCutheon, M., Mclean, D., Miller, J., and Szydlo, J. (1990). The development and functioning of the sense of shame. *Psychoanalytic Study of the Child* 45:377–409. New Haven, CT: Yale University Press.

Zander, A., Fuller, R., and Armstrong, W. (1972). Attributed pride or shame in group and self. *Journal of Personality and Social Psychology* 23:346–352.

Zimbardo, P. G., Pilkonas, P. A., and Norwood, R. M. (1974). The silent prison of shyness. Office of Naval Research Technology, Report Z-17, Stanford University.

NAME INDEX

Subject Index

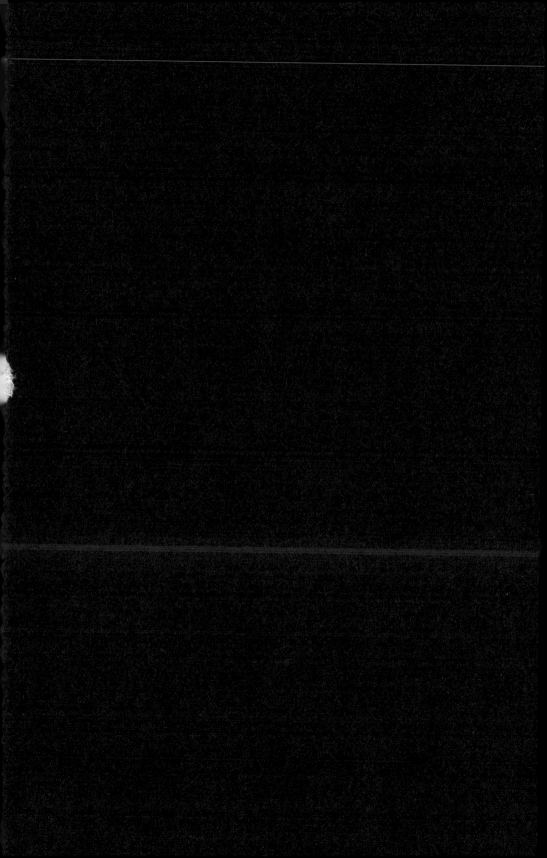